W9-CZV-075

THE BEDFORD SERIES IN HISTORY AND CULTURE

The Urban Underworld in Late Nineteenth-Century New York

The Autobiography of George Appo

WITH RELATED DOCUMENTS

Related Titles in
THE BEDFORD SERIES IN HISTORY AND CULTURE
Advisory Editors: Lynn Hunt, *University of California, Los Angeles*
David W. Blight, *Yale University*
Bonnie G. Smith, *Rutgers University*
Natalie Zemon Davis, *University of Toronto*

THE BEDFORD SERIES IN HISTORY AND CULTURE

The Urban Underworld in Late Nineteenth-Century New York

The Autobiography of George Appo

WITH RELATED DOCUMENTS

Edited with an Introduction by

Timothy J. Gilfoyle

Loyola University Chicago

BEDFORD/ST. MARTIN'S   Boston ◆ New York

For Bedford/St. Martin's

Publisher for History: Mary V. Dougherty
Executive Editor for History: William J. Lombardo
Director of Development for History: Jane Knetzger
Senior Editor: Heidi L. Hood
Developmental Editor: Debra Michals
Production Supervisor: Victoria Sharoyan
Marketing Manager, U.S. History: Amy Whitaker
Editorial Assistant: Laura Kintz
Project Management: Books By Design, Inc.
Permissions Manager: Kalina K. Ingham
Text Designer: Claire Seng-Niemoeller
Cover Designer: Marine Miller
Cover Photo: George Appo, ca. 1897, from *The American Metropolis*, by Frank Moss (1897)
Composition: Achorn International, Inc.
Printing and Binding: RR Donnelley and Sons

President, Bedford/St. Martin's: Denise B. Wydra
Presidents, Macmillan Higher Education: Joan E. Feinberg and Tom Scotty
Director of Marketing: Karen R. Soeltz
Production Director: Susan W. Brown
Associate Production Director: Elise S. Kaiser
Manager, Publishing Services: Andrea Cava

Library of Congress Control Number: 2012945086

Manufactured in the United States of America.

7   6   5   4   3   2
f   e   d   c   b   a

For information, write: Bedford/St. Martin's, 75 Arlington Street, Boston, MA 02116
(617-399-4000)

ISBN 978-0-312-60762-3

Acknowledgments

Foreword

The Bedford Series in History and Culture is designed so that readers can study the past as historians do.

The historian's first task is finding the evidence. Documents, letters, memoirs, interviews, pictures, movies, novels, or poems can provide facts and clues. Then the historian questions and compares the sources. There is more to do than in a courtroom, for hearsay evidence is welcome, and the historian is usually looking for answers beyond act and motive. Different views of an event may be as important as a single verdict. How a story is told may yield as much information as what it says.

Along the way the historian seeks help from other historians and perhaps from specialists in other disciplines. Finally, it is time to write, to decide on an interpretation and how to arrange the evidence for readers.

Each book in this series contains an important historical document or group of documents, each document a witness from the past and open to interpretation in different ways. The documents are combined with some element of historical narrative—an introduction or a biographical essay, for example—that provides students with an analysis of the primary source material and important background information about the world in which it was produced.

Each book in the series focuses on a specific topic within a specific historical period. Each provides a basis for lively thought and discussion about several aspects of the topic and the historian's role. Each is short enough (and inexpensive enough) to be a reasonable one-week assignment in a college course. Whether as classroom or personal reading, each book in the series provides firsthand experience of the challenge—and fun—of discovering, recreating, and interpreting the past.

Lynn Hunt
David W. Blight
Bonnie G. Smith
Natalie Zemon Davis

To Maria and Danielle

Preface

In mid-nineteenth-century America, crime emerged as a major urban problem. From pickpocketing and prostitution, to assault and murder, to counterfeiting and graft, city dwellers in the United States confronted unprecedented levels and forms of antisocial behavior. At this time, criminal behaviors and "informal economies" became common and visible elements of urban life. The growing concerns and fears associated with crime generated the first professional police forces and detective agencies, the rapid expansion of penitentiaries, and multiple reform movements that culminated in the Progressive Era. *The Autobiography of George Appo* presents a rare first-person account of the emergence of crime, criminal subcultures, and the underground economy as a major social phenomenon in American cities in the post–Civil War era from 1865 to 1900.

George Appo's memoir moves beyond his personal world as a notorious pickpocket and con man and illuminates the evolving social structure of the larger urban universe. It explores how crime changed over time; how convicted felons experienced and reacted to the criminal justice system and carceral institutions; the masculine codes of honor and homosocial (and sometimes homosexual) behavior of convicts; and how incarceration differed among various penitentiaries, prisons, and jails. Appo's memoir also reveals the emergence of the first drug trade, epitomized by opium dens; the fluid and uncertain boundaries between cops and criminals; the convergence of political reform and criminal behaviors; and how the new underworld increasingly permeated popular culture at the turn of the twentieth century.

The Autobiography of George Appo challenges much of the literature on nineteenth-century crime, which frequently depicts the criminal as part hero or part dreadful moral exemplar. Appo was hardly a "primitive rebel" intent on righting social wrongs. He never displayed a prerevolutionary or reformist ideology built on a tradition of resistance. Nor was he an inveterate criminal violating the law without qualification or simply for its own sake. He was neither Robin Hood nor Jack the Ripper. Appo was caught in a world not of his choosing and committed certain crimes because of very specific social conditions—urban poverty, rapid industrialization, massive immigration, and violent nativism. His memoir attempts to portray that world in his own words.

Designed for assignment in undergraduate courses, this volume is composed of three parts. The introduction in Part One provides a brief overview of Appo's life and a broad outline of the criminal underworld and the informal economies operating in late nineteenth-century American cities. It situates Appo within the social milieu of the Gilded Age and explains how the new criminal economy, activities, and networks intersected with the dominant institutions and culture of the time. For the first time, the professional criminal became a fixture in American life. The institutions of modern law enforcement—professional police forces; private detectives; penitentiaries, prisons, and jails; and specialized courts such as family court and women's court—were created or expanded during these years to address problems associated with urban disorder. Fascination with illicit exploits even transformed American popular culture. Nineteenth-century stage impresarios created and produced melodramatic entertainments that both glamorized and vilified criminals. In the twentieth century, those entertainments evolved into a major genre of American filmmaking. The introduction illuminates these developments.

The heart of this volume is the abridged autobiography of George Appo in Part Two. The original manuscript has been edited as a chronological, firsthand account of criminal and working-class life in late nineteenth-century America. Appo describes his impoverished childhood in New York's Five Points neighborhood, his violent experiences in prison, his life in Chinatown, his addiction to opium, his successes and failures as a pickpocket and confidence man, his brief theatrical career, and his successful efforts to go straight. Such firsthand accounts of criminal life are rare. Appo's story challenges traditional narratives of crime "from the bottom up."

Finally, Part Three provides a dozen primary source documents relevant to George Appo's life. They include investigative accounts of crime, other descriptions of crime and punishment, a letter from Appo to Governor Theodore Roosevelt requesting release from a state mental hospital, and Appo's obituary. These documents illustrate how the informal economies intersected with urban politics, the rise of the penitentiary, immigration, policing and concerns regarding urban disorder, and the emergence of the criminal in popular culture and entertainment.

The volume concludes with several features designed to facilitate student learning. A chronology offers a detailed overview of the major events in Appo's life and times. Questions for consideration raise issues that can stimulate class discussion or further research. A selected bibliography suggests the most useful texts for those interested in pursuing the subject of criminal life and the underground economy in the late nineteenth and early twentieth centuries.

A NOTE ABOUT THE TEXT

Appo learned to write late in life, and it showed. The typed, ninety-nine-page manuscript on which Part Two is based follows a first-person, stream-of-consciousness style with only thirteen paragraph breaks. The text is marred by grammatical and spelling errors, run-on sentences, and awkward colloquialisms. Unnecessary capitalization and abbreviations appear throughout the document. When quoting, Appo inverted punctuation marks and regularly omitted commas, periods, and quotation marks. In short, Appo needed an editor.

I revised Appo's original manuscript by breaking long, run-on sentences into shorter, more easily understood ones; eliminating abbreviations; standardizing capitalization and correcting spelling; adding missing words (in brackets) when necessary; and removing distracting colloquialisms. More significantly, Appo was frequently confused about when the various events in his life occurred. To clear up this confusion, I reorganized his narrative so that the text more accurately follows the chronology of his life. Purists may be dissatisfied; they are invited to read the complete and unedited version available to the public.

ACKNOWLEDGMENTS

Like crime itself, writing about the underworld is full of unexpected turns and hidden adventures. The documentation that substantiates the details in George Appo's autobiography is found primarily in two manuscript collections. First, I am especially grateful to Jean Ashton, Bernard R. Crystal, and Jennifer Lee at the Rare Book and Manuscript Library of Columbia University. They helped preserve the original autobiography, generously gave me access to Appo's other manuscripts, and allowed me to quote extensively from them. Second, I never would have been able to locate and examine the sources that verify the details in Appo's autobiography but for the dedication of the librarians and staff at the New York City Municipal Archives and Records Center. For more than two decades, Ken Cobb, Leonora Gidlund, and Evelyn Gonzales shared with me their unsurpassed knowledge of the many hidden stories of New York history. Without their help, it would have been impossible to authenticate Appo's autobiography. I remain forever in their debt.

Other historians, librarians, and archivists offered invaluable assistance and support. Ursula Schultz of Loyola University Chicago and James D. Folts, William Gorman, and Richard Andress of the New York State Archives helped locate some of the sources that appear in this volume. At the Newberry Library in Chicago, I profited from the numerous conversations and criticisms generously offered by curators, staff, and fellows, particularly Richard Brown, Elliott Gorn, James Grossman, Sidney Harring, Fred Hoxie, and Alfred Young. Christopher Ramsey accurately transcribed and helped edit the documents. For more than twenty years, my colleagues at Loyola University Chicago offered ideas, support, and friendship. I am especially grateful to Mark Allee; Dina Berger; Robert Bireley, S.J.; Robert O. Bucholz; Anthony Cardoza; Patricia Clemente; Sheldon Cohen; David Dennis; John Donoghue; Leslie Dossey; Lewis Erenberg; Frank Fennell; Elizabeth Fraterrigo; the late Joseph Gagliano; William Galush; the Reverend Michael Garanzini, S.J.; Zouhair Ghazzal; Walter Gray; the Reverend William Grogan; Theresa Gross-Diaz; Edin Hajdarpasic; Lillian Hardison; Ann Harrington; Jo Hays; Elizabeth Hemenway; Susan Hirsch; Theodore Karamanski; Suzanne Kaufman; Michael Khodarkovsky; Tom Knapp; Christopher Manning; the Reverend John McManamon, S.J.; Patricia Mooney-Melvin; Prudence Moylan; Michelle Nickerson; Janet Nolan; Paula Pfeffer; John Pincince; Harold Platt; Kyle Roberts; Barbara Rosenwein; Sylvia Rdzak; Kim Searcy; Stephen Schloesser, S.J.; Elizabeth Shermer; Marek Suszko; and Elena Valussi.

Several institutions provided financial and other support. Loyola University Chicago provided two paid leaves of absence. Fellowships from the Newberry Library, the National Endowment for the Humanities, the National Museum of American History of the Smithsonian Institution, the John Simon Guggenheim Memorial Foundation, and the Minow Family Foundation gave me both time and money.

Several individuals read the introduction and edited version of Appo's autobiography, especially Elliott Gorn, Timothy Spears, and Brad Verter. Their suggestions and criticisms have made this a better book, as have those of other reviewers: Jeffrey Alder, University of Florida; Daniel Czitrom, Mount Holyoke College; Kenneth Heineman, Angelo State

University; Andrew Kersten, University of Wisconsin–Green Bay; Alan Lessoff, Illinois State University; Allen Steinberg, University of Iowa; and Matthew Avery Sutton, Washington State University. I am especially indebted to developmental editor Debra Michals for her lengthy summary of suggestions made by others and for her detailed positive criticisms at a critical stage of revision. The team at Bedford/St. Martin's was supportive in guiding this project from its inception to the finished product, especially William Lombardo, Mary Dougherty, Jane Knetzger, Heidi Hood, Laura Kintz, and Andrea Cava. Nancy Benjamin of Books By Design shepherded the book through its final stages.

As I have written elsewhere, my greatest thanks belong to my family. Jerry Gilfoyle, Linda Pattee, and Adele Alexander opened their homes and shared their cars in my research trips. Reyna Cerrato played with and cared for my children when I was away. My mother and father helped me locate the physical sites described in George Appo's autobiography and waited patiently outside libraries and historical societies throughout New York while I perused old manuscripts and local newspapers. I regret that neither lived long enough to read the books that resulted from their personal sacrifices. I do not regret that my children, Maria and Danielle, interrupted me to fill the pool or drive them to soccer, ballet, swimming, or ice-skating practice. My wife, Mary Rose Alexander, has lived with (and tolerated) George Appo as long as I have. Only a spouse would have put up with him for all these years.

Timothy J. Gilfoyle

Contents

Illustrations

THE BEDFORD SERIES IN HISTORY AND CULTURE

The Urban Underworld in Late Nineteenth-Century New York

The Autobiography of George Appo

WITH RELATED DOCUMENTS

PART ONE

Introduction: Cultures of Crime

George Appo (1856–1930) was one of America's first "good fellows"[1] — a criminal who considered his illegal enterprise to be an entrepreneurial craft and shared an ethic of loyalty, male honor, and camaraderie among his fellow outlaws. As the United States industrialized during the nineteenth century, crime emerged as a major urban problem, and social networks of men and women immersed in the "informal economies" of American cities appeared. Pickpocketing, prostitution, counterfeiting, opium use, and gambling were daily reminders of new forms of illicit behavior and urban disorder. More important, criminal establishments — unlicensed saloons, opium dens, gambling halls, and brothels — became common, tolerated, and often visible parts of urban life and popular culture. Such places created fluid communities and safe havens for men and women who experienced frequent arrests and incarcerations, shared criminal enterprises, and indulged in illicit drug consumption. Law enforcement officials were convinced that these so-called good fellows were "professional" criminals. George Appo epitomized this new kind of criminal character.

The growing concerns and fears associated with crime transformed America. Efforts to address the illegal activity generated the first professional police forces; the birth of the detective (the "private eye") and detective agencies; the rapid expansion of penitentiaries, jails, and other custodial institutions; and even Progressive reform. Yet we know little about the early criminal subcultures. Popular films and television shows — William Wellman's *The Public Enemy* (1931), Francis Ford Coppola's *The Godfather* (1972), Martin Scorsese's *Gangs of New York* (2002), and HBO's *The Sopranos* (1999–2007) — have not only glamorized the underworld of the nineteenth- and twentieth-century metropolis but also have frequently defined how Americans think about crime. Still, the actual social environments and networks of criminals and other participants in the nineteenth-century underworld remain elusive.

In one significant way, George Appo was no ordinary convict. Though lacking any formal education and illiterate into his adult years, he wrote an autobiography.[2] Appo's reminiscence offers a rare window into the hidden and forgotten underworld of Gilded Age (1870–1900) America and the beginnings of Progressive Era (1890–1920) reform. What social forces, for example, encouraged certain men and women in late nineteenth-century cities to resort to crime? What role did race, class, and gender play in the choices individuals made to engage in certain criminal activities? Did massive urbanization and industrial capitalism create new types of crime? How did the new and expanding nineteenth-century penal system treat convicts? How did convicts react to incarceration? What forces created opium dens and the nation's first drug trade and allowed that trade to flourish in American cities? Did social networks exist that bonded male criminals together in distinct and organized subcultures? Can contemporary social structures and institutional supports of organized crime be traced back to the late nineteenth century? Appo's autobiography addresses all these questions.

WHO WAS GEORGE APPO?

Appo was the offspring of a racially mixed marriage. Born on the Fourth of July 1856, he was the son of Catherine Fitzpatrick, an immigrant fleeing famine in her native Ireland, and Chang Quimbo Appo, one of the earliest Chinese immigrants in New York City. Quimbo was convicted of manslaughter in 1859 and sent "up the river" to New York's Sing Sing Prison. Shortly thereafter, Catherine reportedly died in an accident at sea. Effectively orphaned by the age of five, George was raised by informal foster families (neighbors who took him in) in America's most notorious ghetto—New York's Five Points neighborhood in lower Manhattan. He claimed he never spent a day in a classroom; instead, the streets of Gotham were his school. George's childhood resembled that of the fictional characters created by Charles Dickens (Oliver Twist) and Victor Hugo (Jean Valjean in *Les Misérables*). But his tale was hardly fiction; his was the life of a burgeoning American underclass—what some considered a criminal proletariat—in the new industrial city.

Figure 1. *George Appo as a Teenager or Young Adult*

This undated photograph was probably taken by New York police officials after one of his earliest arrests and then publicly displayed in the "Rogue's Gallery" of Police Headquarters, a collection of hundreds of photos of convicted and suspected criminals in the city. The Rogue's Gallery was popularized by chief detective Thomas Byrnes after 1880, and reflected the growing anonymity of New York's rapid nineteenth-century urbanization.

Source: George Appo folder, Box 32, Society for the Prevention of Crime Papers, Rare Book and Manuscript Library, Columbia University, New York.

The first half of George Appo's life confirmed the maxim, "Give me the child for his first seven years, and I will give you the man." Under the informal and sometimes neglectful care of a variety of Five Points families, he worked and scave[...] [...]bers and living by his [...] d of pickpocketing, a [...] heir meager earnings. [...] n in excess of $500 (t[...] fer- ing the pockets [...] [...]er, more lucrative for

Appo's success [...] ro- duced him to opiu[...] [...]to adulthood. He spe[...] nd asylums. His teeth [...] nd he was subjected t[...] nt outside prison. He[...] [...]is throat was slashed [...] [...]a- sions. One shooting[...] [...]4, Appo was forced to[...] g police corruption ii[...] y front-page news in [...] [...]. For years thereafter [...] the target of numerous retributive assaults.

*[Handwritten annotations: • pickpocketing → changes of urban economy; • violent; • violence in jail; * Society for Prevention of Crime → turned over a new leaf]*

When Appo was in his mid-forties, the combination of unemployment, his violent lifestyle, and his advancing age convinced him to renounce his life of crime. After 1910, he became an employee of the Society for the Prevention of Crime, a private anticrime organization in New York. He worked briefly as an actor and was an aspiring poet. For a time, his transformation was held up as a model by certain Progressive reformers, who labeled him "the finest crook that ever turned a new leaf"[4] (Document 5). He died in 1930.

THE RISE OF THE PICKPOCKET

George Appo's life coincided with the era when crime became a major problem in American cities. The most frequently punished serious offenses (excluding intoxication and similar forms of disorderly conduct) in nineteenth-century cities were crimes involving some form of property, such as larceny, robbery, and burglary.* By 1830, more

---

* Larceny is the unlawful taking and carrying away of a person's personal property, robbery is the illegal taking of property from a person by violence or intimidation, and burglary is breaking into another's dwelling with the intent to commit a felony.

than half the punished offenses in Boston, New York, and Philadelphia were larceny cases. For the remainder of the century, law enforcement officials noted the rising number of forgery, fraud, counterfeiting, shoplifting, and other property crime cases. The growing disparity between the rich and the poor as the United States industrialized and urbanized, combined with the increasing availability and display of consumer products in department stores and elsewhere, likely contributed to the rise of purloined property. In 1886, New York's chief detective, Thomas Byrnes, began his best-selling book *Professional Criminals of America* (Document 9) with the statement, "Crimes against property are of . . . frequent occurrence in the cities and towns of this country."[5]

The most sophisticated of those who regularly engaged in property theft were pickpockets. Allan Pinkerton, the most influential private detective in American history, conceded that "of all the departments of crime as now practiced, there is not one which contains a larger number of adept operators than that of pickpockets." One pickpocket described the post–Civil War period as "the halcyon days for us."[6]

The rise of pickpocketing (especially by young boys) and other new criminal activities were, in part, products of the changing urban economy. After 1840, teenage apprentices virtually disappeared from urban workshops across the United States. Young males, previously trained and supervised in craft and household environments, were increasingly employed in more impersonal factories. The decline of craft employment occurred at the very moment that New York experienced a growing demand for various street trades—peddlers, hucksters, scavengers,* bootblacks, and newsboys—and an unprecedented flood of European immigrants. Between 1840 and 1855, an estimated two-thirds of all U.S. immigrants passed through Gotham, most serving as a source of cheap labor in the growing industrial and commercial economies. By 1860, half the city was foreign-born, a pattern replicated in growing urban centers nationwide. Increasingly, certain parts of the working class, especially those trapped in the casual and unskilled labor market, were pushed into street trades and the informal, underground economies. Many were youths between eight and eighteen years of age with parents of rural or peasant origins who relied on every family member's contributions for their economic survival. Appo was one such example.

Pocket-picking teenagers reflected this dramatic economic transformation. In New York, less than 10 percent of teenagers arrested as

---

* A huckster is a retailer of small articles, especially a peddler of fruits and vegetables or an aggressive peddler. A scavenger is someone who searches through and collects items from discarded material.

pickpockets worked in factories, served in apprenticeships, or attended school, indicating the lack of access to education or more formal employment opportunities (because of their age) of many low-income or immigrant youths. Most young pickpockets were recruited into the activity by peers who, like themselves, worked in nonindustrial, low-paying, service-sector jobs such as selling newspapers, shining shoes, or peddling goods. The overwhelming majority of these youthful larcenists were between the ages of fourteen and seventeen (more than 80 percent), native-born (more than 80 percent), and male (more than 90 percent). Many, like Appo, were the offspring of immigrants. Most never considered themselves to be children; the vast majority identified themselves as adult wage earners because of their early entry into the workforce. In fact, more claimed to be "unemployed" than students in school. To so-called child pickpockets, the term was an oxymoron.[7]

The changing social ecology of the street also facilitated such behavior. By the mid-nineteenth century, city thoroughfares served multiple functions for urban youths: workplaces, amusement centers, even homes. During the 1850s, New York police chief George W. Matsell and the Reverend Samuel B. Halliday separately estimated that 5,000 to 10,000 boys lived on Gotham's streets. Another minister believed that between 10,000 and 30,000 unsupervised children roamed the city's streets. In 1870, New York's Children's Aid Society provided various services to more than 24,000 children, including nearly 6,000 orphans and 15,000 homeless youths. In 1876 alone, Gotham's police force "recovered" 5,593 "stray" children. In fact, approximately 150 children in New York were abandoned by their impoverished families every month during the 1870s. One 1886 report claimed that 12,000 homeless youths could be found nightly "wandering in the street."[8]

In this context—youthful poverty, rapid urbanization, declining apprenticeship opportunities, and immigrant and labor market competition—Appo's childhood evolution from newsboy to pickpocket was nothing out of the ordinary. Contemporary observers surmised that most of the city's pickpockets learned the trade as youths working as newsboys and bootblacks. Charles Loring Brace of the Children's Aid Society openly feared that the majority of child peddlers, newsboys, and other youthful street workers became pickpockets, petty thieves, or prostitutes. "A boy can get next to a woman in a car or on the street more easily than a man can," one former pickpocket said, "and if he is a handsome, innocent-looking boy, and clever, he can go far in this line of graft." Children, teenagers, and other young panhandlers and pickpockets migrated to the most heavily traveled and crowded streets to hawk—and sometimes pilfer—goods. In Manhattan, lower Broadway even earned the nickname "pickpockets' paradise."[9]

Conditions in the new industrial city contributed to the emergence of this criminal class. First, the physical intimacy of densely packed sidewalks made picking pockets easy. Second, nineteenth-century pedestrians carried valuables in their coats and outer garments, in part for convenience and also because men's trousers sometimes lacked pockets. Most coats included external pockets with no flaps, a pickpocket's dream. Watches, wallets, and other possessions were there for the taking.[10] Third, nineteenth-century businessmen, bank messengers, and ordinary pedestrians routinely carried large sums of cash and valuables on their person. Credit cards did not exist until the twentieth century, and only a few Americans had personal checking accounts. Such accounts were largely irrelevant, however, since many merchants did not accept checks, especially from strangers, and most purchases were cash transactions.

Pickpockets shared a certain sense of their identity and a camaraderie. Detective Allan Pinkerton lamented that pickpockets considered themselves to be part of a "profession" and had "just as high a regard for their reputations as have the most *au fait* [expert] gentlemen in society." He acknowledged that some preferred to work alone but most traveled in groups numbering between two and five. Accomplices moved ahead of the pickpocket himself, jostling oncoming pedestrians and identifying potential victims, then signaling to the pickpocket behind them. Boston detectives Benjamin P. Eldridge and William B. Watts believed that the more skilled pickpockets relied on dexterity and nimbleness, rather than rude shoving, to remove money, watches, and wallets.[11]

This fraternity of thieves shared a distinctive, arcane language. Novelist Herman Melville described this vernacular as "the foulest of all human lingoes, that dialect of sin and death, known as the Cant language, or the Flash." Indeed, the lingo was hard to comprehend. Pickpockets referred to their accomplices as "mobs." The actual larceny was a "touch," which was performed by a "wire," a "pick," a "bugger," or a "tool," while "stalls" or "pushers" distracted or bumped the victim. The "cover" made sure no one was watching. The streets, parks, or trolleys where they worked were "beats." Pocketbooks were "leathers," and money was a "roll." Former police chief George W. Matsell's *Vocabulum; or, The Rogue's Lexicon* (1859) was among the earliest national exposés of this distinctive oral culture (Document 6). Overhearing one conversation, a reporter confessed that he found pickpockets impossible to understand, as if they spoke in a foreign tongue.[12]

DRUGS AND CRIME

What did Appo and his associates do with their stolen earnings? Appo succinctly explained: "I lay around the Opium Joints and Dives of the City, . . . where I would pass the nights in these dance halls making a good fellow out of myself, spen[d]ing the dishonest money I made grafting during the day."[13] In American cities, new leisure institutions — "dives," such as concert saloons, opium dens, and ordinary saloons — emerged in the mid-nineteenth century to meet the recreational and consumer demands of the growing population. There pickpockets, con men, and other criminals spent their ill-gotten profits. There they went upon release from jail or prison. There they got reacquainted with former associates and met future accomplices. There they socialized within a wider network of those engaged in illicit activities. And there "gangs" and criminal confederates congregated to relax and plan their enterprises. This was the milieu of the good fellow.

After 1860, opium dens were also an integral part of the first drug and bohemian subcultures in American cities. Often located in the back rooms of tenements or concert saloons, opium dens provided a physical space for patrons in search of the relaxing euphoria that came with smoking the drug. Proprietors prepared and served opium, while patrons reclined on beds or platforms that extended the length of the rooms. On crowded nights, smoke filled the dens, sometimes so thick it was impossible to see more than a few yards away. Initially organized by Chinese immigrants and commonly associated with "Chinatowns" in New York and other American cities, opium dens were commonplace by the end of the nineteenth century. "It is a mistake to assume that Chinatown is honeycombed with opium 'joints,'" journalist Jacob Riis wrote in 1890. "There are a good many more outside of it than in it."[14]

Opium dens were also controversial because of the diverse array of people who gathered there. Within the smoke-filled spaces, respectable actors and actresses, artists, and wealthy clubmen interacted with thieves, con men, and prostitutes. Middle-class, native-born Euro-Americans mingled with Asian and other foreign-born immigrants. An exotic and erotic "Orientalism" merged with a rough-and-tough male hedonism. While these socially integrated spaces and hidden subcultures never developed the intellectual vitality, middle-class consciousness, or large female participation characteristic of urban bohemias in the twentieth century, opium dens nevertheless promoted an ethic of cosmopolitan fantasy and dangerous pleasure. They surely challenged the dominant American values of self-sacrifice, hard work, sexual abstinence, and postponement of pleasure. Prophetically, one reporter predicted that "in the next century, instead of the old-fashioned temperance agitation, we shall have a great moral and religious battle with opium smoking."[15] He was half-right; in the twentieth century, the opium subculture would be supplanted by cocaine, crack, and other narcotic subcultures.

For men like Appo, the opium den served as a "school," much as the street had earlier in their lives. An addict by his teenage years, Appo admitted that opium dens offered not only relaxation and escape but also the opportunity to meet like-minded associates interested in alternative and safer forms of graft. "The different systems" or "sure thing graft," as Appo described them, were confidence (or con) games* with very high rates of success. "Criminal occupation," concluded detective Thomas Byrnes, "is, like everything else, progressive." The opium den offered Appo the opportunity to progress to more lucrative criminal endeavors.[16]

GREEN GOODS

Opium dens were where Appo was introduced to the "green goods game." When Appo was invited to join Eddie Parmeley's criminal gang, he ascended to perhaps the most lucrative confidence game in nineteenth-century America. For the first time, he avoided the "tough graft" of pickpocketing, with its many risks, most notably the threat of frequent incarceration. Confidence games such as bunco, dice, short cards, flimflam,† and selling fake jewelry were much less dangerous. Although they required bankrolls and large sums of cash immediately available they qualified as "sure thing graft" because of their higher rates of success.[17] The most successful of these cons was the green goods game (Document 11).

The green goods game was creative. Operators sent letters to individuals throughout the United States offering genuine-looking counterfeit cash, or "green goods," manufactured from stolen U.S. Treasury currency engraving plates. Prospective buyers were offered cut-rate prices: $1,200 of counterfeit currency for $100, even $10,000 for $600. For purchasing the maximum amount available, the individual was promised a monopoly of the sale of green goods in his region. Interested parties were instructed to rendezvous at certain hotels in the New York

---

* Swindles in which the victim is defrauded after his or her confidence has been won.
† Bunco games and flimflam were various swindles in which the perpetrator cheated while gambling or persuaded a person to buy worthless property.

metropolitan area, where they met a "bunco steerer," who directed, or "steered," them to the goods at another hotel or office. There the steerer introduced the interested party to "the old gentleman," who displayed the goods. The buyer examined the alleged counterfeit money, which was actually genuine legal tender. When the buyer agreed to purchase the greenbacks and turned to make his payment, a "ringer" standing behind a movable wall substituted an identical bag for the one containing the money. The buyer usually express-mailed the package home to avoid suspicion from railroad and other detectives. When he eventually opened the bag at home, he would find only worthless sheets of blank paper, a brick, or even sawdust instead of the counterfeit cash. Humiliated and empty-handed, the victim had no legal recourse, since he himself was guilty of attempting to defraud the U.S. government.[18]

The green goods game was a sophisticated con. The most successful operations required considerable finance, elaborate hierarchies, and political protection. Leading financial backers, called "capitalists" by their confederates, supplied bankrolls of $3,000 to $20,000 to display before potential victims. That was a huge sum of money in an age when an unskilled worker earned less than $1,000 a year. Collusion and a "working partnership" with the police were necessities, according to reformer and journalist William T. Stead (Document 11). Financial backers generally earned 50 percent of each successful scam, out of which they paid the police for "protection."[19]

The green goods game was an unintended product of the new national, market-based economy. Indeed, in the decades following the Civil War, few issues spawned more social conflict than national finance. Debates over paper money, federal debt repayment, national banks, and the silver versus the gold standard occupied the attention of American political and business leaders. These controversies ultimately generated new political movements, embodied the Greenback party and Populism.[20] The increasing reliance on greenbacks as the nation's paper currency inadvertently gave new life to the crime of counterfeiting and related confidence games. It also generated a new urban underworld with an emerging class of professional criminals such as Appo. Although Appo worked as a cigar maker, hatter, barber, and even an actor at various points during his life, he was at heart a pickpocket and con man. By the 1880s, he was enmeshed in an informal but complex system of pickpockets, fences, opium addicts, and, most important, green goods operators.

The world of the green goods operators was inextricably rooted in the era's male underworld of pleasure. Illicit activities such as prostitution, gambling, and opium use overlapped and fertilized one another

(Documents 7 and 10). By some accounts, "nearly all" green goods men were "opium fiends." News, municipal, and other reports mentioned finding opium-smoking materials on the premises of green goods offices during police raids. Other green goods establishments were described as "virtual opium dens." The "Haymarket* pimps" Adolph Saunders and Harry Hilton, who invited George Appo to join one green goods gang, were identified as "opium fiends." New York police captain James McLaughlin summarized the common belief that most green goods participants were opium addicts: "They all hit the pipe."[21]

The green goods game exemplified the emergence of a new criminal phenomenon: organized crime. Although the term was popularized with the illegal economies associated with Prohibition after 1920, the label "organized crime" was initially applied to both the green goods business and Tammany Hall, New York City's Democratic party political machine in the 1890s.[22] More significantly, the green goods business was an early example of a national, market-based criminal network organized to distribute illegal goods to willing customers. Green goods organizations required substantial capital, high investment returns, an ongoing hierarchical organization, the threat of violence to achieve monopoly power, and talented, or "professional," operatives. Such characteristics later defined organized crime in twentieth-century America. Similarly, the green goods game was facilitated by new transcontinental transportation technologies such as the railroad, mass communication systems including the telegraph and transcontinental postal service, novel financial instruments such as greenbacks, and changing patterns of leisure in the form of dives and opium dens. Appo's criminal activities were, for the first time, national in their scope.[23]

POLICING THE INDUSTRIAL CITY

George Appo's criminal career also coincided with the emergence of modern policing, the detective (both public and private), and new forms of criminal justice. The population of the three largest U.S. cities—New York, Chicago, and Philadelphia—increased twentyfold or more between 1800 and 1890. (By contrast, between 1900 and 2000 the population of these cities increased by a factor of less than three.) Although homicide and violent crime rates in the largest U.S. cities

---

*The Haymarket at 29th Street and Sixth Avenue was a prominent concert saloon known for promoting prostitution.

declined after 1865 and cities by some measures actually grew safer, fear of crime increased due to the social changes resulting from the rapid population growth and immigration. Newspaper editors and other writers described New York City, for example, as a "carnival of crime."[24] Periodic riots—New York in 1834, 1837, 1849, and 1863; Boston in 1834 and 1837; Philadelphia in 1844; Baltimore in 1856, 1857, and 1858; and New Orleans from 1854 to 1856—spawned nationwide fear of increasing lawlessness. These and other forms of disorder contributed to the adoption of professional police forces at mid-century: New York and Philadelphia in 1845, New Orleans and Cincinnati in 1852, Boston in 1854, Chicago in 1855, and Baltimore in 1857.[25]

Even with professional law enforcement agencies, American cities had smaller police forces than their European counterparts. New York, for example, had fewer officers per capita than either London or Paris. European cities usually provided one police officer for approximately every 250 to 350 residents; New York hired only one officer for every 400 to 550 citizens.[26] By 1890, New York's police force of approximately 3,400 was dwarfed by the 12,000 gendarmes in Paris and the 14,000 bobbies in London.[27] As Table 1 shows, New York in the nineteenth century compared to the twentieth century was poorly policed.

The minimal number of police officers and the reluctance to establish large, government-controlled law enforcement agencies was hardly unique to New York. Early nineteenth-century Americans were very suspicious of armed central authority. Fear of arbitrary armed power in cities dated back at least to the Boston Massacre of 1770, in which British soldiers shot and killed members of a group of unarmed colonists.

Table 1. *New York City Police Force*

YEAR	NUMBER OF POLICE	BUDGET (MILLIONS OF DOLLARS)	POPULATION	RATIO OF POLICE TO RESIDENTS	PER CAPITA COST (DOLLARS)
1850	901	.488	515,547	1:572	.95
1860	1,473	1.395	813,669	1:552	1.71
1870	2,325	2.901 (1869)	942,292	1:405	3.07
1880	2,159	3.227	1,164,673	1:539	2.77
1890	3,410	4.588	1,441,216	1:423	3.18
1900	7,426	11.993	3,437,202	1:463	3.49
1950	19,789	101.965	7,891,957	1:399	12.92
1975	42,165	—	7,483,000	1:177	—
1990	26,911	1,627.488	7,322,564	1:272	222.26

Many equated a professional, uniformed force with monarchy and anti-republican violence. Still others believed that municipal institutions such as the police should reflect community concerns. In 1839, for example, New York mayor Isaac Varian said the police should be "but a part of the citizens."[28] Consequently, most cities in the first half of the nineteenth century were policed by a small number of nonprofessional (by later standards), unarmed constables or marshals.

Even as large American cities adopted professional law enforcement agencies during the mid-nineteenth century, the low number of officers reflected the historical ambivalence regarding police power. Most U.S. cities had even smaller police forces than New York. In 1890, several of the ten largest cities had well over 500 residents for every police officer, notably Chicago (589), St. Louis (686), Cincinnati (634), and Cleveland (900). Other large cities exceeded 700 residents per officer, including Buffalo (843), St. Paul (747), Minneapolis (772), Columbus, Ohio (784), Pittsburgh (816), Toledo (984), Milwaukee (1,025), and Rochester, New York (1,106).[29] The scarcity of police officers challenged their ability to monitor and control criminal activities and networks.

Police departments did, however, enjoy distinctive powers. Most notably, vagrancy statutes enacted by most states after the Civil War made the process of justice "summary"—that is, defendants were arrested "summarily" without a warrant and without due process of the law. Police were not compelled to inform a defendant of his or her civil or legal rights upon arrest or interrogation. (The so-called Miranda warning, or Miranda rights, was not required until 1966.) They could arrest suspicious people on sight or based on a complaint and lock them up without bail until trial. Police called such tactics "preventive arrests." Suspects were usually tried without a jury and assumed guilty unless they could rebut police testimony with "a good account of themselves," supported with alibis or witnesses. Police officers' frequent use of the nightstick and other forms of sanctioned violence led one observer to describe them as "the autocrats of the sidewalk."[30]

Some police officials aggressively exploited their power. In 1880, for example, New York's chief detective, Thomas Byrnes, established a "dead line," authorizing police to arrest any criminal suspect south of Fulton Street (Document 9). The action transformed Byrnes into a hero among Wall Street businessmen. The threat of preventive arrest enabled Byrnes to force visiting "professional criminals" to appear before him upon entering New York City and promise not to engage in any criminal activity while there. Byrnes also employed and defended the "third degree"—violent interrogation methods that included punching suspects in the face, whipping them with a hose, squeezing their testicles, and other forms of physical intimidation.[31]

By the 1870s, New York's police courts disposed of more than 84,000 cases annually, equivalent to one of every twelve New Yorkers or one of every nine male residents. The overwhelming majority of these defendants (95 percent by 1895) were arrested summarily and without due process. During the final quarter of the nineteenth century, the total number of men arrested over each five-year period was roughly equal to New York City's entire adult male population. So many men passed through jails such as the Halls of Justice, nicknamed "the Tombs," that public officials often negotiated with inmates regarding their treatment, dispersing benefits to those possessing political, economic, or some other influence.[32]

Appo's experience with arrest reflected this distinctive form of nineteenth-century urban law. Arrest and incarceration, however, were common experiences not only among lawbreakers but also among transient working-class males (sometimes defined as "vagrants"). Individuals unable to find a secure footing in the boom-and-bust urban industrial economy, especially those excluded by background, race, unemployment, or misfortune, were subjected to an aggressive and often harsh system of justice.

POLITICS AND CRIME

Police and law enforcement officials sometimes tolerated certain forms of crime. During the second half of the nineteenth century, professional criminals operated "within reason" in return for bribing the right officials. In New York, well-known burglars and pickpockets reportedly paid police officials in central headquarters on a weekly basis to avoid prosecution. Leading pickpockets divided specific blocks or areas among themselves, giving each a monopoly, and reported on competitors who violated such agreements. The most successful pickpockets even hired clever attorneys who fought any arrest with a writ of habeas corpus (a court order releasing a prisoner from unlawful detention). "The old system," wrote journalist Lincoln Steffens (Document 10), "was built upon the understood relations of the crooks and the detective bureau."[33]

The most visible example of municipal toleration of criminal activity was the "vice economy" associated with prostitution. In the early nineteenth century, theater operators in New York, Chicago, Philadelphia, Boston, St. Louis, Cincinnati, New Orleans, and Mobile, Alabama, routinely permitted prostitutes to solicit and conduct business in the balcony—the so-called third tier—of their establishments. By mid-century, the brothel was the preeminent institution in urban America's underground economy. New York had more than five hundred of them, and other large cities counted several hundred as well. None of this was legal; rather, commercial sex thrived in the streets, saloons, and entertainment areas (sometimes called red-light districts) of cities via an informal system of citizen toleration, municipal bribery, and weak policing. The considerable amount and public visibility of prostitution begot legalization movements between 1850 and 1920. New Orleans (1857–1859 and 1897–1917) and St. Louis (1870–1874) legalized some forms of commercial sex. San Francisco (1911–1913) instituted a system of medical inspection of prostitutes.[34] These were exceptions, however. Most calls for regulation, including one by a New York Assembly committee in 1876 (Document 7), proved unsuccessful.[35] More often, an informal, corrupt, decentralized de facto system of regulation emerged in cities. "In most of the precincts of the city," complained a New York Senate committee report in 1895 (Document 8), "houses of ill-repute, gambling houses, policy shops, pool rooms and unlawful resorts of a similar character were being openly conducted under the eyes of the police." It was little more than a system of "licensed crime."[36]

George Appo personified how the subcultures of commercial sex, entertainment, drug use, pickpocketing, and other "licensed" criminal activities intersected with urban politics and law enforcement. As a child growing up in Donovan's Lane in lower Manhattan, he described how gambling, alcoholism, robbery, and the fencing of stolen goods were part of his everyday life. The opium dens he frequented as an adult were filled with professional entertainers from the theater, as well as men and women involved in the business of commercial sex. Appo's introduction to the lucrative green goods con game occurred in an opium den by criminals he described as "Haymarket pimps"—well-educated men involved in the sexual underworld of Gotham's most popular concert saloons. His greatest success came as a green goods steerer. His employer, Jimmy McNally, began "as a bully who was kept by a prostitute," according to the evangelical reformer William T. Stead, before going on to run a restaurant, saloon, and political club allied with Tammany Hall (Document 11). The *New York Tribune* even equated New York Democrats with the underworld: "As the grog shop is the Democratic nursery, so . . . bawdy publications are their fairy stories."[37]

Numerous municipal reformers, church leaders, and honest public officials were outraged by this systemic toleration of street-level crime and political extortion. Government investigations, often instigated by Republican party officials, repeatedly demonstrated the pervasive and seedy connections between public officials and outlaw activities. This was especially true in North America's largest metropolis. In 1875, New York City mayor William Wickham and a state assembly committee investigating the causes of crime in New York concluded that much of the police force was corrupt (Document 7). In 1884, a legislative committee chaired by future U.S. president Theodore Roosevelt confirmed that police officials not only tolerated but actually promoted certain forms of gambling and prostitution. In the 1890s, New York State investigatory committees — the Fassett Committee in 1890, the Lexow Committee in 1894 (Document 8), and the Mazet Committee in 1899 — documented numerous ongoing examples of police collusion with multiple kinds of criminal commerce. Law enforcement officials used their power "not to enforce the laws," argued critics, "but to wring from lawbreakers a share of their booty."[38] To many, the line separating law enforcement and criminal activity was nonexistent.

THE PENITENTIARY

The fear of increasing crime contributed to the expansion of prisons and the penitentiary system throughout the United States. Pickpockets such as Appo rarely avoided arrest and clashes with the law. Appo himself was arrested more than a dozen times and spent more than a decade in at least eight different prisons, jails, and asylums. Within these different institutions, he encountered an astonishing diversity of incarcerations: a year of juvenile reform on the school-ship *Mercury*; three sentences in the workshops of Sing Sing; part of a prison term in the wood and hat shops of Clinton; more than a year in Blackwell's Island; at least six incarcerations in the Tombs; several weeks in Philadelphia's Moyamensing Jail, followed by the isolation of Eastern State Penitentiary; and more than two years in the Matteawan State Hospital for the Criminally Insane.

Appo's penitentiary and jailhouse experiences reflected the variety of prison punishments. For example, he was trained in the techniques of seamanship on the school-ship *Mercury*, where he served his first sentence. The vessel was used as a municipal training and nautical school to counteract juvenile delinquency and child abandonment, as well as to deflect criticism of the Children's Aid Society's policy of sending such youths to farms in the West. The municipal program presaged future

Progressive Era reforms designed to combat teenage criminality. In the early 1870s, the *Mercury* made five or six 10-day trips annually, as well as a three- to four-month winter cruise. Upon release, the male charges were qualified to serve in the Navy or merchant marine.

The *Mercury* was a unique experiment (cost and criticism led the city to abandon the program in 1875). More common was the inconsistent, inadequate, and often corrupt supervision Appo witnessed in county prisons such as New York's Blackwell's Island Penitentiary, where criminals sentenced to prison terms of one year or less were sent. Lax security allowed for frequent and easy escapes, euphemistically called "elopements" by some. Inmates mockingly referred to the facility as "the Old Homestead."[39]

Large penitentiaries such New York's Sing Sing and Clinton prisons, however, were not homesteads. Inmates in those institutions were subject to hard labor, frequent physical punishment, and repeated torture by officials. Beginning in the 1820s, New York State pioneered a new system of contractual penal servitude that was later adopted almost everywhere in the United States. Under this system, states allowed private manufacturers to establish factories in prisons. This would ensure that inmates engaged in hard labor, while also generating income to cover the costs of their incarceration. By the 1870s, Sing Sing housed the world's largest stove-manufacturing business in the world. Private contractors not only converted penitentiaries into profitable workshops (for themselves) but also exerted extensive control over the disciplinary and punishment regimes there. Such practices were reinforced with the passage of the Thirteenth Amendment to the U.S. Constitution in 1865, which outlawed slavery but protected punishment in prison as a form of legal involuntary servitude. The amendment stated, "Neither slavery nor involuntary servitude, except as a punishment for crime whereof the party shall have been duly convicted, shall exist within the United States, or any place subject to their jurisdiction." Convicts became, in effect, "slaves of the state."[40]

The combination of legal servitude and privatized contractual labor led to even harsher punishment by prison officials. Flogging and whipping with a cat-o-nine-tails (a multitailed whip) were common before being outlawed in 1847. In short order, they were replaced with equally terrifying mechanisms of pain: the yoke, the buck, and the shower bath. The yoke, sometimes called the crucifix, required strapping a thirty- to fifty-pound iron bar on the back of the outstretched arms and neck of an inmate, forcing him to bend forward and hold the bar's total weight on his lower vertebrae. The buck required tying an inmate's wrists

His community of clandestine commerce valued loyalty and consumption. A good fellow was "a money getter and spender," Appo insisted. He brandished his profits and shared his successes with his comrades in crime. Above all, he was trustworthy and dependable. When push came to shove, a good fellow suffered "the consequences and punishment of an arrest for some other fellow's evil doings both inside and outside of prison."[45]

Most reformers considered this to be a perverse ethic of loyalty, but to Appo a good fellow's values were rooted in shared suffering and riches. He endured solitary confinement in prison for refusing to identify an official who gave him a newspaper. He pickpocketed and schemed his way to Canada to bring an ailing accomplice back to his childhood home. He traveled more than 450 miles to bring news of a penitentiary cell mate to the man's family. He refused to implicate police officials with whom he conspired in various confidence games. He balked at pressing charges against men who violently assaulted him. He even forgave the man who shot out his eye.

Appo, however, lived in a violent world. He may have resorted to violence only in self-defense, but as much as he tried, he could not escape it. Indeed, Appo was more often a victim, exemplified by the multiple scars and missing eye visible to any observer. For him, a good fellow endured violence inflicted by others. Rather than strong-arming opponents to assert himself, Appo relished risk and avoided force. If one could not inflict pain, the ability to suffer it was a quintessential virtue. His honor, manhood, and masculinity revolved around duplicity, not muscle. Brains, not brawn, made a good fellow.[46]

PROGRESSIVE CRIMINOLOGY

Appo's final incarceration placed him in the forefront of Progressive Era criminology. In 1896, he was arrested after a violent saloon confrontation. His attorney, Ambrose H. Purdy, feared for Appo's safety in prison in light of his testimony before New York State's Lexow Committee two years earlier (Document 8). Purdy's solution: convince the judge to declare his client insane. Appo thus became one of the first individuals subjected to a psychological examination before sentencing. Only a few months earlier, New York judges had been given the power to send indicted but unconvicted individuals to a state psychiatric hospital, rather than a penitentiary, if they were deemed mentally ill. For nearly three years (1896–1899), Appo was held in the Matteawan State Hospital for the Criminally Insane in upstate New York (Document 3).

Appo's "indeterminate sentence" (that is, a sentence of no definite duration) reflected the growing desire by Progressive reformers, legal authorities, and social scientists to treat criminal behavior in new ways that were sensitive to the environment in which criminals lived and were raised. In addition, after 1890 judicial and Progressive reformers were increasingly critical of the absence of careful mental and physical examinations of defendants and convicted felons prior to sentencing. Legal reforms focused on the social causes of crime, not simply punishing deviant individuals. Urban courts and penitentiaries, argued reformers, should transform criminal behavior, eliminate child abuse, "Americanize" immigrants, and improve public health. Consequently, court magistrates, police justices, and justices of the peace became less independent in sentencing and fell under the centralized control of new legal authorities. Municipalities created specialized courts to address problems associated with women (prostitution), juveniles (child crime or abuse), and family disputes (divorce). Criminal law merged with social work, welfare reform, medical and psychiatric evaluation, and new sentencing options.

Appo's placement in Matteawan illustrated this more "socialized" approach to criminal behavior and legal remedy, which demanded greater intervention in the lives of defendants and convicted felons. In nearly a dozen previous arrests and run-ins with the law, no official ever questioned Appo's psychological health or social environment. Now, for the first time, urban courts adopted new evaluation techniques associated with psychiatry, medicine, and social work, often with the expressed purpose of preventing future criminal behavior. Compulsory medical and psychological examinations combined with new sentencing options—probation, parole, the indeterminate sentence, hospitalization of the insane, and eugenic sterilization* —to address urban crime. These legal reforms were the tangible products of the Progressive Era, as the urban legal system became a laboratory for democratic change.[47]

These changes extended into the penitentiary. Later Sing Sing wardens Thomas Mott Osborne (1914–1916) and Lewis E. Lawes (1920–1941; Document 4) heralded the rehabilitative potential of the prison and maintained that distinctions between prison culture and the culture

---

* Medical intervention by the state to remove or render unusable the reproductive organs of individuals defined as "inferior."

at large must be minimized. Both rejected the notion of a distinct "criminal class," arguing instead that criminal behavior originated from multiple causes and that criminals originated from all classes of society. Osborne created the Mutual Welfare League to encourage internal self-government within the prison and thereby transform convicts into citizens. Lawes established sports teams, music groups, and educational programs for inmates. Prisons failed, argued Osborne and Lawes, because they treated inmates as different from society at large, hence creating "artificial" and "unnatural" environments. Criminals did not constitute a separate class, but rather were similar to law-abiding members of society.[48]

THE CRIMINAL MEMOIR

The thin line between deviant and law-abiding citizens was a common theme in a new and popular nonfiction genre of the late nineteenth century—the criminal autobiography. Popular interest in the criminal underworld was hardly new. Urban crime narratives enjoyed considerable popularity throughout the nineteenth century. Beginning with Edgar Allan Poe in the early nineteenth century and continuing with George Foster, George Lippard, George Thompson, Ned Buntline, and George Wilkes, writers exploited the public's fascination with the "mysteries and miseries" of the antebellum underworld of New York, Philadelphia, New Orleans, San Francisco, and elsewhere.[49] These explorations into the dark side of city life, at times lurid and gruesome in tone, emerged from journalism, especially the penny and flash presses.* Many authors of criminal lore began their careers as reporters, frequently providing the first crime coverage in American newspapers. In most cases, they depicted the city as a polarized dichotomy, divided into areas of darkness and daylight, sunshine and shadow, respectability and unrespectability.

This method of crime reporting continued for the remainder of the century. Matthew Hale Smith's *Sunshine and Shadow in New York* (1868), Edward Crapsey's *The Nether Side of New York* (1872), and James D. McCabe's *New York by Sunlight and Gaslight* (1881) portrayed Gotham and other American cities as places of division and danger. Criminal attorneys such as William F. Howe and Abraham H. Hummel

---

* In the 1840s, the flash press covered and sometimes sensationalized the brothel underworld.

exploited similar fears with *In Danger* (1888), warning readers about "the snares and pitfalls of the crime and vice that await the unwary in New York."[50] And prominent reformers such as Charles Loring Brace, Anthony Comstock, and Helen Campbell resorted to the same literary devices in their descriptive accounts. James Buel's numerous publications, including *Mysteries and Miseries of America's Great Cities* (1883) and *Sunlight and Shadow of America's Great Cities* (1889), reflected the national scope and popularity of this genre.[51]

Law enforcement officials joined this literary fraternity late in the century. Police chiefs and detectives turned writers—such as George Washington Walling, Thomas Byrnes (Document 9), and William Mc-Adoo of New York; Benjamin P. Eldridge and William B. Watts of Boston; and Allan Pinkerton of Illinois—chronicled the most organized forms of crime. The detective became a fixture in true crime (nonfiction) narratives, a real-life American version of Sherlock Holmes. Nonfiction writers paid close attention to the structure, operations, and lifestyles of the criminal underworld. As firsthand but outside observers, these writers possessed a unique authoritative voice that gave their tales a sense of legitimacy and urgency. Crime, they argued, was increasingly professionalized, almost an art form. "The ways of making a livelihood by crime are many," warned Byrnes, "and the number of men and women who live by their wits in all large cities reaches into the thousands." The only way to counteract crime, these writers argued, was better law enforcement.[52]

Interest in criminal subcultures extended to the stage and popular culture. For example, shortly after Appo's controversial testimony before the Lexow Committee (Document 8) in 1894 and several failed attempts on his life, he and convicted concert saloon proprietor Tom Gould were invited to play themselves in a stage production about the underworld. *In the Tenderloin* opened in New Haven, Connecticut, before moving to Brooklyn, New York, and then the People's Theatre on the Bowery in New York, one of the three largest theaters in the city. The show eventually traveled to Syracuse, New York; Youngstown, Ohio; and Indianapolis before closing. Appo played to mixed reviews, but that mattered little (Document 12). His appearance in the melodrama marked the first time convicted felons appeared onstage, a reflection of the growing attraction of criminal life in popular culture.[53]

Appo's portrayal of himself onstage was simultaneous with the earliest memoirs of American criminals. George Bidwell's *Forging His Chains* (1888) and Langdon W. Moore's *His Own Story of His Eventful Life* (1893) were among the initial attempts by former convicts to recount their experiences. These were written as moral warnings, "to restrain that inordinate thirst for gold which seems fully as insatiable to-day as it was a score of years ago," according to Bidwell.[54] More often, criminal memoirs were evangelical sermons. In *A Pardoned Lifer* (1909), Opie Warner expressed his intention to help fathers guide their sons, especially those "who may think that the life of the bandit leads to greatness, a short cut to fame." Thomas Maslin's 1912 account of his criminal exploits culminated not only in his conversion to Christianity but also his entrance into the ministry. W. H. Flake's *From Crime to Christ* (1915) offered the predictable and formulaic text of the evangelical Christian. And in his prison conversion, Wellington Scott insisted that little separated the criminal from the honest citizen. "The idea that the denizen of the underworld is a character different from the rest of society is a fallacious one," he insisted. The lawbreaking and the law-abiding citizen were one and the same.[55]

Even those who explicitly rejected evangelical conclusions nonetheless emphasized that crime did not pay. The publisher of female pickpocket Sophie Lyons's autobiography in 1913 claimed that "her new life as a respected woman is the only one that is really worth while." Lyons herself pointed out that even prominent criminal masterminds served as lessons on the futility of crime—they died alone and penniless. "If crime does not pay for the really great criminals," she concluded, "how can the small criminals have any hope?" Lyons's contemporary Eddie Guerin expressed similar sentiments, observing that men who lived much of their adult lives engaged in criminal activity made little money. "Certainly no one has ever died a rich man," Guerin said. He characterized his life as one of "incredible foolishness," adding, "Only a man out of his senses, or inherently wicked, could waste his life as I have wasted mine."[56]

Some criminal accounts articulated an openly political and oppositional viewpoint. Donald Lowrie's *My Life in Prison* (1912), Alexander Berkman's *Prison Memoirs of an Anarchist* (1912), Julian Hawthorne's *The Subterranean Brotherhood* (1914), Jack Black's *You Can't Win* (1926), and Eugene V. Debs's *Walls and Bars* (1927) treated incarceration, if not as a form of capitalist and class control, at least as a system that should be abolished. As their titles suggest, such accounts concentrated on the prison experience and devoted little attention to the complexity of the criminal subcultures of most inmates.[57]

A new type of criminal memoir appeared alongside these evangelical proclamations and political critiques. Josiah Flynt's *The World of Graft*

(1901), based on actual interviews with underworld figures, and Hutchins Hapgood's *The Autobiography of a Thief* (1903), the life story of a petty thief named Jim Caulfield, were devoid of any religious agenda and presented more authentic and sociological renderings of criminal life. Both underscored the environmental roots of crime, their attraction to certain criminal activities, their lavish spending habits, the horrors of prison life, the widespread collusion between public officials and criminal entrepreneurs, and the absence of economic opportunities for most felons. These complicated and subtle accounts did not entertain readers with adventure tales or provide warnings against dissipation and decadence. They were also pessimistic. George Appo's autobiography emerged from this school of confessional realism.

APPO TRANSFORMED

To turn-of-the-century, white, middle-class Americans, men like Appo personified "the dangerous classes." When Louis J. Beck wrote the first book-length account of New York's Chinatown in 1898 (Document 1), Appo embodied foreign-bred lawlessness (even though he had been born in Connecticut), "the new hybrid brood" of "half-breeds" and "pig-tailed aliens," whose lives were a war against all that was good and true in the world. Immigrants and their children—the majority population in the largest American cities—were vilified in such accounts as the progenitors of lawlessness and moral turpitude. Lawbreakers such as Appo did nothing but harm and were "born to crime." Simply put, "in all fairness, such a man is better dead."[58]

Even Appo's sympathizers held out little hope for such men. "What could be expected of the children of criminals," asked reformer and Appo ally Frank Moss of the Society for the Prevention of Crime in 1897, "growing up in an atmosphere of crime, taught crime by their parents and associates, and compelled to shift for themselves in tender youth?" Lawbreaking was a seemingly insoluble problem. "It is," lamented Moss, "almost impossible for the criminal to reform."[59]

Appo was most likely influenced by Hutchins Hapgood's *The Autobiography of a Thief*. Appo never acknowledged Hapgood, but both authors emphasized common themes: the environmental causes of crime, the traumas of prison life, and the desire by longtime criminals to "go straight." Hapgood, in his introduction, admitted that the world of graft was "the most natural thing in the world," given his subject Caulfield's childhood. Both Appo and Caulfield considered prison conditions nothing less than a "systematic crime against humanity." Illegal commerce and the subculture surrounding it were a young man's world. Eventually, the difficulties of such a life proved too much for even the most hardened criminal. "I believe that a time comes in the lives of many grafters," Caulfield opined, "when they desire to reform."[60]

In this context, Appo's relationships with prospective employers such as Tom Lee (a Chinatown merchant and underworld figure) and Frank Taylor (the owner of a woodworking business) or reformers such as Frank Moss assumed a larger meaning. Their efforts to employ Appo—to help him go straight—reflected the limited opportunities available to convicted felons. Appo enjoyed no family connections, craft training, or formal education. Yet these were the social structures that offered upward mobility and economic opportunity for middle-class and skilled working-class men. The employment tribulations and frustrations detailed by Appo in his autobiography reflect how much past criminal behavior affected job employment opportunities. Success was predicated on access to certain social networks and one's ability to exploit them. Appo's primary associations were with former convicts and other underworld associates. For that reason, Appo acknowledged, "I and the other men always returned to a life of a crook as soon as discharged."[61]

Such a series of lifelong frustrations probably contributed to the contrite image Appo presented in his autobiography. Throughout his life, the only steady employment ever offered to him came from evangelical reformers such as Moss. "I really believe were I not fortunate enough to meet good people who took a kindly interest to secure honest employment for me," Appo admitted, "I don't know what would have become of me."[62] Despite the difficulties of reforming, the loss of income, and the decline in his lifestyle, Appo changed. Remarkably, he displayed little anger or resentment toward those who encouraged the transformation. Indeed, he felt indebted to them. If the first half of Appo's life confirmed the maxim, "Give me the child for his first seven years, and I will give you the man," the second half refuted it.

APPO'S MEMORY

Effectively orphaned as a child, Appo grew up in the most impoverished neighborhood in nineteenth-century America, never attended school for even a day in his life, and only learned to read and write while in prison as a young adult. The criminal underworld was largely an oral culture;

the men who inhabited it were not known for introspection or keeping a personal diary. How could such a person write his own autobiography? In Appo's case, the truth is more startling than fiction. Appo's autobiography was an evolutionary product, the result of more than twenty years of musing on the meaning of the underworld. His literary saga began not in 1915, when he wrote the first pages of his memoir, but rather during his 1895 trial for stabbing a police officer.[63] His attorneys and the Society for the Prevention of Crime officials Arthur F. Dennett and Frank Moss, hoping he might receive a lenient sentence, urged Appo to write a brief autobiographical account of his criminal experiences. The result was "The Full History of My Life," Appo's nine-page, handwritten testimony. The document sketched out the broad details he later expanded on in his autobiography: his birth in 1858 (which is incorrect according to his birth and baptismal records; the correct date is 1856), his father's conviction for murder, the death of his mother, his lack of schooling, and his experiences at Sing Sing. This account presented a stark image of Appo's childhood and teenage years. After being discharged from the *Mercury*, he tried to obtain legitimate work but failed because of his illiteracy and small size. So dire were his circumstances, Appo wrote, that he "was compelled to sleep in hallways, [and] had nothing whatever to eat." He resorted to picking pockets simply, he confessed, "to obtain the means to keep me alive."[64]

Appo's motivation to write an autobiography remains a mystery. Quite likely, he wanted to set the record straight. By the time Appo recounted his life experiences in 1915 and 1916, he had avoided conflicts with law enforcement authorities for nearly two decades. In fact, having abandoned his earlier associations with the underworld, Appo worked as an undercover investigator for the Society for the Prevention of Crime after 1910. This reformed George Appo, however, was unknown to the American public. Perhaps he was determined to present a more accurate account of his life in order to rectify his public image, to correct the biased, inaccurate, and even racist reporting about his earlier life and activities.

One could easily conclude that Appo dictated his life story to another party, most likely a law enforcement official or reformer who placed the document in the files of the Society for the Prevention of Crime, where it languished for years. But the authenticity of his work—that he both wrote it and described verifiable events—is reinforced by at least one of his contemporaries, Sing Sing warden Lewis Lawes. In his historical memoir of the prison, Lawes quoted Appo's unpublished autobiography at length, particularly his descriptions of conditions at Sing Sing during

the late nineteenth century (Document 4). Lawes acknowledged the
originality of Appo's narrative but never revealed the location or origins
of the manuscript.[65]

Appo displayed an uncanny ability to remember seemingly trivial
details about his past. He remembered, for example, being raised in
Five Points by the impoverished Allen family, a detail confirmed in census and prison manuscript records. Appo wrote that he was released
from Clinton Prison on January 9, 1879. He was only one day off. He
described his arrest in the jewelry store of Augustus Kunz on Tenth
Street in Philadelphia. City directories from 1879 to 1891 reveal that a
Gustav Kunz was a watchmaker and jeweler in the firm of Breitinger
and Kunz, which was located not on Tenth Street, but one block over
on Ninth.[66]

Appo enjoyed writing. Though illiterate early in life, he became a
man of letters in his later years. This was hardly unusual, according to
Lawes. "Writing is the prisoner's traditional avocation," he observed in
1932. "Almost every prisoner feels that he has a story to tell, an autobiography that is worth the telling." At different points in his life, Appo
even wrote poetry about his prison experiences. Only a few of his poems
survive, but they may represent a larger body of work that was lost or
discarded.[67]

APPO AND THE EMERGENCE OF
ORGANIZED CRIME

Appo's memoir and experiences foreshadowed the criminal networks
that became commonplace in twentieth-century American cities. By
then, nineteenth-century confidence games such as the green goods
game were labeled "rackets," and the "shyster lawyers" Appo encountered in prison and jail were known as "fixers." Opium smoking and
the popularity of opium dens prefigured the rise of another illicit recreational drug culture. And the "dives" where Appo splurged and blew his
ill-gotten gains were transformed into cabarets and nightclubs. Appo's
activities were less a product of ethnicity, religion, or type of workplace
than they were an outgrowth of the new social and economic structures
of the modern metropolis.[68]

Appo's autobiography portrays a life characterized by no family structure; no formal schooling; an early introduction to crime; an inability to
find, obtain, or sustain legal employment; and little institutional involve-
ment other than law enforcement. The very structures that shaped most

individual behaviors in nineteenth-century America did not exist for Appo. Instead, he was immersed in the subcultures embodied in child street life and later organized around interpersonal violence, antisocial hierarchies molded and bolstered by prison, and an underworld language shaped in part by illiteracy. Criminality in industrializing cities was associated with those segments of society unable to find a secure footing in the mainstream economy. Sadly, the same structural forces that determined Appo's life path and fostered crime a century ago persist in American cities today.

NOTES

All newspapers cited originate in New York City unless otherwise noted.

[1] On the origins of the term *good fellow*, see Timothy J. Gilfoyle, *A Pickpocket's Tale: The Underworld of Nineteenth-Century New York* (New York: W. W. Norton, 2006), 339n5. Appo used this term ten times in his autobiography.

[2] The original typescript "Autobiography of George Appo" (hereafter cited as Appo) is located in George Appo folder, box 32, Society for the Prevention of Crime Papers (hereafter cited as SPC Papers), Rare Book and Manuscript Room, Butler Library, Columbia University, New York.

[3] Inflation rates vary according to different measuring indexes. In 2011, $500 in 1875 was worth $10,600 using the consumer price index; $9,760 using the gross domestic product (GDP) deflator; $68,100 using the unskilled wage; $135,000 using the income value or nominal GDP per capita; and $925,000 using the relative share of GDP. See Samuel H. Williamson, "Six Ways to Compute the Relative Value of a U.S. Dollar Amount — 1790 to Present," MeasuringWorth.com, accessed July 27, 2012, http://www.measuringworth.com/calculators/uscompare/result.php.

[4] *Evening Journal*, May 21, 1930, clipping, George Appo folder, box 32, SPC Papers.

[5] Thomas Byrnes, *Professional Criminals of America* (New York: Cassell, 1886), i. On larceny, see William Francis Kuntz II, *Criminal Sentencing in Three Nineteenth-Century Cities* (New York: Garland, 1988), 114, 129, 155; Lawrence M. Friedman, *Crime and Punishment in American History* (New York: Basic Books, 1993), 108–10. In New York, nearly half (48 percent) of all crimes in 1866–1867 involved some type of larceny. That figure never dropped below 36 percent until after 1887. In 1927, robbery (25 percent) surpassed larceny (24 percent) for the first time. See New York State Senate, *Proceedings before the Special Committee of the New York State Senate* (Albany, 1876), 1192a, and New York State Crime Commission, *Report to the Commission of the Sub-Commission on Penal Institutions — 1928*, table 1 (Albany: J. B. Lyon, 1928), 33.

[6] Allan Pinkerton, *Thirty Years a Detective* (St. Louis: Historical Publishing, 1884), 36; *The Autobiography of a Thief*, recorded by Hutchins Hapgood (New York: Fox, Duffield, 1903), 35.

[7] For more details, see Timothy J. Gilfoyle, "Street-Rats and Gutter-Snipes: Child Pickpockets and Street Culture in New York City, 1850–1900," *Journal of Social History* 37 (2004): 853–62.

[8] Samuel B. Halliday, *The Little Street Sweeper; or, Life among the Poor* (New York: Phinney, 1875), 142–43; Children's Aid Society, *First Annual Report* (New York: Children's Aid Society, 1854), 3–4; Children's Aid Society, *Nineteenth Annual Report* (New York: Children's Aid Society, 1871), 6; Charles Loring Brace, *The Dangerous Classes of New York, and Twenty Years' Work among Them* (New York: Wynkoop & Hallenbeck, 1872), 132–33 (10,000 to 30,000), 344; Helen Campbell, Thomas W. Knox, and Thomas

Byrnes, *Darkness and Daylight; or, Lights and Shadows of New York Life* (Hartford, Conn.: A. D. Worthington, 1891), 112, 153, 213 (15,000 homeless children); *Tribune*, January 17, 1877 (5,593 stray children); Linda Gordon, *The Great Arizona Orphan Abduction* (Cambridge, Mass.: Harvard University Press, 1999), 8 (150 per month).

[9] *Autobiography of a Thief*, 35 ("go far"); unmarked clipping, February 2, 1884, District Attorney Scrapbooks (hereafter cited as DAS), New York County, New York City Municipal Archives and Records Center, Chambers Street, New York ("pickpocket's paradise"); *Tribune*, August 12, 1876; Children's Aid Society, *Seventeenth Annual Report* (New York: Children's Aid Society, 1869), 48 (list of child criminal occupations); Brace, *Dangerous Classes*, ii, 26–27, 344.

[10] *Star*, October 8, 1883, clipping, DAS; Jonathan Slick, *Snares of New York; or, Tricks and Traps of the Great Metropolis* (New York, 1879), 39; *Tribune*, August 12, 1876. On men's pants, see J. Gottfred, "Reproduction Clothing—Men's Pants," *Northwest Journal* 6 (1994–2002): 32–37.

[11] Pinkerton, *Thirty Years a Detective*, 33–39, 48–50; Benjamin P. Eldridge and William B. Watts, *Our Rival, the Rascal: A Faithful Portrayal of the Conflict between the Criminals of This Age and the Defenders of Society, the Police* (Boston: Pemberton, 1897), 17.

[12] Herman Melville, *Pierre; or, The Ambiguities* (1852; repr., New York: Penguin Classics, 1996), 240; George W. Matsell, *Vocabulum; or, the Rogue's Lexicon* (New York: George W. Matsell, 1859). For lists of underworld slang, see Gilfoyle, "Street-Rats and Gutter-Snipes," n. 28.

[13] Appo, 24–25.

[14] Jacob Riis, *How the Other Half Lives* (New York: Charles Scribner, 1890), 94–95.

[15] *Sun*, December 23, 1884, clipping, vol. 10, DAS.

[16] Appo, 8–9, 12–13; Byrnes, *Professional Criminals*, 1.

[17] On sure thing graft such as bunco, dice, short cards, flimflam, fake jewelry, and green goods, see Frank Moss, *The American Metropolis* (New York: Peter F. Collier, 1897), 3:132.

[18] Gilfoyle, *Pickpocket's Tale*, 204–42.

[19] *Tribune*, September 11, 1894; William T. Stead, *Satan's Invisible World Displayed; or, Despairing Democracy: A Study of Greater New York* (London: Mowbray House, 1898), 108.

[20] David R. Johnson, *Illegal Tender: Counterfeiting and the Secret Service in Nineteenth-Century America* (Washington, D.C.: Smithsonian Institution Press, 1995); Stephen Mihm, *A Nation of Counterfeiters: Capitalists, Con Men, and the Making of the United States* (Cambridge, Mass.: Harvard University Press, 2007).

[21] *Bridgeport Evening Post*, September 12, 1894 ("nearly all"); *World*, May 25, 1892, clipping, vol. 98, DAS ("They all"). On Saunders, see *Times*, March 5 and 11, 1887. On Hilton, see *Herald, World, Sun, Times*, and other newspapers, May 25, 1892, clippings, vol. 98, DAS.

[22] On green goods as an example of organized crime, see *Evening World*, editorial, June 1, 1895, vol. 141, DAS. On Tammany Hall as organized crime, see Society for the Prevention of Crime, *Report* (New York: Society for the Prevention of Crime, 1896), 6–7.

[23] R. T. Naylor, *Wages of Crime: Black Markets, Illegal Finance, and the Underworld Economy* (Ithaca, N.Y.: Cornell University Press, 2002), 14–16.

[24] For "carnival of crime," see *National Police Gazette*, August 24, 1867; *Tribune*, February 2, 1896. Examples of the growing fear of crime in New York after 1860 are abundant. The most convincing evidence that American cities were increasingly safe after 1860 appears in Roger Lane, *Violent Death in the City: Suicide, Accident and Murder in Nineteenth-Century Philadelphia* (Cambridge, Mass.: Harvard University Press, 1979); Eric H. Monkkonen, *Murder in New York City* (Berkeley: University of California Press, 2001).

[25] Friedman, *Crime and Punishment*, 68–70; Roger Lane, *Policing the City: Boston, 1822–1885* (Cambridge, Mass.: Harvard University Press, 1967); Allen Steinberg, *The Transformation of Criminal Justice: Philadelphia, 1800–1880* (Chapel Hill: University

of North Carolina Press, 1989), 140–49; Eric H. Monkkonen, *Police in Urban America, 1860–1920* (New York: Cambridge University Press, 1981). On rioting, see Paul Gilje, *Rioting in America* (Bloomington: Indiana University Press, 1996).

[26] Kenneth T. Jackson, ed., *The Encyclopedia of New York City* (New Haven, Conn.: Yale University Press, 1995), 911, 166; Frederick H. Wines, *Report on the Defective, Dependent, and Delinquent Classes of the Population of the United States* (Washington, D.C.: Government Printing Office, 1888), 566, 569.

[27] On the precise breakdown of the New York, Paris, and London police forces, see unmarked clipping, June 13, 1890, vol. 74, DAS; Lisa Keller, *Triumph of Order: Democracy and Public Space in New York and London* (New York: Columbia University Press, 2009), 54.

[28] Wilbur R. Miller, *Cops and Bobbies: Police Authority in New York and London, 1830–1870* (Chicago: University of Chicago Press, 1973), 17.

[29] Sidney Harring, *Policing a Class Society: The Experience of American Cities, 1865–1915* (New Brunswick, N.J.: Rutgers University Press, 1983), 37. Boston had well over 500 citizens per officer prior to 1880. See Lane, *Policing the City*, 173.

[30] Amy Dru Stanley, "Beggars Can't Be Choosers: Compulsion and Contract in Postbellum America," *Journal of American History* 78 (1992): 1265–93; Byrnes, *Professional Criminals*, 34–35 ("preventive arrests"); *Frank Leslie's Illustrated Newspaper*, August 7, 1876 ("autocrats").

[31] Byrnes, *Professional Criminals*, 52a; Gilfoyle, *Pickpocket's Tale*, 247–54.

[32] Mary Roberts Smith, "The Social Aspect of New York Police Courts," *American Journal of Sociology* 5 (1899): 152 (95 percent); Timothy J. Gilfoyle, "'America's Greatest Criminal Barracks': The Tombs and the Experience of Criminal Justice in New York City, 1838–1897," *Journal of Urban History* 29 (2003): 530–31, table 1.

[33] Lincoln Steffens, *The Autobiography of Lincoln Steffens* (New York: Harcourt Brace, 1931), 222–26, 288; Josiah Flynt, *The World of Graft* (New York: McClure, Phillips, 1901), 39, 46–47, 56; *Brother Jonathan*, January 28 and March 24, 1860 (police familiarity); New York State Crime Commission, *Report— 1929* (New York: J. B. Lyon, 1929), 107 (habeas corpus).

[34] Neil Larry Shumsky, "Tacit Acceptance: Respectable Americans and Segregated Prostitution, 1870–1910," *Journal of Social History* 4 (1986): 669–70; Richard Tansey, "Prostitution and Politics in Antebellum New Orleans," *Southern Studies* 18 (1979): 475–77; Duane R. Sneddeker, "Regulating Vice: Prostitution and the St. Louis Social Evil Ordinance, 1870–1874," *Gateway Heritage* 11 (Fall 1990): 20–47; Neil Larry Shumsky and Larry M. Springer, "San Francisco's Zone of Prostitution, 1880–1934," *Journal of Historical Geography* 7 (1981): 79–85.

[35] New York State Assembly, *Report of the Select Committee Appointed by the Assembly of 1875 to Investigate the Causes of the Increase of Crime in the City of New York*, Assembly Document 106 (New York: Martin B. Brown, 1876).

[36] New York State Senate, *Report and Proceedings of the Senate Committee Appointed to Investigate the Police Department of the City of New York*, Senate Document 25 (Albany: James B. Lyon, 1895) (hereafter cited as *Lexow Committee*), 1:21, 24. Timothy J. Gilfoyle, *City of Eros: New York City, Prostitution, and the Commercialization of Sex, 1790–1920* (New York: W. W. Norton, 1992).

[37] Appo, 2–3, 37; Stead, *Satan's Invisible World Displayed*, 108; *Tribune*, April 25, 1868.

[38] New York State Assembly, *Report . . . to Investigate the Causes of the Increase of Crime*, 7 (corrupt); *World*, June 15, 1894, clipping, vol. 126, DAS ("booty"). On the Roosevelt investigation, see New York State Assembly, *Report of the Special Committee Appointed to Investigate the Local Government of the City and County of New York*, Assembly Documents 153 and 172 (Albany: Weed, Parsons, 1884). On the Fassett Committee, see *World*, April 12, 1890, and *Journal* and *Press*, April 13, 1890, clippings, vol. 72, DAS.

[39] New York State Assembly, *Report . . . to Investigate the Causes of the Increase of Crime*, 65, 66.

[40]The term "slaves of the state" appears in the Virginia legal case *Ruffin v. Commonwealth*, 62 Va. (21 Gratt) (1871), 790. See Donald H. Wallace, *"Ruffin v. Virginia* and Slaves of the State: A Nonexistent Baseline of Prisoners' Rights Jurisprudence," *Journal of Criminal Justice* 20 (1992): 33–40; Rebecca M. McLennan, *The Crisis of Imprisonment: Protest, Politics, and the Making of the American Penal State, 1776–1941* (New York: Cambridge University Press, 2008), 100, 116–18.

[41]Gilfoyle, *Pickpocket's Tale*, 53–58, 167–77, 356–57nn34–39, 394nn28–30.

[42]*Tribune*, March 28, 1882 (liquor distilled); *Tribune*, December 14, 1897 (opium); *Times*, August 10, 1893 (whiskey); New York State, *Report of the State Commission on Prison Labor* (Albany: Argus, 1871), 6 (pamphlets); *World*, April 15, 1874 (clay pipes, sugar); Louis Berg, *Revelations of a Prison Doctor* (New York: Minton, Balch, 1934), 44–46.

[43]*Tribune*, January 17, 1877; New York State Prison Commission, *Investigation of the State Prisons, and Report Thereon, 1876* (Albany, 1877), 13; New York State Crime Commission, *Special Report on Penal Institutions* (Albany: J. B. Lyon, 1930), 8–9; Allan Pinkerton, *Criminal Reminiscences and Detective Sketches* (New York: G. W. Dillingham, 1878), 52–55.

[44]*Morning Journal*, November 3, 1889, clipping, vol. 67, DAS.

[45]Appo, 81.

[46]Ibid.

[47]Michael Willrich, *City of Courts: Socializing Justice in Progressive Era Chicago* (New York: Cambridge University Press, 2003).

[48]Thomas Mott Osborne, *Within Prison Walls* (New York: D. Appleton, 1914); Thomas Mott Osborne, *Society and Prisons: Some Suggestions for a New Penology* (New Haven, Conn.: Yale University Press, 1916).

[49]This literature is voluminous; see bibliography.

[50]William F. Howe and Abraham H. Hummel, *In Danger; or, Life in New York: A True History of a Great City's Wiles and Temptations* (New York: J. S. Ogilvie, 1888), v.

[51]See bibliography for examples of this literature.

[52]Byrnes, *Professional Criminals of America*, 1; George W. Walling, *Recollections of a New York Chief of Police* (New York: Caxton, 1887); William McAdoo, *Guarding a Great City* (New York: Harper & Bros., 1906); Eldridge and Watts, *Our Rival*; Allan Pinkerton, *Professional Thieves and the Detective* (New York: G. W. Dillingham, 1880).

[53]Gilfoyle, *Pickpocket's Tale*, 260–70.

[54]George Bidwell, *Forging His Chains: The Autobiography of George Bidwell* (Chicago: Art Album, 1888), 3, 17; Langdon W. Moore, *His Own Story of His Eventful Life* (Boston: L. W. Moore, 1893).

[55]Opie L. Warner, *A Pardoned Lifer: Life of George Sontag, Former Member, Notorious Evans-Sontag Gang of Train Robbers* (San Bernardino, Calif.: Index Print, 1909), 19; Thomas Maslin, *From Salon to Prison, From Prison to Pulpit* (Ashland, Pa.: G. Kyler, 1912); W. H. Flake, *From Crime to Christ; or, 27 Years in Prison* (Binghamton, N.Y.: Business Art Print, 1915), v; Wellington Scott, *Seventeen Years in the Underworld* (N.p., 1916), 112–13.

[56]Sophie Lyons, *Why Crime Does Not Pay* (New York: J. S. Ogilvie, 1913), 9, 61; Eddie Guerin, *I Was a Bandit* (Garden City, N.Y.: Crime Club / Doubleday, Doran, 1929), 1, 74.

[57]H. Bruce Franklin, *Prison Literature in America: The Victim as Criminal and Artist* (New York: Oxford University Press, 1989), 146–50; Larry K. Hartsfield, *The American Response to Professional Crime, 1870–1917* (Westport, Conn.: Greenwood, 1985).

[58]Louis J. Beck, *New York's Chinatown: An Historical Presentation of Its People and Places* (New York: Bohemia, 1898), 250, 259–60.

[59]Moss, *American Metropolis*, 3:118, 143.

[60]*Autobiography of a Thief*, 9, 10, 344.

[61]Appo, 95.

[62]Ibid., 79–80, 95.

[63]Appo claimed he was writing in 1915 and 1916. See ibid., 76, 96.

[64]George W. Appo, "The Full History of My Life" (handwritten), n.d., in *People v. George Appo*, April 19, 1895, New York Supreme Court, box 10100, location 106231 (unprocessed collection), District Attorney Indictment Papers, New York City Municipal Archives and Records Center, 31 Chambers Street, New York.

[65]Lewis E. Lawes, *Twenty Thousand Years in Sing Sing* (New York: A. L. Burt, 1932), 90–93.

[66]On the Allen family, see P. 31, Ward 6, Election District 4, Federal Census Population Schedules, City of New York, 1860; Entry 1056, P. 54, Ward 4, Election District 2, New York State Manuscript Census, 1855, County Clerk of New York Archives, 31 Chambers Street, New York. On the precise date of Appo's release from Clinton, see "George Wilson," December 12, 1878 (deduction date), Reports of Deduction of Sentences by Prison Agents, Wardens and Superintendents (A0601), vol. 2, and "George A. Wilson," January 8, 1879, Diary of the Principle Keeper of Clinton Prison, in New York State Archives, Albany. On Gustav Kunz, see James Gopsill, *Gopsill's Philadelphia City Directory for 1879* (Philadelphia, 1879–81).

[67]Lawes, *Twenty Thousand Years*, 243. The poems and correspondence are in boxes 2 and 32, SPC Papers.

[68]On pickpocketing, confidence games, and other criminal activities described as "rackets," and on the similarity of "shyster lawyers" and "fixers," see Edwin Hardin Sutherland, *The Professional Thief: By a Professional Thief* (Chicago: University of Chicago Press, 1937), 43–99; *Autobiography of a Thief*, 38–42, 243. On the definition and origin of the term *racketeer*, see John Gunther and James W. Mulroy, "The High Cost of Hoodlums," *Harper's*, October 1929, 529–40.

PART TWO

The Autobiography of
George Appo

CHILDHOOD

At two minutes of five in the morning of July 4th, 1858, and in the City of New Haven, Connecticut, at 2 George Street, I was born. My father, a Chinaman, who's right name was Lee Ah Bow, was born in the city of Ning Poo, China, and came to this country in the year 1847 and settled down in San Francisco, California in the tea business until 1849, when the gold excitement broke out in that section of the country. He then went to the goldfields and worked out a claim which was panning out successful, until one night while asleep in his tent with another Chinaman, he awoke and saw two Mexicans in the tent robbing his partner, the Chinaman, who was killed by them. He shot both the Mexicans dead and left the goldfields and traveled over the mountains, day and night, with a gang of Mexicans trying to run him down. He got safely away and came to New Haven, Connecticut, where he again went into the tea business and got married and soon after I was born.[1]

He was offered the position as tea tester for the large tea and coffee house firm of Christainson & Wells at 49 Vesey Street. He accepted the position and came to New York City and went to work at once with Christainson & Wells and then rented apartments for the family in a private house at 45 Oliver Street, where also lived the Fletcher family,

---

[1] New Haven, Connecticut, birth and baptismal records reveal that Appo was actually born on July 4, 1856. Quimbo Appo's establishment was located at 33½ Church Street.

who were the owners of the property.[2] One day [March 8, 1859], Mrs. Fletcher and my father had a quarrel and Fletcher struck him a blow with a mason's trowel. Both of them clinched together and while in that position, Mrs. Fletcher took up a flatiron and struck him on the back with it, and he stabbed her and she died instantly. He was tried and found guilty and sentenced to be executed. The case was appealed and he was granted a new trial and was found guilty of murder in the second degree at this trial and sentenced to imprisonment for life and then the life sentence was commuted to twenty years.[3]

Soon after he received the life sentence, my mother took passage on board the ship *Golden Gate* bound for California to visit her brother at San Francisco. The ship was wrecked in a storm on the high seas [on July 27, 1862] and both my mother and sister went down with the other unfortunates who were drowned.[4]

I cannot explain how I was saved, only that a sailor brought me to New York and left me with a very poor family named Allen.[5] The father of this family was a longshoreman around the docks by occupation and lived in a rear yard which was called by the name of "Donovan's Lane" at 14½ Baxter Street.[6] One entrance [was on Baxter] and the other entrance was on Pearl Street. There lived in this Donovan's Lane poor people of all nationalities and there were four old tenement houses and a large horse and wagon stable and sheds in the Lane. It was a common sight to see every morning under the wagon sheds at least six to ten drunken men and women sleeping off the effects of the five cent rum bought at "Black Mike's" saloon at No. 14 Baxter Street. The rear of

[2]Edward T. Christainson owned the New York and China Tea Company, later Christainson and Company, which operated out of a number of locations in lower Manhattan in the 1840s and 1850s. Appo's correct residential address was 47 Oliver Street, one of the poorest houses in a low-rent district located a few blocks from the East River wharves.

[3]Appo was confused about the events surrounding his father's prosecution. Quimbo Appo was initially sentenced to death by hanging. An appeal and three respites by New York governor Edwin Morgan ultimately resulted in Appo's sentence being commuted to ten years.

[4]The *Golden Gate* was a 2,100-ton, side-wheel steamer that sank on July 27, 1862, just west of Manzanillo, Mexico, killing 198 of 338 passengers.

[5]This was most likely Mary Allen, a thirty-year-old washerwoman residing at 102 Bayard Street, who had two sisters, ages twenty and twenty-five. When Appo was later sent to Sing Sing in 1874, he identified Mary Ann Allen as his stepsister.

[6]Donovan's Lane was also called "Murder's Alley" because of the high crime rate in this tenement-lined passageway. The alley was located in the heart of New York City's notorious Five Points district, sometimes called the "bloody Sixth Ward" and located north of city hall.

this place led into the Lane where all the drunks were dumped out after being relieved of all their cash. Next door to "Mike's" at 14½ Baxter Street, was a secondhand clothing store owned by a man named Cohen who was a "fence"[7] and where all the crooks used to get rid of their stolen goods. Up over Cohen's store was where all the Chinamen of the city lived, and on the top floor was the Chinese gambling and meeting rooms. At that time there were only about sixty Chinamen in all the city and the Lane was then called Chinatown. Such was Donovan's Lane.[8]

It was about the year 1869 when I first met or knew I had a father living. He was released about that time and soon after he secured a position as tea tester with his former employers, Christainson & Wells, 39 & 43 Vesey Street. I was then about eleven years old and soon after his release, he took me from Donovan's Lane to live with him at a rooming house kept by a woman named McNamara, the wife of a policeman. The house was at 5 Park Street. I lived there with him nearly seven months when he again got into serious trouble with a tough fellow named Shay, and during the fight, someone threw a brick and it struck a shoemaker on the head and he died from his injury. My father was charged with the crime and was tried and found guilty of manslaughter and sentenced to a term of seven years.[9] After his conviction [in 1872], I left the McNamaras and went back to live with the Allens again in the Lane.

[I] started out to sell newspapers for a living and remained at this occupation for two years. During the course of that time, I made the acquaintance of two boys my own age who always were well dressed and had plenty of money, earned as I believed, by selling papers. But I soon found out that they were picking pockets on Broadway and used the newspapers as a cover to work their crooked business. After watching them and several other boys, I soon learned the knack, so to speak, of how to pick a pocket. I took one of the boys as a partner. His name was George Dolan and we both worked together for nearly two years and were quite successful.[10]

---

[7]A receiver and buyer of stolen goods.

[8]Appo is probably referring to Jacob Cohen, a clothing worker who resided at 14 Baxter Street. Cohen was convicted of receiving stolen goods and sentenced to one year in Sing Sing in 1876.

[9]The victim's name was Joseph Linkonski, and he survived the assault. Quimbo Appo was eventually convicted of assault with a dangerous weapon and sentenced to five years in prison.

[10]Pickpockets usually worked in groups of two to four people called "mobs." Elsewhere, Appo claimed that he began picking pockets at age seven.

One day in the winter of 1871 [when I was fifteen years old], I was caught in the act while picking the pocket of a downtown businessman, the name of whom I have forgotten. He gave me in the hands of a policeman and charged me with taking $28 from his vest pocket. I was tried before Judge [Joseph] Dowling [who] gave [the victim] a lecture on his carelessness with his valuables, as such was the cause of leading boys into temptation to steal. [I] pleaded guilty and [was] sentenced to the school-ship *Mercury* under the assumed name "George Leonard."[11] I was taken from the boy's prison in the Tombs to Hart's Island, where I was put to work in the grave diggers gang, wheeling a barrow [wheelbarrow] until the ship returned from a cruise from the West Indies, and then I would be transferred aboard of her.[12]

I was about three months on Hart's Island, when one day in April the ship *Mercury* arrived and anchored in the bay and I with twenty-five other boys were transferred aboard of her. On our arrival on board, we were taken and examined by the physician, then given a suit of sailor's clothes and a hammock and a number instead of a name. My number was 182, port watch and stationed as a main topman. We were then turned over to the "master of arms" who took us below and with a rope's end in one hand and a card with the rules and regulations in the other, began to read the rules of the ship to us. After he had finished reading them he gave us a sizing-up look from head to foot, so to speak, and then said: "You understand them now and see that you obey them well. Get up on deck now and learn your ropes."

On reaching the upper deck, the boatswain gave us into the hands of older boys and they teached us all about the ropes and their use and names. Finally about 4 p.m., the boatswain piped "All hands skylark!" meaning all the boys could climb up the rigging and do as they pleased. This was done more to give all the new boys a chance to practice and learn to climb aloft in safety to loosen and furl sail. In about three weeks, I learned everything that a seaman should know, that is, to "box the

[11]Joseph Dowling (1828–1877) was a well-known police court justice who served from 1862 to 1874. He was famous for his common sense and humor. The school-ship *Mercury* was a training vessel and nautical school established by New York's Department of Public Charities and Correction to educate teenage males in the techniques of seamanship. It was in operation from 1870 to 1875.

[12]The Tombs, or the New York City Halls of Justice, was the city jail and modeled on an Egyptian mausoleum, hence the nickname. Hart's Island (Hart Island today) is located in Long Island Sound, just west of City Island and the Bronx. In 1868, the municipality purchased the island in order to establish an industrial school there. Since then, Hart's Island has served as New York's potter's field, where the city's unknown and homeless are buried in mass graves.

compass,"[13] to loosen and furl sail, to make all kinds of knots and to splice ropes, and I took a turn at the wheel.

During the summer months we made short cruises. When September arrived, the ship would sail to the West Indies to St. Thomas, Barbados, the Canary Islands, Rio de Janeiro and to the coast of Africa. This voyage took us eight months and after many hardships, we arrived and dropped anchor in the bay off Hart's Island.[14]

During this long voyage, we came through many severe storms in safety. While anchored in Rio de Janeiro, the "yellow jack fever"[15] was raging there and six boys died out of thirty cases we had on board. To make matters still more worse, while the ship was crossing the equator, we got caught in a calm and we were out for sixty-five days without a sight of land. We had to live on hardtack[16] full of maggots and had to put lime and charcoal in our water tanks. We were allowed one half of a condensed milk can of this filthy water three times a day to drink. Captain Gerard was greatly worried on account of the fever aboard, and the doctor kept us busy burning pitch to fumigate the ship between decks and aft.[17]

The punishment inflicted for disobedience was severe: flogging and the stocks.[18] The latter punishment was very painful especially when the ship is on the high seas rolling about and many boys have broken their wrists and ankles while in the stocks for punishment in the black hold of the vessel.

The ship arrived and dropped anchor in Barbados where we lay for one week and one day, the order given to "Up Anchor for the United States!" The ship arrived at Hart's Island, where we anchored in the bay. I was one of the third cutter's crew and this boat was always used

[13]Nineteenth-century mariners were expected to identify the gradations of the compass card in order, a task called "boxing the compass." The point system of indicating relative bearings survived long after degrees were adopted for compass directions.

[14]The cruise usually lasted from December to May.

[15]Yellow fever, also called yellow jack, is a viral infection common to tropical climates. Symptoms within forty-eight hours of infection include extreme restlessness, inflamed eyes, a high pulse rate, and a white tongue. By the third day, jaundice turns the skin a pale yellow color. In the late 1800s, the disease was a quick killer, with patients dying within three to five days.

[16]A hard, saltless biscuit used for rations by sailors and soldiers.

[17]Appo misspelled Captain Pierre Giraud's name as "Gerard." From January 23 to April 6, 1872 (seventy-three days), the *Mercury* was mired in the doldrums, an area near the equator characterized by calm seas, light winds, or squalls. These conditions are caused by a belt of low pressure on the ocean's surface. The position and extent of this belt varies with longitude and season.

[18]A device used for punishment consisting of a wooden frame with holes in which the feet, hands, or head of an offender were locked.

to carry passengers and provisions from shore to ship or on any special occasion. The crew were all boy prisoners and whenever the cutter was called away for service, a paid sailor, like a keeper, would sit in the stern of the boat and watch us.

One day the cutter was called away and a new German sailor was assigned to guard us. He got into the cutter and ordered us to pull for City Island. When the boat reached there, a man on the dock handed the paid sailor a paper and said: "The goods are down the dock, that's the bill." The sailor jumped on the dock from the cutter to get the goods.

In an instant, one of the boys said, "Give way, let us go home." We all dropped our oars and pulled with might and main, so to speak, for the other end of City Island, where we jumped ashore. We all scattered and left the boat on the beach. I managed to get hold of an old jacket and cap and discarded the sailor's shirt and hat and reached Donovan's Lane where I soon got clothes. After laying quietly under cover for a week, I was out stealing again in the same business.

Now as I look back on the past, I wonder how I ever lived through it all and escaped the many close calls of death from the knife, blackjacks and pistol shots I received.

The first time I received a bullet wound was in the stomach when I was about eighteen years of age. The shot was fired from a pistol in the hands of a detective down in Wall Street, who with a large crowd of excited men were in hot pursuit after me and shouting, "Stop thief." The fact is, I had picked the pocket of a man who had a bank book full of greenbacks conspicuously sticking up from his coat pocket and the detective must have seen me do it, but I seen him before he could grab me, and I dodged through an office building into Nassau Street. Then, seeing the crowd was closing in on me, I threw the bank book and the bills which scattered in all directions among them and they fell over one another trying to secure the money. On reaching the street, I ran down Wall Street to Pearl Street.

As I was turning the corner I heard the report of the gun and immediately felt a burning feeling in my stomach. I ran into the building [at] 300 Pearl Street, where over a cork store lived a family named Maher, with whom I was acquainted. The good woman, Mrs. Maher, hid me between the mattress of the bed where I remained until her son went out, looked around and returned, saying everything was all right. After having the wound attended to by a doctor to whom we told I was accidentally shot, I then got skillful medical treatment at St. Luke's Hospital through the kindness of a gentleman who had some influence there. I believe whoever fired that shot did not know I was hit by the bullet that lodged in a muscle of the stomach and [was] removed.

I soon got well and strong enough to leave the hospital and through necessity was compelled to take up my dishonest life once more and was soon again behind the bars and serving a term of two years and six months.[19]

THE PENITENTIARY

One day [in 1874] I noticed a crowd of people on the corner of Worth Street and Chatham Square watching a street faker.[20] On the surface of the crowd was a big six-foot man with his vest unbuttoned and a heavy gold chain with the bar half out of the buttonhole. I closed gently near him and as he was so tall I had to stand on tiptoe in order to abstract the chain bar and get the whole business. As I released the bar, a fellow in the crowd suddenly jostled me violently by accident. I almost pulled the vest off the intended victim, who grabbed me by the coat collar and my wrist and caught me with his valuable gold watch and chain in my hand, and called the police.

The intended victim's name was John H. Bannon, a city contractor, mason and builder. I was brought to the police station and from there to Police Headquarters where my photo was taken for the [Rogues'] Gallery.[21] Then I was taken to the Tombs Police Court before Judge [Bankston Morgan]. In all three places I admitted my guilt and was held for the grand jury.[22] On April 3rd, 1874, I pleaded guilty before Recorder [John K.] Hackett, who sentenced me to state prison for a term of two years and six months.[23] I was not yet sixteen years of age at the time, but through fear of being sent to the House of Refuge, which place at that time was a house of torture, and feared by the boys who had been there, I gave the name of George Dixon, age eighteen. As the detective

---

[19]Appo's description of being shot appears much later in the original manuscript.

[20]A street swindler or peddler selling something of questionable value.

[21]The collection of criminal photographs on public display at police headquarters.

[22]Appo confused details of this arrest with others in several different passages in the manuscript. I have moved and edited the discussion of Bannon to present a more accurate account of these arrests. For more details, see Timothy J. Gilfoyle, *A Pickpocket's Tale: The Underworld of Nineteenth-Century New York* (New York: W. W Norton, 2006), 352*n*1.

[23]The recorder was an elective officer who served as a judge on the Court of General Sessions, a financial officer for the city, and a trustee of several semipublic charitable institutions. The post originated in colonial times and was abolished in 1906.

had told the judge I was anything but good, he sent me to state prison instead of the Penitentiary.[24]

On my arrival there at Sing Sing, my unfortunate father, who was there at the time, learned from someone of my being sent there, and instead of being quiet about it, got permission from the warden to see and speak with me at his office. The result was: "The son of Quimbo Appo, the notorious murderer is now at Sing Sing, etc.," got into the newspapers and made things in general very unpleasant for me, and I was stamped a bad man and put to work in the laundry contract, ironing new shirts.

I was at work only three days when the paid instructor of the contract put a dozen shirts on my table, saying, "You will have to do these shirts today and see that you do them perfect or I'll know the reason why, if you don't." I told him I would do my best, so I started to do so and finished two shirts, but unfortunately while on the third shirt, I had to go and get a hot iron and before I used it, I had dipped it in water to cool off. Then I started to iron the sleeve of the shirt and accidentally scorched it. The result was I reported the accident to the citizen instructor (Spencer by name) and he went to the keeper (Harris by name) and told him that I willfully burned the shirt. The keeper said to me: "Go and get your hat and coat."

I did so, and he with the instructor, took me to the guard room, where the principal keeper was and reported me to him as willfully and deliberately burning shirts. "What have you to say about that?" said the P.K. [principal keeper].

"It was an accident and I could not help it," said I.

"Accident, hey! Couldn't, hey! Well, we'll make you be more careful after this. Take off your clothes," said he.

"Why, Principal, it was an accident, I could not help it," said I.

"Take off your clothes," he again demanded. As I did not respond quick enough, he shouted: "Seize him" and a big, six-foot keeper and another grasped me by the throat, tore off my coat and pants, knocked out my front teeth by shoving me violently over the paddle board, pulled my hands behind my back, handcuffed me and pulled them up behind my back as I lay across the paddle board, by a small tackle attached to a frame work on [the] sides of [the] paddle board. After securing me, the six-foot keeper took a board shaped just like a canoe paddle with small

---

[24]Appo was seventeen years old. Convicts sentenced to one year or less were usually incarcerated in the Blackwell's Island Penitentiary, located in the East River between Manhattan and Queens. Those sentenced to more than one year were sent to Sing Sing in Ossining, New York. Young offenders were sent to the House of Refuge.

holes in the blade and swung it over his shoulders and brought it down with all his might on my bare back and spine. I counted nine blows and became insensible[25] thereafter.

When I came to, I was lying on the floor and the doctor said, "He's all right now."

The principal keeper said to me: "Do you think you can go back and do your work all right now? If you don't, we have a way to make you."

I replied, "You punished me for nothing and the next time I am brought here, you will punish me for something."

"No insolence, take him back to the shop."

When I got back to the shop with my teeth knocked out and my body black and bruised from the paddle, I took the shirts that were on my table to iron across the shop to the stove, kicked open the stove door and put the shirts into the fire and slammed the door shut again. I was again brought over to the guard room and asked why I did it and I would not answer, and he said: "Put him in again" but the Doctor said: "No, lock him up in the dungeon."

So they took me to the "dark cells" and I lay there for fourteen days on two ounces of bread and a gill[26] of water every twenty-four hours, and when I was taken from the dark cells, I was carried to the hospital injured for life.

When I was released from Sing Sing Prison, I had to go to St. Luke's Hospital to be operated on by Professors [Fessenden Nott] Otis and [George A.] Peters, and after nearly three months under good medical treatment, I left the hospital and as I had no means or way to obtain the necessities of life, I naturally went back to stealing for a living.[27]

Those two years in state prison made me wiser than before so I left New York and went to Philadelphia, where I remained about four months and then returned to New York looking very prosperous. As the year was the Centennial Year 1876 and near to a close, the time being November, New York City was full of strangers from all parts of the world. The crooks were all doing well in general at their business. In fact, New York was overrun with crooks from the West, and Mott Street was being deserted by the good American people on account of the Chinese

[25]Unconscious.

[26]A unit of liquid measure equal to a quarter of a pint.

[27]Fessenden Nott Otis (1825–1900) was a surgeon and professor at the College of Physicians and Surgeons. George A. Peters (1821–1894) was a surgeon at St. Luke's Hospital.

tenants drifting into the neighborhood rapidly.[28] With the Chinamen came many American opium habitués[29] from the West, most of them from San Francisco, and all crooks in every line of stealing brought on to the East by the Centennial Exhibition at Philadelphia. There they worked their different lines of graft[30] and then drifted into New York and made the opium joint[31] in the basement of 4 Mott Street their hangout. This place was the first public opium joint opened for the American habitués and was managed by a Chinaman called "Poppy" and the place was crowded day and night by opium habitués from all stations in life, both men and women, some of good social and financial standing.[32] Most of the rest were crooks in every line of dishonest business, from the bank burglar down to the petty thief.

I soon became intimately acquainted with the crooks and learned many ways and means to earn money dishonestly with not so much risk as picking pockets, but I could not read nor write and my mode of talking was too slangy. Therefore, I could not operate with safety and success as my general appearance was against me, so I had to continue picking pockets. In the month of December 1876, I was again arrested for picking the pockets of Arad Gilbert, of a gold watch. I pleaded guilty on January 9th, 1877, and was sentenced by Judge Gildersleeve to state prison for a term of two years and six months at hard labor.[33]

On my arrival at the Sing Sing Prison, I was assigned to work by the doctor out in the open air, wheeling sand. I worked outdoors for about six months and during the course of that time, I learned to read and write pretty good through the kind and patient teaching of an old German scholar with whom I had the good fortune to be doubled up in the same cell. This man was seventy years old and pleaded guilty to forgery and was sentenced to two years and six months. His name was Louis Stein. I was then transferred from outdoor work to the jail hall as an assistant tier boy. The work was very hard and the confinement and dampness of the place made me very sick after four months' work.[34]

[28]After 1870, the Chinese population along Mott, Pell, Doyers, and Bayard streets, immediately north of Chatham Square and west of the Bowery, grew more predominant. This area, once considered part of Five Points, was increasingly identified as Chinatown.
[29]Frequent or habitual visitors to a place.
[30]Slang for all kinds of theft and illegal practices.
[31]Opium dens were commonly called "opium joints" or simply "joints."
[32]Poppy's opium den at 4 Mott Street was one of the most widely known in New York during the 1870s and 1880s. It was not the first opium den in New York City, but it was probably the first to allow non-Chinese visitors to indulge in opium smoking.
[33]The victim's name is based on police and municipal records.
[34]Sing Sing admission records indicate that Appo could read and write before he served his second sentence there.

I was then taken and sent away in a "draft" with fifty other convicts to the Clinton State Prison at Dannemora [in October 1877] where I was put to work chopping and sawing wood.[35] In those days there was no coal used at the prison. All fires were burning log wood and there were no railroads running from Plattsburgh to the prison, about seventeen miles. It was very tough to be shackled hand and feet, put into an open cart with no springs, and in the coldest part of the winter with no covering and carried from Plattsburgh Railroad Station to the prison over the rough mountain road, those seventeen miles and with nothing to eat or drink save the water on the train from Sing Sing to Dannemora.

I had been working in the wood gang for about two months when a new administration came into power and a petty tyrant named Louis D. Pilsbury[36] became superintendent of prisons, and with him came the contracts of the stove foundry and hat manufactory and his silent system. Every convict when through his task of daily work had to fold his arms, look down on the floor, not to talk even to a keeper. Should you need anything, [you] raised your hand and pointed out to the keeper what you wanted.[37] This man Pilsbury came from Albany and Troy and had a strong political power in that section and he assigned men from both those towns as keepers over the convicts and they were inhuman brutes. In fact, the principal keeper of Sing Sing Prison, by name Archibald Biglin, was an immoral scamp whose immorality which he practiced on convicts was unspeakable.[38]

There were other officials who were robbing the stove contract by the aid of the convict bookkeeper and shipping clerk. Many stoves were shipped out of the prison at Sing Sing and sold to dealers all through the country. I was taken from the wood gang and transferred to the hat

---

[35]Clinton Prison in Dannemora, New York, was established in 1845. It was located seventeen miles west of Plattsburgh, in proximity to iron deposits that state officials hoped would be mined by contract labor convicts. Officials also hoped that this arrangement would initiate a new era of penitentiary reform. Penitentiaries employing contract labor and suffering from labor shortages "drafted" convicts from other prisons to work on certain contracts.

[36]Appo confused his term in Clinton Prison with a later term in Sing Sing. Louis D. Pilsbury was the third generation of Pilsburys involved in nineteenth-century prison reform. He was New York State superintendent of prisons from 1877 to 1879. Appo misspelled his name as Lewis Pillsbury throughout his autobiography.

[37]The silent system sought to isolate inmates from one another and thereby eliminate all potentially corrupting influences. The program of solitary confinement at night and group activity in silence during the day was first attempted at New York's Auburn Prison after 1821 and was sometimes called the Auburn system.

[38]The "unspeakable immorality" that Appo alleges about Biglin (whose name he spelled "Bigbin") was probably homosexual or predatory rape of male inmates.

contract and placed to work running a machine for coning hats.[39] My task was two hundred dozen per day. The keeper of the shop was a French Canadian named Edward Gay. He was too free with his heavy stick and for the least thing, such as turning one's head around from work and other such trivial mishaps, he would come behind one and push the stick into one's back or neck violently, with a threat to take one over to the guard room and that meant punishment.

So one day he pushed his stick into the neck of a convict named Brum who had a twenty-year sentence to serve. After doing so, he told Brum the next time he would take him to the guard room. Then he started to walk away. Suddenly, Brum grabbed an iron lever from my machine and ran up behind the keeper and struck him a blow on the back. Had I not tripped Brum up, the blow would have caught the keeper on the head. Brum again swung the iron lever at the keeper, when a convict named Campbell grasped Brum by the throat, took the iron lever away from him, and held him until the keeper got up. Two other keepers came and took Brum to the guard room for punishment. The man Campbell was pardoned by the governor for aiding the keeper.[40]

I worked in the hat contract up until six weeks before the expiration of my term. Then I was taken very sick from the bad food and the inhaling of the fur dust of the shop and was admitted to the prison hospital where I remained for three weeks. From there I was put to work chopping wood outdoors until my time expired.

On the day I was discharged, I was taken to the state shop and given a cheap suit of clothes made out of stuff resembling salt bagging and dyed black and then taken to the warden's office where the clerk handed me a ticket to New York and five dollars and I left the prison. The date was January 8th, 1879, and it was snowing very hard and I was very cold as the clothes they gave me was of no use in such weather. In fact, the dye was running down the cloth from the wet of the snow melting while on the train to New York.

On my arrival in New York, I went to the editor of the *New York World* in company of a reporter and exposed the brutality and graft that was inflicted on unfortunate men and going on in the state prisons, and made

[39]To make into the shape of a cone.
[40]Clinton Prison principal keeper James Moon presented a different account in his diary. On September 3, 1878, convict Michael Feeney knocked prison keeper D. E. Gay unconscious with an iron pipe. Feeney grabbed and cocked Gay's revolver to shoot him, but another prisoner intervened. Feeney broke away and ran through the shops, calling on the convicts to follow him. Feeney was eventually shot, then later tried and sentenced to ten years, which was added on his previous twenty-year sentence.

particular mention that the prisons should be investigated by a regular live committee formed outside of politicians. The result was the press got after the prison authorities and stopped the paddle and other brutal punishments that has killed and driven many young men insane. I can name unfortunates who were killed and others who were driven insane by brutal keepers in those years of 1874 and 1879.

The first week after I left Clinton Prison, I started looking for work in a hat factory. I went to Garden & Company, 82 Greene Street, and applied for a job. He asked me where I worked last. I told him, in state prison. He got up from his chair, looked at me and said: "We have no vacancy. Our mill room is full."

So I left his office knowing that he told a fib as I had got a "tip" that he needed a young man to run his coning machine. From there I called at the Carroll Hat Company, but failed to obtain work of any kind. I then went to Newark, New Jersey, and applied at two different hat factories, but met with no success. As my money was all spent but about forty cents, I returned to New York and went direct into an opium joint at 4 Mott Street, where I knew I could meet some of my former associates and get financial aid from them.

On entering the place, I was surprised to see so many new smokers. In fact, the joint was crowded with young men and girls. Most of them were strangers to me. I was unable to order an opium layout, still having the prison clothes on.[41] I felt out of place and was about to go out, when a young man called out: "Hello, George! Come over here." As I approached, he got up from the bunk. He shook hands with me, and said: "When did you come down from 'above'" [Sing Sing Prison]? I told him and showed him the clothes they gave me coming out. He laughed and said: "I'll fix you up in the morning with a front [clothes] so that you can get out and make some coin. So lay down here and roll up some pills for me and have a talk." So I lay down, cooked up the card of opium and we both fell asleep. The next morning he bought me a complete outfit of wearing apparel and loaned me five dollars besides. This man was a crook and his business was a confidence swindler, or better known as a "handshaker."[42] His name was Burt Fitzgerald.

Every night I would go to the opium joint and I soon got acquainted with all the habitués of the place and their line of business. Every one of

[41]An opium layout consisted of a pipe, a small lamp with an exposed flame, a small chisel for cleaning out the bowl of the pipe, a needle on which the opium was cooked and rolled into pills over a flame, and a sponge to clean the bowl after every use.

[42]A confidence man known for his outwardly friendly demeanor. Sometimes called a "bunco steerer."

Figure 2. *The Chinese in New York — Scene in a Baxter Street Clubhouse*

Appo was seventeen years old when artist Winslow Homer, famous for his paintings of the Civil War, rural life, and nature, created this lithograph of an opium den in Donovan's Lane, where Appo grew up. One of the earliest images of an opium den in the United States, it depicts the beginnings of the drug subculture. Note the men playing cards, reflecting the connection between opium and gambling.

Source: Harper's Weekly, March 7, 1874, 212.

them with the exception of a few were crooks in every line of graft. As I learned the different systems by which one could earn money easy and with less risk than picking pockets and other rough ways, I started in for myself and was quite successful in making money in "sure thing graft" as it is called by crooks. I had a run of good luck for nearly five months.

In the early part of June 1879, I was arrested on Broadway near Pine Street on suspicion, or rather for being on the Dead Line by Detective [Joseph] Woolsey.[43] As he punched me in the face for demanding why I was arrested, I punched him back. He told the judge I assaulted him and I was sent to the Workhouse [on Blackwell's Island] for six months.

I was about three weeks in the Workhouse [in 1879], when I made up my mind to try and escape from there. I managed to get a little steel saw brought over to another prisoner by a visitor. The night guard made his rounds every half hour and after 9 p.m. he would never count the men in the big cells. I cut the bar of the window and one stormy, rainy night about 1:35 a.m., pulled the bar out and lowered myself from the top window to the ground by strips of my blanket. The other fellow did not come down and I saw him pull the rope blanket up.

I went to the river and tried to swim across to New York, but the tide was too strong for me to swim against, so I swam under the boathouse. As the big sweep boat was pulled up on the davits,[44] I had to climb up to get into the boat as quietly as possible as the crew slept inside the boathouse. I unhitched one pulley at a time, first lowering the bow a little, then belaying the rope[45] and going to the stern, lowering that end down and so on, until I got the big boat on the water. . . . I got the big boat safely across, although I came nearly being run down by a passing steamer.

On reaching New York, I tied the oars to the seat and pulled out the plug from the bottom of the boat and sunk her at the dock. Then I walked in my underclothes to a tenement house and by good luck, I saw a pair of overalls lying on the bedroom window. I took them, put them on, and rolled up the bottoms about ten inches. I then took a Third Avenue car and rode downtown to Mulberry Street where I got some clothes.

---

[43]In 1880, Chief Detective Thomas Byrnes established the "dead line," declaring that any known criminal found in the business district south of Fulton and Liberty streets (the boundary changed at times) was "dead" and subject to immediate arrest. Appo's dating of this incident to 1879 is an error.

[44]A crane that projects over the side of a ship and is used for boats, anchors, or cargo.

[45]Securing the rope by turning it around at cleat or pin on the ship.

JACK COLLINS, TOM LEE, AND FRED CRAGE

On my arrival in New York, I left the depot and went downtown to a saloon called Speigle's at 45 Bayard Street, where I knew many of my acquaintances could be found.[46] On entering this saloon I saw six of them seated at a table playing cards. Two of them got up and greeted me with "Hello, George! Where have you been?"

"I just got in town," I replied. "Let us have a drink."

The six men came up to the bar and the proprietor waited on us. I handed the proprietor a ten-dollar bill to take out the cost of the drinks, and in giving me the change, he laid a five-dollar bill on the bar. As he did so, one of the six men, a bully and a fighter named Jack Collins, picked up the money, put it in his pocket and said: "I'll take care of this."

"Oh, no, you won't, give me that back, you are too funny." At the same time I took hold of his coat collar. He then struck me a violent blow on my neck. I held on to him and had him bent over the bar counter. He reached for a beer glass to hit me and I knew he would do it if I gave him the chance. So I took out my penknife, broke loose from him, got the blade open and as he rushed in at me with the beer glass, I cut him. He fell in a heap on the floor with the glass still in his hand.

I walked out quietly from the place, saw the officer running over to the saloon, went up to him and said: "There's a fellow hurt inside."

The proprietor said to the officer, pointing at me: "This young man must have cut him, I'm not sure, but he is badly hurt and deserves it."

"Did you cut him? Where's the knife?" asked the officer (Gleason by name.) He began to search me, blew his whistle and another officer came and got the ambulance from St. Vincent's Hospital, took me to the station house, and the next morning, to the bedside of Collins at the hospital, and asked him: "Is this the man who stabbed you?"

He would not answer yes or no but said, "Never mind, I'll fix the —— when I get up out of here." Finally, on going out of the hospital ward, he called the officer back and said: "Hold him anyhow, don't let him get out. I'll see about him later on."

"Did he stab you? Answer that question, yes or no," demanded the officer. He would not answer. I was then brought to court and held to await the results of his injuries anyway. Collins got better and I was indicted and charged with felonious assault with attempt to kill and

---

[46]During the 1870s and 1880s, Bayard Street was one of the main thoroughfares in New York's Chinatown. It was marked by houses of prostitution and "tumbler dives" selling stale beer mixed with whiskey.

the newspapers were calling me all sorts of names and bringing up the father's misfortunes.

Finally, I employed [the] lawyer Edmund E. Price, and he advised me to stand trial.[47] I did so and was surprised to see all the witnesses of good standing take the stand in my behalf. Even the good Hospital Doctor Walsh told the judge that Collins was the meanest foulmouthed loafer that ever came under his medical care and how he would insult the good Sisters of Mercy who nursed him back to life.[48] Even the unfortunate girl off whom he lived told the judge and jury of his mean brutality he inflicted upon her if she failed to bring him money. The judge, in charging the jury, told them "that he considered a glass in the hands of an enraged man as deadly a weapon as a knife." The result was the jury went out and returned in a few minutes with the verdict "Not Guilty."[49]

So when I got free [in 1880], I started in the express business. I bought a horse and wagon with the aid of Tom Lee, the then "Mayor of Chinatown."[50] I got all the Chinamen's expressage work and worked steadily for about four months. During the course of that time, I built up a good trade with the laundry supply and foolishly took in a Chinaman, Wong I. Gong, as a partner through the advice of Tom Lee. After I introduced Gong to the wholesale dealers in soap, starch, etc., he got the run of the business and followed my advice and instructions. [Then] Tom Lee sold out the business to Gong for $300 and I was told since he had put up the $300 to start the business, he kept the money. I was again soon in need and destitute and naturally drifted back to the "hangouts" of my former associates, and through dire necessity started on the crooked path once more.

So one cold winter's night, I drifted into a Mott Street opium joint at No. 17 (basement at the time) where a man named Barney Maguire and his "green goods" employers were smoking opium and drinking wine at Maguire's expense.[51] In the place at the time I noticed a young man lying on the bunk all alone smoking opium. As he was an entire stranger and I had never seen him around before, I sat down on the foot

---

[47]Edmund E. Price was an attorney who represented Appo on several occasions.

[48]Appo confused religious orders here. St. Vincent's Hospital was founded by the Sisters of Charity, not the Sisters of Mercy.

[49]Appo believed that this incident and his subsequent adventures with Tom Lee, Wong Gong, and Fred Young occurred in 1886. Other accounts, however, confirm that they happened in 1880.

[50]Thomas L. "Tom" Lee was a deputy sheriff from 1879 into the 1890s. He was the self-proclaimed "Mayor of Chinatown" during the formative years of New York's Chinese community.

[51]Appo misspelled Maguire as "McGuire."

of the bunk near him and without a word between us, he handed me the opium pipe with a pill on it to smoke. I took it and lay down and we soon became acquainted. I asked him where he was from and he said from the *West.* Every evening I would meet him at the joint and soon learned that he was a traveling house thief and robbed wealthy people's homes at supper or dinner hours in the fall and winter.

One evening I went out with him to see how he worked, but he made a failure that evening. He then told me he was going west. I told him I would join him and we would work both ways, that is, I would help him at his work and he would help me at mine. He agreed and the next day we both went to Philadelphia, where we stayed three days. He made no money there, but I was successful and we went to Scranton, Pennsylvania.

On arriving there, I said to him: "Should you ever get arrested, what name would you give in?"

He replied: "Fred Crage."

"Is that your right name?" I asked.

"No, my right name is Fred Young."

I told him I would give the name of George Leonard, so we worked Scranton and many other cities until we reached the city of Chicago, where we made a long stay, about three months, and all the money he made from New York to Chicago was $17. I paid railroad fare and all other expenses from the results of my stealing from New York to Chicago.

So one day, just the beginning of wintertime, Fred said to me: "We will go to St. Paul, Minnesota. I have a good 'thing' up that way and if I am lucky we will be 'away up in G.'"

"Well, all right, any place suits me." So we went to St. Paul. In two weeks, he made $8. Finally, one afternoon we took a train for Minneapolis, only a short ride from St. Paul. That night he took me up to a place called the "Five Corners."[52] Above this section all the rich people live. He went to a house, climbed the porch and opened a window and got in while I was on the lookout for him. He soon came out and when a safe distance away we met and he showed me a silver watch and a cheap stickpin. I told him that was very poor graft and too risky and that he had better give it up.

He replied: "You just wait, I'll get there, good and fat."

---

[52]Appo is probably referring to the Seven Corners district along the west bank of the Mississippi River where Washington, Cedar, and Wine (later Fifteenth Avenue South) streets converged.

"I hope so," said I, so we went back to St. Paul to our room. On the next evening at 5:45 p.m., I was at the St. Charles Hotel in Minneapolis by appointment with Fred, who told me to be sure to be there. I waited for him until 10 p.m. at the hotel, but he did not show up himself, so I went back to St. Paul to my room and waited there all night. As he did not appear, I went and got the morning paper and therein was an article about the house being robbed of jewelry and money to the amount of $37,000 while the family were at dinner. The fact that Fred had tried the night before to rob the house and failed and he disappointed me at the hotel by not showing up to [meet] me, led me to believe that he robbed the house alone and left me out.

I then made up my mind to hunt him up and bring him to account for his mean act, or as the "crook" says—"Putting me in the hole for my share of the coin." I knew that he was deeply attached to a young girl about seventeen years of age who was an inmate of a "parlor house" in St. Louis on Elm Street. In fact, he was all the time talking about her to me, so I got a move on myself, made some money picking pockets that day and then bought a ticket to St. Louis and left St. Paul that night. On reaching St. Louis, I went direct to the fast house where his girl lived. I saw and talked with her and she said to me: "Fred was here and left about an hour ago for New York. See what nice presents he made me," showing me a pair of diamond earrings, a diamond ring and a seal-skin sacque. "Fred is going to send for me and take me to New York in a few days," said she. I commented upon his generosity and bid her goodbye.[53]

After one day's graft in St. Louis, I left for Louisville, and from there to Cincinnati, and kept on going from town to town until I arrived in New York. Then began a search for Fred in the opium joints. I was informed that Fred had been smoking [in one of them] and that he had taken a ship and sailed for Paris, France. This information I found to be true, so I gave up the chase and soon forgot about Fred's meanness until one day about five months after he sailed for Europe, I heard from a friend of Fred's, who got a letter from him, stating that he was sentenced to fifteen years imprisonment in Paris, France for burglary. Then I forgot him entirely.

I then lay around the opium joints and dives of the city, such places as Owney Geoghegan's, Billy McGlory's and the Haymarket.[54] I would

[53]Elm Street and the surrounding neighborhood were populated with prostitutes and pickpockets.
[54]Geoghegan's, McGlory's, and the Haymarket were among the most popular concert saloons in New York.

pass the nights in these dance halls making a good fellow out of myself, spending the dishonest money I made grafting during the day.

SING SING AGAIN

Soon after I arrived in New York, I started to pick pockets again.[55] One day [April 1, 1882] I was standing at St. Paul's Church on Broadway and Fulton Street, when I noticed a very refined-looking man, wearing plenty of diamonds and a heavy gold chain, come along and stop on the curb of the crossing. I stepped beside him and took his watch and chain without him knowing his loss. Then I went to the Crosby Street opium joint and examined the watch and concluded I ought to get at least $30 for the watch alone. I went to [Barney] Maguire who was smoking opium on an opposite bunk and offered to sell the watch to him. He took and examined the watch and said, "No, I got too many of them."

I then left him and the joint and went to a "fence" and sold both [the] watch and chain for $50. The very next night, I was in the Crosby Street joint smoking with a girl acquaintance, when I was tapped on the foot. On sitting up, I found two detectives, [James] Mulvey and [Patrick] Feeney, who told me to get up, as I was wanted at police headquarters. I got off the bunk, put on my hat and coat and asked them what I was wanted for. "You will find out when you get there," said they.

I was brought before Chief [Thomas] Byrnes, who said to me, "What did you do with that watch and chain you got away with on Broadway and Fulton Street the other day?" I denied all knowledge of the charge and after a lot of questions, I was locked in a cell. The next morning, [I was] brought to the police court, where the owner of the jewelry and a witness for him were on hand to prosecute. I sent for lawyer [Abraham] Hummel [and] engaged him as [my] counselor.[56] When my case was called for a hearing, I learned that the complainant's name was Pedro del Valle. He was the ambassador for Mexico and he valued his lost property at $360. The witness merely identified me as being on the corner at the time the crime was committed, and suspected me as the one who picked the pockets of the ambassador.[57]

---

[55]The ensuing discussion appears later in Appo's original manuscript and is placed here for chronological purposes.

[56]Abraham H. Hummel (1849–1926) and William F. Howe (1827–1902) of the law firm Howe & Hummel were prominent criminal lawyers of the late nineteenth century.

[57]Pedro F. del Valle was not an ambassador, but a twenty-one-year-old member of the Mexican legation. He was described in newspapers as "a Mexican gentleman."

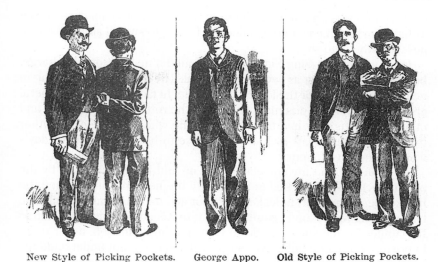

New Style of Picking Pockets.   George Appo.   Old Style of Picking Pockets.

Figure 3. *Appo's Pickpocketing Styles*

Frank Moss, a reformer affiliated with the Society for the Prevention of Crime who befriended Appo in the 1890s, recognized that pickpockets considered their illegal behavior to be part of a distinctive subculture with specific styles, arcane rules, and complex forms of communication. In his three-volume work *The American Metropolis*, Moss sought to convey that the most experienced pickpockets believed that their work was like a professional craft. Indeed, pickpocketing emerged as an underground alternative to the traditional but vanishing forms of apprenticeship in the nineteenth-century urban labor market.

Source: Frank Moss, *The American Metropolis* (New York: Peter F. Collier, 1897), 1:121.

At all events, I learned that Del Valle had offered a $500 reward for the return of his watch and chain, and that the police were searching high and low for the property. I got a word of warning to the fence to whom I sold the articles and by the advice of my counselor, when I was called to plead to my indictment, I pleaded guilty to grand larceny. Judge [Frederick Smyth] sentenced me to three years and six months in state prison.[58]

Now the only person who knew I had that watch and chain, outside of the fence who bought them from me, was Barney Maguire, from whose

[58]Appo incorrectly identified the judge as John Hackett. Frederick Smyth actually sentenced Appo.

opium joint I was arrested. I am certain the fence would not dare to take a chance to give me up to the police, for I knew too much about his business for him to do so.

On my arrival at Sing Sing Prison, I found a new warden in charge, but the discipline just as severe and brutal. The food and everything in general [was] unfit for the lowest animal life. In fact, there was a general epidemic among the prisoners caused by the rotten and filthy meat and other foodstuffs they had to eat. During the whole course of my other two terms, I never saw or knew of a place to bathe after a hard day's work in the stove foundry.

As soon as I had my convict clothes on and [was] examined by the prison doctor, I was locked in a cell until the next morning. When the hall keeper came, [he] unlocked my door and told his convict runner to take me over to section E, south foundry, to Keeper [Patrick] Mackin as his runner for the shop. I realized I was getting a fine job, as a runner in prisons was a graft job. I was surprised and could not understand my good fortune. When the hall runner presented me to keeper Mackin, who was seated at his desk on a raised platform, he said: "This man is sent to be your runner for the shop by the principal keeper, Mr. Biglin."

"All right," said Mackin, "sit down on the platform and fold your arms."

I did so and in about ten minutes, he called me up to the desk, my arms folded and asked me: "What is your name?"

I replied, "George Appo."

"Oh! Oh! I hear you are a bad man."

"You must not believe what you hear, but judge a man as you find him," said I.

"Well, how much time have you got?" I told him three years and six months. "Do you know what you have to do here?"

"I await your orders, sir."

"Now you go to every man in the shop on each floor and take up all the dirty clothes. See that every piece is checked up, count them, put them on a barrow and take them down to the laundry. Be sure you make no mistake in your count and that you get every piece back again. You understand me now?"

"Yes sir." I gathered up all the dirty clothes, counted them, 148 pieces, gave Mackin the account slips, and was surprised to see that he could barely read or write. I brought the wash to the laundry, came back to the shop, sat down on the platform, [and] folded my arms.

Finally, Mackin, who was at the far end of the shop, at the door, signaled me to come there to him, and said: "Take all them buckets down to the water, clean every one of them, bring them back, set them in line as you found them with the lids off and then report to me when you are through." Such was the daily work of a runner.

When the keeper needed a relief keeper, the runner would have to go to the principal keeper and have a relief ticket signed by him and then go in search of one in the prison yard, hand him the signed ticket, and he would go to the shop and relieve the keeper. When I had been under Mackin as his runner for about one week, I found that I was under the care as runner for the most ignorant and brutal keeper in the prison. To make matters worse, the citizen contract foreman was just as bad. In fact, he would report a man for the least damage in his casings after they were shaken out for the mold, and Mackin would take the unfortunate man over to the guard room, make a serious complaint, as willfully spoiling work and the poor fellow would be brought back to the shop almost unable to stand from the paddling he received at the hands of the principal keeper, then made to finish his day's task.[59]

One day, a man named Moran who had a ten-year sentence, and [was] one of the best stove molders in the shop, accidentally spoiled one flask. He was reported and punished. When he returned to the shop, he took a ladle of red-hot iron and burned half of his foot off, and the contractors, Perry & Co. lost a skilled molder as a result.

This incident put me on intimate speaking terms with Mackin. He said to me: "What a d—— crazy fool that fellow was to burn his foot off."

"Well, Mr. Mackin," said I, "the young man has a long term of ten years to serve and he is the best molder you had in the shop. Had you instead of bringing him over to the guard room to be punished, taken him aside and said: 'You had been reported for bad work. I don't want to punish you this time, try and not do it again,' you would then see the good results of your kind words."

I told him that the citizen foreman, Tripp by name, was for the financial benefit for the contractors and would sacrifice a human life every day to get the labor for them. "As keeper, Mr. Mackin, you are in charge of the convicts to look after their interest and welfare and not as a slave driver for the contractors." After many such talks with Mackin, he turned out to be one of the best-hearted keepers in the prison and the men under him turned out the finest of work in appreciation.

---

[59]Patrick Mackin, whose name Appo misspelled as "Macken," was a guard in Sing Sing as early as 1879, when he was stabbed and seriously injured by a convict during an attempted escape. Witnesses testified to his reputation for cruelty during a New York State Assembly investigation in 1881.

When I had about eighteen months of my term served, I was allowed much freedom out of the shop after my work was done and was in a position where I could go into the ladle shanty where the waste hot iron was thrown and cook coffee there for the convict bookkeeper of the stove contract whose office was next door to my shop. This bookkeeper's name was Greenfield and had a five-year sentence.

One day, I had written him a note asking him if he could pay me some coffee if I gave him the money. To my surprise, he stopped me in the yard the next day and asked me if I had written that note myself. "Of course, I did," said I. "Why?"

"Well, tomorrow afternoon, about 3 p.m., meet me in the storage rooms over my office. I'll give you some papers and I want you to copy the writing on them on the blanks I give you as near as you possibly can and return all of them to me in the morning. I'll see you up in the storage [room], when you go for a relief for your keeper. You can copy them in your cell at night," said he.

"All right." The next day he handed me three different bills for stoves that were to be shipped and five blank bills to copy on. I took them to my cell and copied them perfectly. The next morning I handed them to Greenfield, the bookkeeper, and he was extremely pleased. Every night I would copy at least six bills for different kinds of stoves that were to be shipped by rail to the Dakotas and other northwestern towns. Every week I would be paid a pound of coffee for my work.

I [later] found out that this bookkeeper and two keepers, Tierney and Nixon, were robbing Perry & Co., the stove contractors, by shipping stoves to buyers and that my handwriting was exactly like the citizen's shipping clerk[60] for the stove contract. I was used to forge the bills for them unknowingly.

The former keeper Tierney,[61] before he became keeper of the stove shipping office, was the keeper of the jobbing shop where convicts, who were skilled mechanics, were employed by the state to do all the plumbing and other mechanical jobbing work about the prison. In this shop a convict known by the nickname of "Ginger" [who] I believe was there under the name of Thompson with a five-year sentence to serve, had occasion to speak to the convict who worked next to him on the workbench instructing him how to finish a piece of work.[62] The keeper

[60]A clerk who was not a convict but a regular citizen employee.
[61]"Tierney" was probably M. J. Tiernan, who was appointed keeper on May 1, 1878, and was still identified as a keeper as late as 1887.
[62]"Ginger" could have been one of the forty-three inmates who answered to the name of Thompson or Thomson during Appo's three terms in Sing Sing.

Tierney saw him talking to the man and rushed over with his big stick and poked Ginger in the neck.

"Stop your talking, Ginger!"

Being taken by surprise, Ginger jumped from his bench with a hammer in his hand and tried to explain that he had to instruct the other man. But Tierney, with another jab of his stick, told Ginger to shut up, put his hammer down and not give him any back talk. Ginger tried to explain and the keeper raised his stick to strike him, [and] he jumped back. Tierney pulled out his gun and shot him dead and claimed that he shot poor Thompson in self-defense.

Nothing was said or done to Tierney, for Thompson had no relatives or even a good friend in the outside world to take an interest in the case. He was only twenty-seven years of age at the time and was raised up from boyhood in the Fourth Ward. The prison authorities nailed his body in a pine box and buried him up on the hill, or as the graveyard is called by convicts, "25 Gallery," without even a prayer from the so-called chaplain,[63] Mr. Edgerton, who used to delight to be present in the guard room when a poor unfortunate fellow was being paddled and make such remarks as this. When the principal keeper would say to the victim: "So you think the work is too hard for you?" The chaplain: "Ah, maybe he would like to be a clerk in my office."[64]

Keeper Tierney was rewarded by being promoted as keeper in the stove shipping office for Perry & Co. for shooting dead a young man whom I and many others of his outside associates knew would not use a weapon on his worst enemy, let alone a keeper. Such was the kind of officials placed over men to reform them under the Louis D. Pilsbury administration, who introduced the silent system, and fold your arms and look down on the floor, after your hard day's task was done.

Why, the very principal keeper [of Sing Sing Prison], Archibald Biglin was of an effeminate nature and practiced unspeakable crimes on the convict runner he had at his office whose name was Ward and known by the name of Hunt. I accidentally caught Biglin in the act one day, that my keeper sent me to get a relief ticket signed by Biglin. I pretended not to have seen him.

---

[63]Sing Sing's main hall was arranged in twenty-four tiers, or "galleries." Outside, situated on the crest of a hill overlooking the complex, was the burial ground. Inmates called it the "twenty-fifth gallery" because it was geographically higher than the prison.

[64]Silas W. Edgerton served as Sing Sing chaplain from 1880 to 1892. In 1883, he helped found an experimental night school to teach illiterate prisoners how to read and write, the first such program ever created in an American prison.

When I had about one year of my sentence served [in 1883], I was surprised one day when the runner for the P.K. entered my shop and told my keeper that I was wanted over at the guard room by Biglin. I imagined all sorts of misfortunes [were] going to happen to me. I followed the runner to the guard room where the P.K. sat at his desk. As I stood before him with my arms folded and looking down on the floor (as the rule demanded), he said to me: "How much time have you got to serve yet?"

I replied: "Two years and eight months more of a three years and 6 months' sentence."

"Well, I'm going to put you hall runner for Colonel Beattie, and I want you to be trustworthy in all things and behave yourself. Otherwise, out you go into a shop if you don't," said he.

I thanked him and I said I would not abuse his confidence and would do the best I could in all matters. "Well, you go back to your shop and tomorrow I will place you," said he. I left the guard room and wondered at my good luck to get such a fine graft[65] as hall runner. In fact, it was one of the best jobs in the prison, plenty [of] good coffee and something good to eat, a comfortable cell and many privileges were attached to the job.

So the next day, I was assigned hall runner and the man's place I was taking had only two more days to serve of his sentence. He instructed me what to do and I soon got the run of everything. But what puzzled me, I could not understand, [was] why I was trusted with such a fine position. I who had not a single friend that I know of on the outside world would send me much as a paper to read, for I had written to many of my so-called friends to send me some reading matter. But [I] never got a word in reply, so I gave up writing letters and concluded that they were butterfly friends, so to speak, and only fluttered around one for a season, when in prosperity, and when they could make use of one, but the minute misfortune overtakes you they soon forget you are alive. Such is friendship of crooks in general.

I had just made up my mind that I was without a single friend, when I was surprised one day by the warden's runner coming to [the] hall office and telling my keeper that there was a visitor for me at the front office. I went with the runner and as I entered the visiting room, there to my great surprise was a gentleman (Dr. H. H. Kane) to whom I rendered

---

[65]An easy job or task.

a slight service while he was visiting the opium joints to study the evil effects of the drug for publication.[66]

How I made a good friend in Dr. Kane was as follows. One day a man named John Wallace, a confidence operator or handshaker and an opium habitué, said to me: "George, I am to meet a doctor at 6 p.m. in the saloon on the corner (2 Mott Street), but I am to go out of town on business. I want you to meet him for me and get him into this joint (4 Mott Street). The doctor will ask the bartender for me (Wallace) and you will then know he is the doctor."

"All right, I'll be there and meet him for you," said I. So at 6 p.m. I entered the saloon on the northwest corner of Mott Street and Chatham Square and noticed two rough crooks named Dutch Witty and Harmon standing at the bar with a young, well dressed man sandwiched between them. Knowing that the crooks used the knockout drops in their business, I concluded the young man between them was an intended victim. At all events, I asked the bartender if anybody was there inquiring for John Wallace.

"Yes, there, that gentleman," said he, pointing at the young man between the crooks.

I approached, and in a familiar voice said: "Hello! Doctor! Wallace can't be here this evening. I will see you to the joint." Turning to Dutch Witty, I said, "This is a friend of mine. Nothing doing." At the same time, I accidentally upset the drink that was in front of the doctor, and said to him, "We had better hurry up and get to the joint." After excusing myself to Dutch, I took the doctor to the opium joint and explained everything to him about Dutch and Harmon's business. He appreciated my act and I often met the doctor in different opium joints throughout the city.

It was through Dr. Kane that I was so fortunate as to fall into such good positions as hall runner in Sing Sing Prison, for the doctor had put in [a] good word for me with some high official who placed confidence in me during my whole term. When I had about eight months more to serve [in 1884], I was placed as [a] warden's runner for the front office. This position was the best job in the prison. In the meantime, Dr. Kane went to Europe with his family and I never heard from him again, although I made every effort to find him after my release from prison.

[66]Dr. Harry Hubbell B. Kane (1852–1906) was among the first American physicians to study the addictive effects of opium and to document the dangers of narcotic usage for even therapeutic purposes. Kane's books included *Drugs That Enslave: The Opium, Morphine, Chloral and Hashisch Habits* (1881) and *Opium-Smoking in America and China* (1882).

I was certain that he would have assisted me to obtain employment had I met him.

PHILADELPHIA

I tried hard to get work but failed, and in the course of about one month, I drifted, through necessity, back to the opium joints and stealing for a living again. I was not so reckless and foolish as in former days because during my last term of imprisonment, I studied hard and thought a great deal to prepare myself in case I had to steal again for a living, to work more safely and keep out of prison. So when I had got hold of a bankroll, I gave up the rough graft of picking pockets and started in what was called at that time "sure thing graft" such as the "flimflam," or more properly speaking, shortchanging with a ten or twenty dollar bill. I worked this graft for about six months and was very successful.

I left New York for Philadelphia, and began picking pockets in that city. I was very successful for two months and saved enough money for a bankroll to work a more easy and less risky graft called the flimflam (or more plainly speaking, making people make mistakes in giving change for a large bill).

I was successful at this flimflam business until one day, being in need of a ten dollar bill to work with, I entered the jewelry store of Gustav Kunz on Ninth Street with the honest intention to obtain a ten dollar bill for ten ones. He did not have the ten bill, and I was about to leave the place when I noticed a little gold locket I fancied and asked him the price of it. He put up the tray before me and handed me the locket to examine. As I looked at it, he said: "I'll let you have that for $7.50."

I put the locket back on the tray and said, "That's too dear for me."

He suddenly grabbed my hand and said, "You didn't come here to buy, you came here to steal." I told him he was crazy and another man in the store went out and got an officer and I was charged with an attempt at petty larceny.[67]

I, of course, was as innocent as the very judge who sentenced me. Therefore, I stood trial and the jury found me guilty without leaving their seats [on April 8, 1886]. I was sentenced to one year at solitary confinement in the Eastern Penitentiary or "Cherry Hill" as it is commonly

---

[67]The jeweler, Gustav Kunz of Breitinger and Kunz (identified as "Augustus Kunze on Tenth Street" by Appo), believed that Appo was attempting "penny-weight" or "substitution," a confidence game in which a thief inspected jewelry and surreptitiously substituted bogus gems when the clerk looked away.

called by crooks.[68] I was entirely innocent even in thought, let alone in action, of any intention to steal from Kunz the jeweler. Before my trial, I lay in the Moyamensing Jail for six weeks before my case was called for trial. With the filth and food and having to sleep on the floor of the cell during all them six weeks, I suffered terribly, both physically and mentally.

On my arrival at Eastern Penitentiary, my name, age, height, weight and all marks of description was taken and then I was brought to the bathroom. After the bath, I was given a suit of prison clothes and a pair of slippers. Then the keeper threw a monk's robe with a hood and mask around me, pulled the hood over my head and face, and then led me along the jail hall to the center and up one flight of stairs and along the cell tier and unlocked the two doors of cell P, North 3rd. He told me to stoop and bend my head and pushed me gently into the cell, where I took off the robe and handed it out to the keeper, who said to me: "Your number is 9082, Cell, P.N. 3rd. You will find the rules and regulations of the place on the wall, *read them*." He then slammed both doors, locked them and went away.[69]

I then looked around the cell. There was an opening in the ceiling about eighteen inches long, four inches wide and tapering down cone shape, an apology for a window. The ceiling was ten feet above the floor and nothing but the four bare walls to look at, and a canvas cot to sleep on and a bread bag hanging on a little bookshelf in a corner. I sat down on the cot and said to myself, "This is a tough deal for an innocent man. If I were guilty, I would not mind it so much."

Just then the door opened and my block keeper (Mr. Howard by name) said to me: "I'm going to put you to work at toeing stockings tomorrow. Did you ever work at it before?"

"No sir, I don't even know what kind of work that is."

"Well," said he, "I'll put a good fellow in here as a cell mate who will instruct you in the business tomorrow. How much time have you?" I told him one year. "Oh, that will slip around soon," said he and slammed the door and went away.

About ten minutes later, another keeper came to the door, opened the wicket and pushed in to me a soup pan and cup and a spoon, saying, "The dinner will be along soon, so be ready to hand out your pan for soup." He closed the wicket and left. Soon after, I heard the rumbling of

[68]Eastern State Penitentiary was located on the site of a former cherry orchard.
[69]Appo was arrested and sentenced under the alias George Leon. The indictment listed the value of the locket at $3.50. According to the prison register, Appo's number was 3178, not 9082.

[the] grub wagon and stood ready with the pan. The wicket flew open and a large piece of bread was pushed through at me. I handed out the pan which was passed back filled with greasy water and a piece of tough meat that smelled anything but good. Nevertheless, I sat down on the cot and ate enough to satisfy my hunger. As there was nothing to read, I lay down and went to sleep. I was awakened by the rumbling noise of the grub wagon. I got up and took my tin cup and stood at the door. The wicket opened and a ration of bread was pushed through and my cup filled with so-called tea sweetened with molasses.

The next morning after breakfast, the keeper came, opened my doors, threw the robe and hood at me, told me to put them on and come with him. I stepped out on the tier and the keeper led me a short distance, stopped and unlocked a cell door and said, "Jack here is a partner for you, show him how to do his work." As I stepped into the cell, I took off the robe and hood and found myself in a cell with two cots, a table and two stools, a bookshelf and a canvas bread bag and a cell mate, whose name was John Northcross, convicted for grand larceny and sentenced for two years. He had only five more weeks to serve out of the two years. He began to instruct me how to toe stockings and in two days I was turning out my task (eighteen dozen per day). The keeper, Mr. Howard, was greatly pleased and rewarded Jack and me with a paper of chewing tobacco each.

Finally, Jack's time expired and the keeper came one morning, threw the robe and hood at Jack and said to him, "Come on! Time expired."

Jack, after shaking hands with me, said to the keeper, "That's the last time I'll ever put on this monk's robe," and out he went.

The reason they put the robe and hood on a convict is [that] whenever one is taken out of his cell, no one can see his face and recognize him in the future in the outside world. After Jack went out, I remained alone in the cell for about three months and no one can realize the bitterness of one's life in that prison. The ever continuous, unvarying monotony, unrelieved by never the slightest change was almost enough to drive one mad. Were it not for the few good books and the work I had, I don't know what I would have done for relief.

Finally, one morning the keeper opened my doors and surprised me saying to me: "Here's a good partner for you." After the robe and hood was taken off, the keeper said to him: "Now, John, see if you can behave yourself up here and stop trying to dig yourself out."

He then closed and locked the doors and I said to the new partner: "How much time have you?"

He said, "Ten years," and that he had been there fourteen months already, and had been locked on the ground floor cell block where all "long-time men" were. Each cell had a little ten-foot yard in the back where each convict got a half hour of exercise. As a result of John trying to butt his way out to liberty, he was transferred to an upper block and lost his yard exercise as a punishment. This young man was very quiet and reserved and very seldom had much to say.

When I had but two months more to serve, I said to him, "Now Johnny, my time's nearly up and if there is any reasonable favor I can do for you when I go out of here, let me know and you can rely on me to keep my promise." He then began to give me his confidence and told me that he was entirely innocent of the crime for which he was convicted and the circumstances of his arrest and charged with burglary in the first degree. His right name was John Cronin and he was the brother of old Sandy Cronin, a Cincinnati fireman and chief of Fire Engine No. 5 on Hamilton Street in Cincinnati. He had run away from home and his folks had heard nothing of him in nine years. He asked me to get word to this brother so that the prison authorities would not know who his folks were. I promised him I would go to Cincinnati and see his brother personally and tell him the facts of his case and unfortunate position.

So time rolled on and the end of my term of servitude came [on March 9, 1887] and the keeper opened my cell doors, threw the robe and hood at me, and I said goodbye to Cronin. Then I was led to the dressing room, put on my citizen clothes, (the clothes I had brought with me to the prison on my first arrival there), and they were all pressed and as good as new. Then I was brought to the front office and my watch and chain and money they took from me on entering the prison was returned, but not one cent was given me by the state. So my money, $16 and a gold watch came in very handy after I passed through them big iron prison gates and heard them slam behind. I then went to a bookstore and bought some good reading matter, some tobacco and brought them to the gate and sent them in to Cronin. I then went to a pawnshop and got a loan of $10 on my watch and bought things I needed.

That night I drifted into an opium joint on Tenth and Arch Streets, where I met a young fellow with whom I had a slight acquaintance in a New York opium joint. After a talk with him, he told me his name was Tom Wilson and that he was on the road bound for the West all by himself. I told him that I too was going west, so we both made up to travel together. The second day after my release from prison, I was grafting again from town to town and city to city until I finally came to Cincinnati, where I left the train at about 9 a.m. and went directly to No. 5 Engine on Hamilton Street. I asked one of the firemen sitting outside the door if I could see Sandy Cronin on a very important matter. The fireman called out "Sandy!" and an old man came sliding down the pole from above and I asked him if he was Mr. Cronin. He said: "Yes, what can I do for you?"

I replied: "If you will come across the street to the saloon, I will explain. In fact, I bring you news of your young brother John, and what I have to say is private." He became excited and asked if John was alive. When we got to the saloon and seated at a table, I told him the facts of his brother's case and conviction and how entirely innocent he was of the crime. The facts were [that] his brother had tramped from Scranton and on nearing the city of Philadelphia, he picked up a small leather pouch from the ground. On opening it, he found some Mexican gold pieces. He put them back in the bag and into his pocket and then went to a railroad station and sat down to rest himself. He had not been seated ten minutes when in came two detectives, questioned him, took him to the lockup and on searching him found the bag of gold pieces on him which were a part of the swag of a burglary committed in that section of the country that night. He was convicted and sentenced to ten years.

After I had explained everything to his brother, he thanked me and said he would send a lawyer to look after John, his brother. I said good-bye to the fireman and left the city the next day for Columbus, Ohio, where my partner [Tom Wilson] and me put up at a hotel for the night.[70]

The next day we started to work the "flimflam" graft, and in about an hour's work, I made $20. Not being satisfied, I went into a large shoe store, bought a half dozen pair of shoelaces, and handed a ten dollar bill in payment to the salesman. I was leaving the store with five dollars the best of him in making the change, when he jumped over the counter and shouted: "Here you, just a minute." I stopped and asked him what was the matter. "I'll show you," and he sent the other clerk out for an officer and would not allow me to explain or rectify the mistake. When the officer came in, he said: "This fellow is a skin[71] and has cheated me out of some money." I explained to the officer and said if there has been any mistake, it was done unintentionally so far as I am concerned. "The trouble is this man is all upset and excited. Let him count his money and if he finds I have one cent belonging to him, I'll make him a present of ten dollars."

---

[70]The chronology of Appo's relationship with Tom Wilson, whose real name was Thomas Woods, is confusing because the narrative combines several disparate events.
[71]Someone who fleeces or extorts another.

He and the officer went to the money drawer. He counted, after telling the officer, the amount he ought to have and said: "I'm short of five dollars" and as he closed the drawer, he stooped down and found his five dollars on the floor behind his counter, where I had thrown it without him seeing me do so. Still he persisted to have me locked up, so I was taken before Chief [John E.] Murphy at police headquarters, who wanted to know my business. Not being satisfied with my answers, he locked me up and sent his men around the town looking for complaints of a similar kind of graft, but could find none. At all events, he took my photo and I was brought before a magistrate, who discharged me at once.[72]

. . . I left Columbus that night with Wilson for Cleveland, Ohio, where I was very successful. After a week's stay in Cleveland, I left the city with about $600 in my pocket for Buffalo, New York. As my partner, Tom Wilson, objected to come east with me, we separated and he went west. I remained in Buffalo a few days and left there for Rochester and then to Syracuse and then to Albany for New York City and arrived here with about $800 saved over all expenses.

THOMAS WILSON

I then went directly down to the opium joint at 4 Mott Street, and was agreeably surprised to meet my former partner in grafting, Thomas Wilson, smoking opium. I told him I had just got out of prison after serving a year. Wilson got up from the bunk and we both went to lunch at his expense, and then back to the opium joint where I sat watching him and ten other girls and men smoking the drug and listening to the plans of Wilson's intentions about leaving New York. Finally, I agreed to go away with him on the road stealing again. We left the opium joint about 2 a.m. and slept in Wilson's until after 9 a.m. . . . We separated and I walked down to Broadway and Fulton Street.

The first thing I saw was a young man with a wad of bills almost falling out of his vest pocket as he passed me near the crossing. I reached and got the money, walked through Fulton Street to Nassau Street and counted the money in an entrance hall and found I had $48. I then bought a suitcase and some clothes. I rented a room just to put my

[72]John E. Murphy served as superintendent or chief of Police in Columbus, Ohio, from 1887 to 1893. He later founded Murphy and Co.'s Detective Agency and Merchants' Police Bureau.

"grip"[73] and things for safekeeping and then went to the opium joint on Mott Street and found the place full of habitués, all lying down beside the opium layouts, both men and women smoking opium. I then went to where Wilson was smoking and lay down beside the layout, and began to smoke opium once more with Wilson. I told him I was going to leave New York for Philadelphia in the morning. He said he would go with me and we became partners again. The next morning we both got our grips and started on the road to graft together once more.

We remained about two weeks in Philadelphia. From there we traveled from town to city until we arrived at Kansas City, where my partner, Wilson, was taken very sick with a hemorrhage of the lungs.[74] Consequently, he wanted to reach Denver, where he believed he would recover by the good effects of the climate there. So I hustled about to get the money for necessary expenses and we left Kansas City for Omaha, Nebraska.

That night on the train Wilson took a severe hemorrhage and fell unconscious. The conductor brought a doctor from the "sleeper" who stopped the hemorrhage and told me I had better take him off at the next stop and bring him to a hospital, as he would probably not live if he got another attack. I then said to Wilson: "Now, Tommy, the doctor says you are in a bad condition. We have been together for some time. You are a well-educated man and you must come from good people. Tell me your right name and where your folks are and home is, and I will bring you safely there if I have to carry you there myself."

He replied: "My name is Thomas Woods and my home is in Lindsay, Canada."

The morning brought us to Omaha, where I put him in a room, as he would not go to a hospital. To make matters worse, we both had an opium habit. As he could not leave the room, I had to get an opium outfit and smoke the drug in the room with him, instead of going to a joint (a Chinese laundry).[75] At all events, he seemed to improve and gained strength. After a two-week stay, we left Omaha for Kansas City and kept on going from town to city without any mishaps, until we reached the town of Lafayette, Indiana, where there was no opium to be obtained at any price. Consequently, we had to leave that town, and when I got to the railroad depot at 7:30 p.m. in wintertime, I found I had but enough money for one fare to Logansport, Indiana. So I had to use my wits, so to speak, and get us both there on one fare. I went to the telegrapher in the

---

[73]A small amount of luggage wrapped in a sack and held together by a strap, or "grip."
[74]Wilson was probably suffering from an advanced case of tuberculosis.
[75]After 1870, opium users claimed that if a town did not have an opium den, interested parties could often purchase opium from local Chinese laundrymen.

station and asked him in a railroad employer's way for the conductor's name. I said: "Who goes out on the 7:45 this evening?"

He replied: "Edmonds."

"Johnny Edmonds?" asked I.

"No, Eddie Edmonds," said the telegrapher.

So I got the full name of the conductor and went out on the platform of the station where I saw the conductor standing with a lantern in his hand by his train. I approached him and said: "Mr. Edmonds can I speak to you?"

"Yes, what is it?"

I replied: "I'm taking a very sick friend home and unfortunately I am run short of money, so if you will kindly take us over your division with one fare, you will do me a favor and when I see you at Logansport sometime, I will make good the balance. Eddie, there's my sick friend sitting on the windowsill."

He looked at Tommy, and said: "I don't like to do it, but under the circumstances, board the train and meet me on the platform of the smoker, when the train starts." I thanked him, and Wilson (Woods) and I took our grips, boarded the train and took a seat in the smoker car. When the train got in motion and some distance from the station and the conductor came to punch and collect the tickets, I met him on the platform, as instructed, and handed him the money, $8. He checked my hat with two slips and I gave one to Woods. The next morning we arrived in Logansport, where we stopped at the St. Charles Hotel and got a supply of opium at a Chinese laundry and remained four days in the city, and I was financially successful during the course of that time.

We left Logansport and kept on going from town to town until we reached Buffalo, New York, where we stayed two days only. From there we went to St. Catherine, Canada, then to Hamilton and then to Toronto, Canada, where I was very successful, as there was a big county fair going on. I left the fairgrounds with $600 and twenty-two watches.

When we got back to Toronto, Woods and I bought new clothes. I said to him: "Tommy, you and I had better leave here tonight for your home in Lindsay, Canada, and I won't do any more grafting (stealing) until I land you there safe. You ought to telegraph your people you are coming home," said I.

He replied, "No, it is best not to." That night we took the train for Lindsay and when we arrived there we went to the only hotel in the place—the Gibson House. After Woods got rested, we both started to go out to the farm where his folks were. When Woods entered the dairy where he knew his mother and sisters were, I remained down the road. The meeting between Woods and his mother was both sad and joyful.

I remained in Lindsay five days and had a very good time there with Tommy Woods's two brothers, who drove me all about the country, and on Sunday, took me to church where their sister belonged to the choir and was an excellent singer. I then bid them all goodbye, and left Lindsay for Toronto, where I stayed three days and then went to Montreal and stopped three weeks at the Rosin House. I was very successful during the course of my line of grafting. I then came to New York City by way of Buffalo, and on my arrival in New York, I went directly from the depot to an opium joint and found the place crowded with American men and women of all professions in life — high, low and degraded — all smoking opium in the Crosby Street joint. The proprietor of this place was Barney Maguire, the green goods financial backer at that time. . . . The place was located just across the street from the rear of Niblo's Garden Theatre. The place was soon advertised throughout the country as Maguire's Hop Joint.

GREEN GOODS

In the meantime, I became acquainted with the men in the green goods business and was employed by one of the "writers," that is a man who sent out thousands of green goods circulars throughout the United States and Canada, as his "steerer" or messenger. My part of the business as steerer was to go and meet the "come-on," or victim, at the hotel where he was instructed to come and do business. Then I told him that I was the confidential messenger of his friend "the Old Gentleman" and sent to conduct him safely to where he could transact business with impunity and safety.

I worked as a steerer for over eight years and was very successful. Everyone I steered to the "turning joint" always made a deal from $300 to $1,000. I received only ten percent of the money, while the "writer" and the man who put up the bankroll of $20,000 each received 45 percent of the deal. The man who put up the bankroll would have as many as fifteen writers on his staff and each of these men would bring on at least one or two victims per day.

I was then working for Eddie Parmeley who was the boss and financial backer of the business at that time.[76] I worked for Parmeley about

[76]Edward Parmeley, alias Edward Parmeley Jones, moved to New York in the 1870s and was befriended by Chatham Street saloonkeeper Patrick Divver. Parmeley operated four gambling dens on Chatham Square and Chatham Street before entering the green goods business in the 1880s. He became rich, moved to Bridgeport, Connecticut, and fled to Europe during the Lexow Committee hearings in 1894.

eighteen months and he had his headquarters at the time at the Point View Hotel at 110th Street and Central Park.

One day I was sent to the Ryan House in Elizabeth, New Jersey, to bring a "come-on" from Alabama. When I arrived at the Ryan House, I looked at the register and found two men instead of one. So I went up to their room, knocked on their door and walked in. I gave them the password (All is well) to show them I was the right man to talk business with. I told them I was simply the confidential messenger of their friend, the Old Gentleman, and was sent to conduct them safely to Mott Haven, where the Old Gentleman was waiting patiently with the goods for them.

"We expected to meet him and [the] goods right here," they said.

"Well, you understand the nature of the business and you certainly cannot expect the Old Gent, who is seventy-eight years of age to come here with twenty thousand of the goods and display them in a public hotel to two strangers," said I.

"How far is Mott Haven from here?" they asked.

"Only a short distance, and the place is very handy for you to make your train back home after you do business, whether you do business or not. All your expenses, hotel bills and railroad fare are paid to and from your home," said I.

"All right, we'll go at once."

So I got them to New York and brought them to 110th Street, planted them in the sitting room off the bar and went upstairs and told the salesman, Paddy O'Brien, or "Paddy the Pig," that there was two guys together downstairs.[77]

"Where are they from?" asked Paddy.

"Alabama," said I.

"Bring them up in ten minutes and I'll be ready for them."

So I went down and in ten minutes I brought them up and introduced old Bill Vosburg as the Old Gent and Paddy as the son of the Old Gent.[78] Paddy said to them: "Why, there are two of you here."

Then turning to me, he said: "Don't you know that I do business with but one man at a time? Take one of them out. I don't care which one it is."

[77]Thomas "Paddy the Pig" O'Brien (1846–?), alias John Allen or David Harman, was a "salesman" and a "bunco steerer" for the green goods operation of Eddie Parmeley. O'Brien was arrested in 1891, fled to England, and was captured, tried, convicted, and sentenced to ten years in prison. A few weeks after his conviction, he escaped and was never heard from again.

[78]Bill Vosburg (1826/1828–1904), alias "the Old Gentleman," "Old Bill," William Watson, or John Lee, worked for Eddie Parmeley and was also a prominent bank robber, safe blower, pickpocket stall, and green goods turner. Some claimed he was arrested fifteen to twenty times in New York City alone and stole a total of $2 million during his lifetime.

The biggest one of the two said, "I'll do the business and you wait outside."

So I took his partner down to the barroom, left him there and returned to the "turning joint" (salesroom) and took a seat at the table beside the "guy." Paddy was displaying the "goods" to him in ones, twos and fives, all spread out on the table.

After the "guy" had examined them, he said, "I'll take ten thousand of these goods."

So Paddy put the money in $1,000 packages, put $10,000 in the satchel, locked it, and at the same time cautioning the victim about being careful of giving his confidence to friends. A lot more talk [transpired] when suddenly the guy grabbed the satchel and $10,000, pulled out his gun and covered Paddy. I jumped up and snatched the gun from the guy, covered him with the gun and took the bag of money from him and threw it out the window into the stable yard where Eddie Parmeley's brother was always on the lookout for just such an event. I then emptied the slugs out of the gun and threw them outdoors and handed the empty gun back to the guy, saying to him: "Now sit down and do business like a man."

Turning to old Vosburg who was standing at the door, I said to him: "This man is all right and is not connected with the United States detectives. I will be responsible for him, knowing he will make a good and safe agent to handle the goods throughout his section of the country."

Old Vosburg shook his head in a doubtful manner and said to the guy: "I am surprised. I didn't think you would do anything like that. After our long correspondence, I had the utmost confidence in you, but no matter. What are your expenses to and from your home, your railroad fare, hotel bills and everything in general? I promised you your expenses whether you did business or not and you will find me a man of my word."

"Well," said the guy, "let me tell you. I and my partner was talking with a man on the train while coming here and he told us that the last time he was in New York he was swindled out of $200 and warned us to be mighty careful, so when you would not let my partner here with me to do business, I became suspicious that things were not all right. I am on the level in this business and you place the goods in my hand and I'll pay for them and pledge you my word that I'll handle them safe enough."

Old Bill Vosburg turned to Paddy the Pig and ordered him to go down and bring up $10,000 of the goods. Paddy went down for the goods and Vosburg said to the guy: "Remember, I am giving you the state rights. You will be the sole agent throughout your section of the country."

After a lot more encouraging talk, up came Paddy the Pig with the bankroll. He opened the bag and threw out the money carelessly on the table, counted out one package of five dollar notes, containing $1,000 in each package, and saying to the guy: "There is $1,000 in each package." As he picked up each package, he would pull off the end elastic and rip the money package up like one would a deck of cards showing the guy the money was there so as to save time instead of counting it all out. He put the $10,000 in the bag, and locked it up.

After giving the guy instructions and warning about making confidential friends and how to handle the goods, he said to the guy, and pointing to me: "My messenger will see you safe to the depot and see that you get your train and get away all right, so I'll bid you goodbye and, above all, follow my instructions to the letter." Paddy handed me the bag of money and while he was shaking the guy's hand and cautioning him, I was at the door and opened it about twelve inches. In a second, the fellow outside took the money bag from me and handed me a bag of paper. Paddy said he had better let me carry it to the railroad station.

"Oh, no, I'll take care of it, never fear." He therefore pulled out a roll of $650 and paid it to Vosburg for the goods.

When I got him and his partner near the depot, I advised him to express the goods to his home by the Adams Express Company, telling him that in case of a railroad accident, the goods would be found. By shipping them, they would reach home safely. I merely suggested this, fearing he would open the bag in the depot and discover that he was done and then make trouble. I was glad when he took my advice and expressed the bag of paper to his house. . . . They boarded their train and that was the last I ever saw of them.

I mention this incident merely to show the risk a green goods steerer takes in that business. He has to keep his wits about him from the time he meets his victim until he puts him safely on the train. After he has done business and believed that he has the goods safe in his possession, should the victim become the least suspicious that he has not the goods in the valise or box, he would open and see to make sure and the result would be a bullet for the steerer when he found blank paper instead of the greenbacks he paid for. In fact, every victim or "come-on" I ever met always carried a gun and would use it on the least provocation. At all events, I worked steadily for Eddie Parmeley for about fifteen months and during the course of that time, I was very prosperous and successful.

One day, for some cause or reason unknown to any of the employees (who were old-time "crooks," bank burglars, sneaks, pickpockets and sure thing grafters), Eddie Parmeley was forced to close up the business and make room for Jimmie McNally to operate the business with his bankroll.[79] Consequently, most of the crooks who worked for Parmeley had to go back to their rough line of business. Some of them still worked the green goods game under their own system and without giving up protection money to the police. Jim McNally had the police protection, not only in New York, but in New Jersey as well. He took money [from] the Haymarket pimps (men who lived off the shame of girls) and made it a business, putting them to work sending out a mail[ing] of green goods circulars and guaranteeing them protection from arrest.

In a very short time, McNally had the country flooded with his circulars and the victims coming on to do business in droves of fifteen and twenty per day. The ex-pimps would not take a chance as steerers, [so] McNally and his writers or correspondents got some of the steerers who worked for Parmeley and Barney Maguire to go after and bring on their victims to do business and then see them safely on board their train for home.

I went to work for two of McNally's correspondents [in 1891]. Their names were Harry Hilton and Dolph [Adolph] Saunders, both former Haymarket pimps and both well educated and confirmed opium habitués. I became acquainted with them in an opium joint owned by McNally on Forty-Sixth Street and Seventh Avenue.[80] This place was a regular meeting place for all McNally's green goods workers. I used to go there to find out what hotels they were using for their victims to stop at and when they expected a "come-on." When I would get the necessary information, I would go to the hotel and watch for the victim to register. When he would get to his room, I would call and say to him, "The Old Gentleman is waiting patiently for you with the goods. Follow me and I will conduct you safely to him. I am the messenger for your old friend, the Old Gentleman." I would then take him to another man with a bankroll and have the come-on do business with him instead of McNally. Therefore both the writer and McNally are the losers. That is called "stealing a guy." I would get 50 percent of the guy's money, whereas if I was working as a steerer, I would get only about from $10

[79]James "Jimmy" McNally (ca. 1861–?) was regarded as "the king of the green goods men." He allegedly began his criminal career as a pimp, later operated an opium den, and eventually ran a green goods operation (with a staff of thirty-five) earning more than $3,000 per day. McNally later lost his wealth, served time in an Illinois state prison, and was reportedly impoverished by 1907.

[80]Appo mistakenly identified this location as Forty-Second Street and Seventh Avenue.

to $20, no matter how big a deal this victim made. Anyway, I became well acquainted with Hilton & Saunders. As they offered me 10 percent for my service and gave me protection, I went to work for them and McNally. I worked for McNally and Saunders for nearly two years and was very successful as a steerer as most every victim I was sent after made a deal.[81]

POUGHKEEPSIE

One day in the month of February 1893,[82] Jim McNally had some misunderstanding with a police officer named [Michael] Morgan, up in Poughkeepsie, New York, to whom he paid money each week for the protection of his men from arrest, and to allow them to operate without molestation. In fact, during the course of the two years I worked to and from Poughkeepsie, I often met Officer Morgan in the barroom of the New York Hotel and talked and drank with him at the bar there. He knew what my business was.[83]

One night about 10 p.m., I met Dolph Saunders, the writer for Jim McNally and the man I was steering guys for, by appointment on Sixth Avenue and Twenty-Eighth Street in New York. Saunders said to me: "Now, George, you will have to get up to Poughkeepsie tonight by the next train out. The guy is there now I am sure. Take this letter and pointers and be sure to land him (the victim) because he is a thousand dollar deal and I don't want to lose him."

I said, "All right, I'll land him safe enough. Give me the pointers," which were the passwords — "safe and sure one hundred." These passwords were for me to say as an introduction to the victim on meeting him to convince him that he was meeting and talking to the right man. The letter was merely a message stating to the victim that I was merely the confidential messenger of the Old Gentleman who would conduct him safely to where he could transact the business with impunity.

I took the next train out and arrived in Poughkeepsie after midnight, February 12, 1893.[84] It was a very cold and stormy night. On reaching

---

[81]Appo claimed to have worked for McNally for five years. West Forty-Sixth Street was noted for the large number of brothels between Sixth Avenue and Broadway.

[82]Appo erroneously remembered the date as January 1894.

[83]Police officer Michael Morgan (1856–1921) joined the Poughkeepsie police force in 1891 and remained on the force and a court officer until his death in 1921.

[84]Appo erroneously remembered the date as January 11, 1893.

the New York Hotel, I looked over the hotel register for the name of the guy (Hiram Cassel) to see if he had arrived from North Carolina, but his name was not there on the book. So I asked the bartender, who knew all about the business. He said no guys had arrived in nearly a week and he wanted to know why they were coming on so slow. I then went to bed and got up at 5 a.m., took a look at the register and not seeing the guy's name, I went to the railroad depot and learned that all the trains were delayed by the snowstorm. I then returned to the hotel, where I waited until 8 a.m. As the guy did not arrive yet, I went skating with the hotel proprietor's son on the Hudson River.

At 9:15 a.m., I returned to the hotel and found the names of Hiram Cassel and Ira Hogshead on the hotel register. I went up to the room they were assigned to, knocked on the door and went inside. I found two, big, six-foot men (mountaineers), one sitting on the bed and the other standing by the washstand. As I entered, I said: "Safe and sure, one hundred. I'm glad to meet you." They both put out their hands and gave me a hearty handshake. I then handed them the sealed letter which introduced me as the messenger of this friend, the Old Gentleman, with whom they had been corresponding about the business. I then told them that the Old Gentleman could not understand what had delayed them so long. As he had other very important business that had to be attended to, he told me to wait here for you, and when you arrived, to bring you to Mott Haven, where you could examine the goods and do business with safety.

After a lot more talk with them, they said, "Well, how far is that place from here?"

"Oh," said I, "not far, only a short distance. I will get your tickets and go with you. After you are through business with the Old Gentleman, I will see you safely aboard the train for your home. When we go down to the depot, you and your friend keep together and follow me about ten feet behind and don't talk to and ask questions of anybody, not even me. Remember the nature of the business, and three is a crowd. Don't board the train until you see me get on board. Then take a seat near me. When the train starts, I will hand you your tickets and have a talk with you and give you other instructions. Do you want some lunch?"

"No, we have had plenty," said they.

"Well, our train for Mott Haven leaves in twenty minutes, so if there is anything you need, let me know and I'll get it for you."

"No, there's nothing, but we want to get to business as soon as possible," said they. "So let's go and take the cars and get there."

I then took them downstairs and outside the entrance and walked toward the depot which was only a block away. On reaching there, I bought three tickets for New York. When I got out on the platform of the station, I saw only one of the men standing there. I approached him and asked where his friend was.

He replied: "He stopped to talk with a man up the road."

"Oh," said I, "that will never do. I instructed him not to talk with anybody. You wait here. Don't board this train until I go and see what is detaining him and bring him here."

I left the station and when I reached the end of the street, I saw the guy (Hogshead) standing on the viaduct over the tunnel trying to attract his friend's attention to come back from the depot. On looking further ahead, I saw Officer Morgan about thirty feet away, walking with his head turned toward me. I thought nothing of this action at the time, so I approached the guy and said, "What seems to be the trouble? Do you want to lose this train?"

"I don't care to do business. I've changed my mind," said he.

"Well, I'm sorry to hear you talk in such a manner. You go back to the hotel and I'll bring your friend there, and we will talk the matter over. If you are still dissatisfied, I will wire your friend, the Old Gentleman and explain your actions. I am simply the messenger in this matter."

He started with me to the hotel and I left him there and brought his partner from the station and up to the bedroom of the hotel. His partner (Hogshead) stood by the washstand with his small satchel opened on it. Cassel sat down at the foot of the bed and there was space just wide enough between the side of the bed and the wall against which the washstand stood for a person to walk through sideways to get to the door or window. Hogshead opened his satchel and took a large flask of whiskey from it and took a large drink of the liquor and put the flask back again.

I then said, "Well, Mr. Hogshead, what seems to have changed your mind? I know that the Old Gentleman is really in need of an agent throughout your section to handle his goods. I will tell you what I will do to convince you that everything is just as he has represented to you. I will go to Mott Haven and explain to the Old Gentleman that you do not care to go any further and have him bring the goods here to you in this room where you both can examine them. If you find that they are not just as represented, whether you do business or not, all your expenses to and from your home, railroad fare, hotel bills and the loss of your time will be cheerfully paid you both by the Old Gentleman. I am simply his confidential messenger and I cannot do nothing further in the matter. You understand me, don't you?"

The guy, Mr. Cassel, who was sitting on the bed said, "That's fair and square, Hiram! What in h—— is the matter with you? Let's wait and have the goods brought here."

"I tell you! I know what I'm doing. I've changed my mind and that settles it," said Hogshead.

"Well, Mr. Hogshead, I'm very sorry to hear you talk in that manner. You are leaving an opportunity of your life go by unheeded, so I will bid you goodbye," said I, putting out my hand for Hogshead to shake. But he refused to shake hands. Instead, he again took a drink of whiskey from the flask.

I, in the meantime, turned my back to him in order to shake hands with Mr. Cassel, who got up, took my hand, and as I was about to say, "I'm sorry you will not wait here," Hogshead sneakingly took from his satchel a big Colt revolver. While I was shaking hands with Cassel and my back turned to him, he cowardly put the revolver to the back of my right temple and shot me. By a sudden turn of my head, I fortunately saved my life.

I don't remember even hearing the report of the gun and did not know anything for ten days after, as I lay unconscious during the course of that time. But I was told by a patron of the hotel who happened to be on the landing, that when he heard the report of the pistol, he saw the two guys rush out of the room and me staggering out after them and saying to the patron of the hotel: "Just hold him one minute. Oh, never mind." At the same time, Hogshead, who was halfway down the stairs, turned and fired another shot, but missed me. I fell to the floor at the head of the stairs.

When I came to, I found myself in the hospital and a nurse at my bedside to whom I asked, "What is the trouble with me?"

"Keep quiet, now," and off he went for the doctor.

In the meantime I tried to get my senses about me. When the good doctor came, I asked him what was the matter and how long I had been asleep. When I tried to get up I fell back again on the pillow and blood came from my wounded eye. The nurse fixed me all right again, gave me some medicine and I went to sleep. The next morning I awoke and found the sun shining bright and I in full possession of my senses. I then missed my right eye and remembered the two "guys" Cassel and Hogshead and concluded that Hogshead had shot me cowardly from behind. When the doctor came and he asked me how I felt, I said all right, and asked permission to get up, but was told to keep quiet and I would be all right in a day or so.

While I was propped up in bed that day, I was surprised by a visit from the policeman Morgan, who came to my bed and asked me, "How are you feeling, George? I did not think that 'guy' would shoot you. Too bad you've lost your eye."

I realized at once, remembering seeing Morgan walking with his head turned toward me and Hogshead just before the shooting, that he was the man who spoke and warned Hogshead to have nothing to do with me.

I said to Morgan: "That's poor consolation to give me now. If you and my backer (McNally) had any grievance or falling-out, why didn't you come to me and say, 'Get out of here! You can't do no business here.' I would have taken heed and left the town."

"Well," said he, "it is done and it can't be helped any now, so the less you say about the matter, the better it will be. Keep quiet, and everything may come out all right. I will see you again."

On the next day, the doctor gave me permission to get up and sit at the window. On the following day, I was taken from the Vassar Hospital to the jail where I was put in a hospital cell and remained there for about ten days when I was released under $1,500 bail.

During the course of those ten days in jail, the keeper came to me one day and asked me if I wanted to see and have a talk with the man who shot me, as he was very anxious to see me. I said to the keeper, "I don't want to see him in particular, but if he wants to see me, and you have no objection, why, all right, I'll see him."

So the keeper unlocked the room door and led me across the tier to another room like the one I was in and unlocked the door and there was the two big "guys" seated on the cots, looking the most forlorn of all God's creatures, men without a single friend in all the world. I approached Mr. Cassel and, shaking him by the hand, said, "I am sorry to see you locked up here for this shooting, but you need not worry for I will make no complaint. Therefore they will merely hold you as a witness at my trial and then release you."

Cassel said, "I tell you, I'm mighty glad to see you alive and well. I can't understand how that darn fool yonder (pointing at Hogshead) could shoot down a little fellow like you. Why, the whole town's talking mad about him."

I motioned him not to talk and said to him, "It could not be helped. The shooting was an accident, you understand?"

"Do you know," said he, "this darn affair has cost me over $3,000 already for lawyer's fees and 'fixing things up' as they call it around this section."

I told him not to pay out one cent more and that whoever told them "he was fixing things up" to have him released was a fraud and skin. I then turned around to his partner, Hogshead, and said in a whisper, "Well, you meant business that time, but accidents will happen and they can't do anything to you for an accident. You understand me? So you need not worry anymore and above all don't pay out another cent of your money to the lawyer."

I then shook hands with them, bid him goodbye and said, "I hope you will get out of this soon and I forgive you."

The keeper then came to the door and I returned with him to my room, and he said to me, "Them two fellows are big husky mountaineers and it's a wonder your head wasn't carried completely off your body with the big gun that was found on Hogshead." I left the jail soon after this on $1,500 bonds and in about three weeks after my case was called for trial.

I appeared at court with my lawyer, pleaded not guilty and stood trial. The jury found me guilty without leaving their seats and I was sentenced to three years, two months and to pay a fine of $250 to Sing Sing Prison. I went to Sing Sing Prison and my lawyer appealed the case to the general term of the supreme court and two judges decided against me and one, Judge [Calvin E.] Pratt, decided in my favor. With this encouragement, I appealed to the court of appeals and the seven judges rendered a favorable decision for me and said my conviction was an outrage. I was released at once, after serving nine months and two weeks in the Clinton Prison at Dannemora.

CLINTON AGAIN

During the course of that time, I had a tough deal from being hounded and punished by a keeper named [Michael] Haggerty, who had charge of the jail hall.[85] This keeper in 1878 and I had trouble with each other. In fact, he was the most inhuman brute that ever existed in my estimation and many a poor, unfortunate convict was driven insane and made sick unto death from this brute's inhuman treatment. He had charge of the

---

[85]Appo misspelled keeper Michael Haggerty's name as "Hagerty."

dark cells and did most of the paddling of convicts under punishment at that time.[86]

I had been reported for having a piece of a New York newspaper (the *Herald*) and reading it in my cell on a Sunday. The guard who caught me reading it unlocked my door and took me and the piece of newspaper to the guard room and the deputy warden asked me where I got it. I told him the truth, that I found it in the officers toilet. He demanded to know which one. I refused to tell him, not wishing to get my shopkeeper or the contract foreman into trouble. Consequently, he ordered me locked up in the dark cell and kept there until I told where I got the newspaper. I was then taken and put in the "cooler," as the dark cells were called, and as it was on a Sunday, keeper Haggerty was off duty for that day, but on Monday morning he came to the dark cells to feed the men in the "coolers" on two ounces of bread and a gill of water.

When he came to my door, he swung it violently open and shouted at me. "D—— you! Get up here and take your ration."

"I don't want it," I replied.

"You don't, hey? I'll bet you will before I get through with you," and he threw the little piece of bread at me and the gill of water on the cell floor, and then slammed the door and locked it.

In about an hour the deputy came with Haggerty, opened my door and said to me: "Have you made up your mind to tell me where you put that paper?"

"I have told you all that is necessary and I have nothing more to say," said I.

"We will see about that," said Deputy Warden [James] Moon.[87]

Keeper Haggerty said to him: "You see he has thrown his ration of bread and water on the floor."

"What did you do that for?" asked Moon.

"I did not throw it there. The keeper did and threatened me because I told him I did not want it."

"You lie!" said Haggerty and violently pushed me back from the door into the cell and slammed the door. Haggerty every morning came. When I refused to accept the punishment rations, he would swear at me and throw the bread and water on the floor, where he would find

---

[86]Appo had been incarcerated in Clinton Prison from October 13, 1877, to January 8, 1879, under the alias George Wilson. Haggerty was later investigated for cruelty.

[87]James Moon began working at Clinton Prison in 1876 and was quickly promoted to sergeant of the guard. He was appointed principal keeper in 1877, serving until at least 1882 before being succeeded by John Parkhurst. By 1891, Moon was principal keeper again and brought up on charges of brutality.

the bread still lying there each morning on the floor where he threw it. For fourteen days, I never even drank a drop of water or ate a crumb of bread.

Finally, on the fifteenth day, he came and found me lying on the floor weak and sick. He came in the cell, gave me a kick and said: "Get up on your feet." I got up and as he stepped out from the cell, I picked up the wooden pail and threw it and all its contents at his head, and I fell helpless on the floor. The doctor, [E. D.] Ferguson by name, came and gave orders to remove me to the screen cell.[88]

These cells are not so bad as the coolers as there is a cot and one gets two meals a day. In these screen cells at that time, there were three other poor fellows gone insane from brutal treatment. One poor fellow, named Mike Hicks, was chained down to a ring bolt on the floor where he died. I used to hear keeper Haggerty cursing and kicking this poor fellow every day. I reported it to the doctor who told me to "shut up."

One day the doctor came and took Mike Hicks up to a room in the hospital, a dead man, and put me in confinement to a light cell. This all happened in 1878.[89]

So when I came back to Dannemora, many years later for being shot in the green goods business, Haggerty remembered me. To my misfortune I was placed to work in the jail hall under his charge. The first thing he said and did to me, was: "So you are back again, how much time have you got?" I told him. "Well, you better behave yourself or you'll never live to do it. I'll put you as a helper on a tier and you do what the other man tells you to do, you understand?"

I simply said: "Yes, sir."

He called the convict I was to help and work with on the tier, and said to him: "Take this fellow and show him what you want him to do and see that he does it all right." "Now, you go with him," said he to me. I worked with this convict named Quinn, a burglar by profession and as I found out later a handyman for Haggerty who put him up to make trouble for me. I was warned by the other convicts to look out for him.

Sure enough, one day he began by ordering and shouting loudly at me whenever Haggerty was near. Still I paid no attention to him until one day he ordered me to put the water kits out by the cell doors on the top tier. I started to do so and when I got about half the tier done, he

[88]E. D. Ferguson was the Clinton physician from 1876 to 1878. Appo misspelled his name as "Furgeson."

[89]Appo erroneously remembered the year as 1879. The prisoner Appo described is probably Thomas Hicks, who was involved in an unsuccessful escape attempt on April 17, 1878. Sixteen men died in Clinton during Appo's term there.

came running and shouting at me to get down on the lower tier. I told him I would as soon as I finished the tier that I was on, and told him it was [not] necessary for him to shout at me, that one would think he was under a salary of a keeper. He then rushed at me and I struck him a blow on the nose making it bleed. During this mix-up, Haggerty, who was on the tier below us, came running up with his heavy stick upraised. I saw that I was in trouble, so I went at Quinn and began to punch him, and get punished for something.

In the meantime, Quinn ran toward Haggerty, shouting: "Look out, he's got a knife!" Haggerty demanded me to hand over the imaginary knife. I told him I had no knife. He then took me to the guard room before the deputy warden McKennon, who asked Quinn what the trouble was about. He replied that I without any cause came behind him and struck him on the nose and threatened to cut him. I denied Quinn's statement and tried to explain the truth, but I stood no show. The consequence was [that] I was locked up in the dark cell where I remained for twelve days and nights.

Every morning Haggerty would throw the two ounces of bread at me and say: "Here, d—— you, drink this," handing me a gill of water which I refused. He would then say: "I'll bet you drink it before I get through with you," and then he would slam the black door with a bang, the same as he did in 1878, with a curse.

On the afternoon of the twelfth day of my dark cell confinement, the deputy came to me and said: "Why don't you behave yourself?"

I replied: "Why don't you give me a chance and put me to work with a man and not a scheming inhuman brute who has had it in for me ever since 1878, when I was here under punishment, and exposed his brutality to the public through the press when I got free and I will do so again." The deputy then asked me if I knew Eddie Parmeley (the green goods financial backer). I told him, yes, and that Parmeley was a resident of Troy, N.Y.

"Well," said he, "I'm sorry you had this trouble. I'll put you in a light cell for a few days and then place you in a shop where you will not be bothered." So he took me out of the "cooler," gave me a fine cup of coffee and a big ham sandwich and placed me in a light cell. In three days I was assigned to work in the wrapper shop, folding women's wrappers, where I worked for nine months.

One day, unexpectedly, the keeper came to me and said, "Get ready, you are going home."

I left everything I had to the convict who worked next to me on the bench and went with the keeper to the state shop, took off the "stripes" and put on a suit of salt bag citizen's clothes, furnished by the state, by the way. The $40 suit of clothes I brought to prison I never saw again. Anyway, I had $60 in the front office that I brought with me, and as soon as I got to New York, I bought a nice suit of clothes and gave the "salt bags" to a poor fellow who needed them, and went down to my lawyer's office and thanked him for his untiring efforts in my behalf. Then, of course, I called on my financial backer, Jim McNally. In three days I was again working as steerer for the green goods business for him and continued working for about six weeks, when McNally had to close up.

STEALING GUYS

I went to work for Mike Ryan, who had his green goods headquarters down on West and Liberty Streets.[90] He had everything right in that precinct and worked the business without interference or molestation of the police. In fact, Mike Ryan was the political boss of that district and had big influence with police captain Richard O'Connor.[91] When attached to the district attorney's office some years before he became a police captain, O'Connor told Recorder Hackett, before whom I pled guilty to grand larceny, that I was a notorious thief. Consequently, I was sentenced to two years and six months in state prison. When he heard that I was working for Mike Ryan, he told Ryan to keep me away from his precinct. One morning, when I came to work, Ryan took me aside and said, "George, you are the best little fellow I have working and I cannot go into details. In fact, I am forced to tell you not to come down here anymore to work."

So I left Ryan, and as there was no other green goods financial backer working under police protection, I hunted up a man named "Dutch Gus" who had a bankroll. I told him I had a scheme to steal all of Ryan's "guys" (victims) if he would take their orders and "beat" them for the money.

Gus said: "You bring the guys and I'll get their coin."

The next morning, I watched the side entrance of the North River Hotel barroom on West and Barclay Streets. One of Ryan's steerers

[90]Michael Ryan (1843–?) was an ex-convict, professional gambler, and green goods dealer in lower Manhattan who once worked for James McNally. During the 1880s and 1890s, he was McNally's rival, controlling territory south of Fourteenth Street and west of Broadway. Before the Lexow Committee in 1894, Ryan described himself as a bookmaker, gambler, and "speculator in anything."

[91]Richard O'Connor was appointed to the police force in 1873 and promoted to the rank of captain in 1887. After his transfer to the Twentieth (Tenderloin) Precinct in 1892, he tolerated the many gambling and prostitution activities in the district.

came along with a guy and entered the sitting room. He sat the guy at a table and told him that he was going to tell the Old Gentleman of his arrival. The steerer left the place and walked down toward Liberty Street to tell Ryan to get the turning joint ready for business.

In the meantime, I entered the sitting room, walked to the guy at the table and said to him, "The regular messenger won't be back and the Old Gentleman is waiting patiently for you with the goods, so follow me."

The guy got up and I took him on a fast walk to Gus. He made a $300 deal, and I then took him to the Grand Central Station, saw him safe aboard his train and then returned to Gus and received my share of the deal—$150.

I then went down to Mike Ryan. . . . I told him that I was sorry for his loss, and again asked him if there was any chance for me. He said no, so I left him abruptly and stole two more guys from him at two different times and brought them to Gus who made successful deals with each one separately at $500 apiece. My share was 50 percent of both deals.

I would have continued to steal Ryan's guys every chance that came my way, but one morning an unexpected event happened to me as I left the house where I lived.

THE LEXOW COMMITTEE

On reaching the sidewalk, I was approached by two men, Arthur Dennett and [Thomas] Carney, who represented themselves as officers of the Lexow Committee.[92]

After I demanded their authority, Mr. Dennett handed me a subpoena, saying, "This will explain matters."

I read the paper and as I had no idea what the Lexow Committee was or meant, I became suspicious and refused to accompany them.

Then Carney said: "We are sent up here to take you dead or alive."

"Well," said I, "if that's the case, I'll go down with you, but I assure you there is no information of any importance that I can give that would be of any interest or value to you or the committee. So you are only wasting time bothering with me."

"Well, we will see about that," said Mr. Dennett. "All that is wanted of you is to tell how you come to get shot up at Poughkeepsie."

[92]The Lexow Committee was a privately financed (by the New York Chamber of Commerce), Republican-led investigation of municipal corruption in New York City in 1894. The committee was chaired by state senator Clarence Lexow. The highly publicized hearings and final report exposed the depth of police and political malfeasance in New York City.

When we arrived at Judge [John] Goff's office, I was interviewed by him and then taken before the Lexow Committee and put upon the witness stand.[93] For three hours I was questioned by the counselors, Mr. Frank Moss[94] and Honorable Judge Goff. When they got through with me, there was nothing else I could say about the systematic grafting of the then police. The press then began to write me up in all kinds of characters,[95] representing me to the police and the underworld associates in anything but a favorable light to them.[96] They began to look on me as a dangerous fellow to them.

The consequences were that one morning [on September 28, 1894] on leaving the office of Judge Goff, I was met on Broadway and Barclay Street by Mike Riordan, who was then the confidential man for police captain Richard O'Connor and Mike Ryan. Riordan stopped me and said: "How are you? Mike Ryan would like to see and have a little talk with you. He is down at the North River Hotel. Come on down with me."

So I walked down with him to the North River Hotel, entered the barroom where Riordan met and spoke to the proprietor who went upstairs and returned in a few minutes and said: "Come back here," and led the way to a private sitting room.

"Mike will be here shortly. What will you have to drink?" said he. I ordered a cigar and Riordan said: "Bring me a whiskey. Why don't you drink something, George?"

"No, thank you. I'm just after eating." Instead of the proprietor going to the bar to serve the order, Riordan went out and brought me a cigar and a glass of whiskey for himself. Just then in Ryan [entered] and we all sat down at a table.

I said: "I will take a little whiskey," knowing that Riordan would drink the same from the same bottle, and the proprietor and Ryan ordered a

[93]John William Goff (1848–1924) was an Irish immigrant who grew up in poverty in New York City. After being educated at Cooper Union, he was admitted to the New York State Bar Association and became associated with numerous Irish independence organizations. In 1888, he became assistant district attorney for New York City, and in 1894 he was elected to the office of recorder against the Tammany Hall–backed incumbent. He served on the New York Supreme Court from 1906 to 1919.

[94]Frank Moss (1860–1920) was counsel for the Society for the Prevention of Crime, first gaining notice when he prosecuted the proprietors of brothels in 1887. He succeeded Theodore Roosevelt as president of the board of police commissioners in 1897 and continued his attacks on public prostitution, at one point characterizing Oscar Hammerstein's Olympia, one of New York's largest theater complexes, as a brothel. Moss served as an assistant to the New York City district attorney from 1909 to 1914. He wrote about Appo in his three-volume work *The American Metropolis* (1897).

[95]Appo is referring to the negative characterizations of him in the newspapers.

[96]New York newspapers published stories several weeks earlier that Appo would betray his green goods associates when he appeared before the Lexow Committee.

small bottle of wine. Riordan then went out for the drinks and said to me: "George, I am surprised at you going before that committee and saying what you did. Did the committee ask or say anything about Captain O'Connor?"

"No, not that I know of, but they were very much interested about you from the way they questioned me while on the stand. In fact, they know more about your business and yourself than I do. Anything you read in the papers about me and what I said on the stand you must not believe or pay any attention to it. It is all lies and exaggeration. I believe you have some fellow now associated with you, or someone working for you, who is giving information to some reporter who is publishing all that stuff about your doings and making it look as though I was responsible for it," said I.

Just then, Mike Riordan came in with the drinks on a tray. He set the bottle of wine and the wineglasses on the table. I noticed that he was very careful in selecting one of the two glasses containing the whiskey, setting it down in front of me and saying: "Well, drink up George." I took the glass and as I raised it, I noticed an almost imperceptible whitish color floating on the top of the whiskey, but said nothing. I began to talk to Ryan so as to delay drinking it. When Riordan said, "Why don't you drink up?" I raised the glass and tasted the whiskey. Sure enough, I tasted the drug or the poison that Riordan had put in the whiskey to do me harm. I got up from the table as though to finish the drink, and as I noticed the both doors of the room were closed, I let the glass of whiskey fall from my hand as though by accident. Riordan jumped at me and struck me on the head with a blackjack, but I grasped the wine bottle and smashed him on the nose with it and upset the table so as to give me time to get at the door leading to the barroom. I made a punch at the proprietor with the broken bottle, who was in my way and reached the barroom, when I received another blow on the head, making a bad scalp wound. Before I became unconscious, I smashed the glass on the street door to attract attention. That was all unnecessary because an officer, named O'Connor, who was a relation to the Captain O'Connor, was and had been waiting about the entrance all the time I was in the sitting room with Ryan and the other two.

I was then taken to the Chambers Street Hospital. When I came to, I found myself in bed and my head all bandaged up and Captain O'Connor's relative sitting at my bedside in a uniform. I asked him what hospital I was in. "Shut your mouth up, d—— you!" was his reply to me. I saw the doctor in the ward and called him, and told him I was well enough to get up.

That same afternoon, I was taken to the private room of Captain O'Connor at the Church Street Police Station, who said to me: "What was all the trouble about?" I explained everything just as it happened and my grounds for suspecting their bad intentions to injure me.

"I don't think so, but I'll look into the matter," said the captain. "By the way, what had you to say about me before that committee?" asked he.

I replied: "Nothing. I don't remember your name even being mentioned by any person I know of connected with the investigating committee."

He got up from his chair and said to the policeman O'Connor: "All right, take him to court." I was then brought to the Centre Street Court, where Mr. [William] Travers Jerome pleaded my case as counselor and I was released.[97]

About two weeks after this affair, I met a man named Mahoney who was a frequenter of Sam Pettit's saloon on West Street, just south of Liberty Street, where Mike Ryan and his green goods men used as a meeting place.[98] Mahoney said to me: "You were very lucky. Ryan and Riordan meant to 'croak' (kill) you and put your body in a bag. Johns the expressman was to drop it into the river."

"How do you know that?" I asked.

"I overheard it in Sam Pettit's. I advise you to keep away from around West Street."

I told him, "I have no fear of Ryan or anyone else connected with him, and you can tell him so when you see him." I had no more trouble from Ryan.

The daily papers kept continually writing articles about me exposing the evil doings of the police and many other exaggerated lies about crooks being allowed by them to ply their crooked business with impunity by paying the police protection money. The consequences of all this newspaper talk made many bad and dangerous enemies for me, especially among my former associates and friendly acquaintances among the political ward "heelers"[99] in the different parts of the city. The reporters would write and publish articles about me criticizing the high police officials and their administration and a lot of other things

[97]William Travers Jerome (1859–1934) was one of the leading trial lawyers in New York by the early 1890s and served as counsel for the Lexow Committee in 1894. As New York City district attorney from 1901 to 1910, he led an ongoing campaign against gambling in the city.

[98]Pettit's saloon, at 87 West Street in lower Manhattan, was considered one of the best locations for green goods operations because of its proximity to ferry stations along the Hudson River, allowing for the quick movement of potential victims in and out of New York.

[99]Low-level workers for local politicians.

I never mentioned, that were lies from beginning to end. In fact, these same reporters I had never seen or met or talked with any person on the articles that were published. I mention this to show why I was assaulted so frequently by the police and others and forced to defend myself after the Ryan affair and the publications of the press.

IN THE TENDERLOIN

One day [in September 1894] I was standing on Centre Street near Leonard. Suddenly I was tapped on the shoulder and greeted with: "Hello! You are just the fellow I want to see. What are you doing now?" asked the lawyer Edmund E. Price.

"Nothing, can you get me something to do?" I replied.

"Yes, come with me to my office." I went with him and on entering his office, he said, "Now, George, take a seat." I sat by a center table and the lawyer said to me: "I have written a play and am about to have it staged. The name of the play will be *In the Tenderloin* and will be under the management of George W. Lederer.[100] Now I would like to have you take a principal part in the green goods scene where Tom Davis gets shot dead by the Texans Holland & Hill, who came on to steal the bankroll from Davis. You remember, George, I had their case in court and had them discharged," said Price.[101]

"Yes, I remember both the shooting and the trial of the Texans who shot Davis dead."

"Well, George, I want you to take the part of the steerer and be in the turning joint scene when the shooting comes off, and the minor parts in the play. If you are satisfied to do this, I will arrange with Mr. Lederer to pay you $50 per week and expenses while on the road."

"All right, I will accept your offer at once," said I. He made up the written contract. I read it and signed it and we both went up to the Bijou Theatre on Broadway where we met Geo. W. Lederer and his theatrical Manager, Dunlevy. . . .

The next morning at 9 a.m., I arrived at the Bijou Theatre and met Dunlevy and all the actors who were to take a part in the play. I was handed my part in writing and we then began to rehearse each [of] our parts. At the end of the rehearsal I was told that I did fine and to always

---

[100]George Lederer (1862–1938) was a Broadway actor, stage manager, and director.

[101]Price's melodrama was based on the murder of green goods operator Tom Davis. He was killed by James T. Holland of Texas on August 31, 1885, at the Rapid Transit Hotel at 113 Reade Street in New York.

continue to do the same and make no change in my talk or actions in the future. We rehearsed morning and night for one week.

The play was produced at the People's Theatre on the Bowery for the first time after much advertising in the daily papers and my picture plastered on the bills of the dead walls of the city.[102] On this first night of my appearance as an actor, I stood behind the scenes with an actor beside me who was told to prompt me so that I would make no mistake. When my turn came to go on the stage, he kept saying, "Watch your cue." All of a sudden he gave me a push between the two other actors, saying: "Introduce Holland & Hill." Now that was all unnecessary for him to do that and he came near causing me to slide in on the stage. Anyway, I controlled myself and as I appeared on the stage with the two Texans (Holland & Hill) I was given a great encore by the audience and the house was packed.

After the play was over, Mr. Lederer said to me: "George, you did splendid. I am satisfied."

The two first weeks I played at the People's and Brooklyn Theatres, I was paid my salary of $50 per week. But when we started on the road, I never got one cent of my salary for three weeks, nor did any of the others of the company get paid. Yet we were drawing full houses wherever we played and Lederer was making good sums of money. When we disbanded at Indianapolis, Indiana, and after much anxiety and waiting, our hotel bill and railroad fare was paid. After all the scenery and baggage was put aboard the train and the hotel bills paid, we all took the train bound for New York and I was told by the manager of the company that the show was disbanded and that I would be paid my three weeks salary ($150) as soon as I arrived in New York. . . .

When I arrived in New York, I went direct to the Bijou Theatre to get my money and found two of the actors of the company there ahead of me, waiting to see the treasurer for their money. I asked them if they had been paid yet. "No! Nor do we expect to be paid a cent. It seems to me that Lederer intends to do us all," said one of the actors to me.

"Well," said I, "you as a professional actor can make him pay you what he owes you for your labor by bringing him into court."

They both began to laugh at me and said: "Let me tell you something. There is not an actor in the business who has nerve enough to make a

[102]Appo erred in remembering the precise chronology of these events. He erroneously believed that his encounter with Price occurred in 1899 and that the production *In the Tenderloin* opened at the London Theater on the Bowery. The production opened at the Grand Opera House in New Haven, Connecticut, in November 1894. In December, it moved to the Star Theatre in Brooklyn, and then it opened in New York on December 17, 1894, at Henry C. Miner's People's Theatre, 201 Bowery.

Figure 4. *Scene from* In the Tenderloin

Appo's testimony before the Lexow Committee in 1894 and his shooting a year earlier briefly made him a minor celebrity. He was invited to play himself in a melodrama about the New York underworld, an early "reality-based" play called *In the Tenderloin*. The production, which included this concert saloon scene, lasted only two months. The show's popularity, however, illustrated the public's ever-growing fascination with criminal life.

Source: "Plays and Players," *Illustrated American,* January 5, 1895.

complaint when he gets beat out of his salary. Every one of us gets the worse end of it quite often and we dare not complain. If we did, we would find attached beside our names in the books of the dramatic agency a big 'K' which denotes '<u>Kicker.</u>' When a company is being formed, the manager looks for actors to fill parts in the play, and sees the big 'K' beside the name, that actor will never get a date, as he is put down as a "Kicker."

While he was telling me this, in walks the treasurer, bowing and smiling, and said: "Well, gentlemen, what can I do for you?"

I said: "I was sent here by the manager, Mr. Dunlevy of the play *In The Tenderloin* to be paid three weeks' salary now due me ($150)."

"Oh, yes, you are George Appo. Well, Mr. Lederer is in the city today and you come here tomorrow and I will let you have five dollars to see you through until then." He handed me five dollars and a receipt for the same for me to sign. I signed it and went away.

As I got to the street, I met another actor of the company who asked me if the treasurer was inside. I said: "Yes, and he paid me five dollars."

"Did you sign a receipt for the five dollars?"

"Yes, of course," said I.

"You were foolish to do so. Now you won't get another cent out of Lederer and no matter how hard you kick, he has the best of you for six years on that receipt," said the actor to me.

Well, I called every day for one month but was told always that Mr. Lederer was out of town and from that day until this present day (July 17th, 1915) and naturally have given up all hope of ever receiving the balance of that three weeks' salary ($150) still due me.

Such was my experience on the stage in my efforts to earn an honest living. I found that the system of cheating the actors out of their hard-earned money was a common practice with such men as George W. Lederer who financially back the shows they take on the road. The poor actor dare not complain for fear of the loss of a future date with some other show. In fact, I tried time and again to see Lederer and obtain at least a portion of the money owed by him, but failed. I even consulted the lawyer, Edmund E. Price, who got me to sign the contract and take the part needed in the play. The only encouragement he gave me was: "I can't do nothing in the matter. Wait until you see Mr. Lederer and I guess he will settle up with you all right then." So I got tired and disgusted in my efforts to connect with Lederer.

VIOLENCE

One day [April 9, 1895], soon after the first article published about the police with my name signed to it, I was on the northeast corner of Sixth Avenue and Twenty-Eighth Street to meet an actor named Theodore Babcock.[103] When he appeared, I invited him to have a drink, and on entering the saloon, I noticed a young fellow whom I knew as a Haymarket "cadet" (pimp) standing in front of the side door of the saloon talking

[103]Theodore Babcock was a minor actor who performed in New York in the 1890s. Appo erroneously believed the ensuing events in this passage transpired before his performance in *In the Tenderloin*. Since they took place after, I have moved them to this part of his narrative.

with an officer in uniform. I saw him nudge the policeman and point at me. As Babcock and me had our drinks placed before us, this young cadet came and stood beside Babcock and gave him a push, saying, "What's the matter, do you want the whole bar to yourself?" Of course, Babcock became surprised and indignant and the cadet struck him a violent blow in the face.

I immediately smashed the cadet and he clinched me. In a moment, the policeman ([Michael J.] Rein by name) rushed in from the side door and struck me a violent blow on the head, splitting the scalp open about three inches.[104] I held on to the cadet and grabbed a glass from the counter and struck him with it, and took all the fight out of him. In the meantime, the officer kept hitting me on the back and sides with his club. I managed to get my penknife out and opened. In order to protect myself from the club, I rushed in on the policeman and give him all he deserved. He laid on the sidewalk after he sneaked out of the saloon.

I remained there and two other policemen came and locked me up after the doctor sewed up the wound on my head. My sides were bruised and painful from the beating I received. The next morning I was brought to court and charged with felonious assault and held for the grand jury under $1,500 bail. When my case was called to plead to my indictment, I was forced to plead guilty *in self-defense* before Judge [Rufus B.] Cowing who presided at the General Sessions Court. I was sentenced to a term of one year in the penitentiary, Blackwell's Island.[105] I was put to work in the carpenter shop making coffins.

On reaching the island, I was asked by the deputy warden what I worked at outside. I told him I was a carpenter by trade, when in fact I knew nothing about the trade. I had been posted[106] by old-time crooks to say that I was a carpenter so as to get to work in the best shop there and avoid the hard quarry labor out in the cold. I was assigned to the carpenter shop and put to work on the coffin bench, beside old Ike Vail, the confidence man and handshaker, as his assistant, making coffins for the city. Of course, Ike and me were well acquainted outside when at liberty and when he put a saw in my hand and told me to groove the sides and saw them even, he noticed my embarrassment, and said: "How did they come to put you here as a carpenter?" I told him how I was posted to say I was a carpenter. He laughed and told me he would

[104]Michael J. Rein was appointed to the police force in 1886. In 1901, he was a patrolman (with Joseph Petrosino) in the Headquarters Squad.

[105]Appo remembered a harsher punishment than he received. His bond was not $1,500 but $500, and his sentence not one year but six months.

[106]Advised.

make a boss carpenter out of me before my time would expire. He then posted me—"Whenever the screw (keeper) comes near our bench, keep sawing wood, any old piece, and I'll square you up with him if he should get next to you." Anyway, in about two weeks I was an expert coffin maker and remained in the shop until my time expired, with a clear record.[107]

On my discharge, I did not have one cent and was fortunate to have returned to me my good clothes I had brought with me, as at that time convicts with a year sentence or more, seldom got back their clothes that they brought up with them. There was lots of graft going on in the clothes room. In fact, in all penal institutions, it is the same. The convict who is assigned to take charge of the clothes room is very fortunate and the keeper is sure of him knowing what to do for his own interest.

My time expired [on April 5, 1896] and I was roaming about the city in search for some honest employment. I accidentally met the policeman [Michael] Rein on Sixth Avenue and Twenty-Ninth Street in citizen's clothes. He greeted me with: "Hello there! When did you come out?"

I replied, "About eight days ago."

Then said he: "Do you know, I felt d—— sorry after you got 'settled' (sentenced). If I knew as much then as I do now, that trouble between us never would have happened."

I replied: "Well, it's all over now, but you were to blame and you ought not to have paid any attention to that pimp from the Haymarket who pointed me out to you in order to curry favor of you, for himself and his girl."

"Let us have a drink. I want to have a talk with you," said he.

"No thank you, I'm not drinking anything. I am on some business now and will see you again. Goodbye," said I, and walked away and never saw him again.

In the meantime, I tried to get some work to do and after about six weeks' search, I gave it up and through necessity, I began to drift back to my former crooked life and to associate with some of my former acquaintances, who nevertheless were seemingly afraid to be seen in my company for fear of being put down as a "squealer" by the police.

<hr>

[107]Isaac S. "Handsome" Vail (1835–?), also known as "Old Ike," was a well-known confidence man and bunco steerer from Poughkeepsie. By 1897, he was so well-known to police officials in New York and New Jersey that it was impossible for him to carry on his confidence games. This paragraph appears earlier in Appo's manuscript in conjunction with an earlier sentence to Blackwell's Island.

MATTEAWAN

One morning [July 10, 1896], about three months after my release from the penitentiary, I was on the corner of Mott Street to meet a friend by appointment. Not seeing him around, I entered the saloon on the corner of Mott Street and Chatham Square, thinking he might be there, but he was not in. After buying a drink and a cigar, I said to the bartender: "Eddie, did you see Frank Tuttle around this morning?" This bartender, Eddie Erwin by name, gave me an ugly, sneering look and with a filthy remark, told me to take a sneak out of the place.

I was surprised at his ugly disposition as we were always on friendly terms. I said: "Why, Eddie! What is the matter? Are you mad at me? Explain why."

He snatched up a bottle from the back counter and said to me: "If you don't get out, I'll knock your brains out with this."

I laughed at him and said, "You better not try it." I left the saloon by the side door and took a seat on the iron railing just outside to the left of the side entrance of the saloon. I had just seated myself and [was] about to read the paper when the side door opened and Erwin rushed at me and struck me a violent blow on top of my head with a blackjack. I jumped for him as he ran into [the] side entrance, but was stopped and grabbed by the throat by a ward heeler named [John] Atwood. I took a tight hold of him and got my penknife out and cut him badly in self-defense, but before he let go [of] my throat and fell, I was struck on the head by a policeman named Stephen Loughman.[108]

My scalp was sewed up, [and] I was pushed violently into a cell by the policeman Loughman, who said to me after closing the cell door: "Your hash will be cooked up well this time, d—— you." I remained in the cell without food all that day and night and [was] then taken to police court and held to await the results of Atwood's injury. I was informed that the bartender Erwin had three manufactured witnesses besides himself to swear falsely that I was drunk and cut Atwood for no provocation whatsoever. When my case was called for trial, there was the five men sitting together on the front bench in the courtroom ready to take the witness stand to commit perjury. These men were all friends and associates of Erwin's and were not even in the neighborhood at the time of the assault on me. I was personally acquainted with two of these witnesses,

---

[108]Appo confused this incident with his earlier confrontation with police officer Michael Rein. All references to Rein have been changed to arresting officer Stephen Loughman, whose name was misspelled in court and newspaper records as "Lockman," "Lochman," "Loughran," and "Laughlin."

their names were Mike Walsh and——Hartigan. Both of them were bartenders by occupation.

At the time I was brought into court, I was still suffering from the two blows I received on the head by Erwin and the policeman Loughman. As I stood before the court bar to plead to the indictment, I was very weak. As the charge was read to me, I was surprised to see a lawyer named O'Reilly, a brother of Dan O'Reilly, step up beside me and say to the judge, "Your Honor, I will take this case."

Suddenly, Ambrose Purdy jumped up, and in an indignant tone of voice said: "Your Honor, please, this is my client. My client is insane and devoid of reason and I demand Your Honor to form a commission and investigate his mental condition." His Honor agreed with Purdy and I was taken back to the Tombs Jail Hospital.[109]

Soon after Purdy had me brought out to the counselor's room and said to me, "Who employed or assigned Counselor O'Reilly for you?"

"I do not know."

"Well, no matter, I'm glad I was there to stop him. You are in a bad fix and they are bound to put you away for a long term. They have four witnesses besides the complainant Atwood, so the best way I can see out of it is to have you sent to the hospital for a short while and then everything will come out all right in the end. You understand me, don't you?"

"Yes, but Counselor, this is all a frame-up job. I am the victim in the case."

"I know it, but what can we do? Everything is against you and I can't see any way out of it but the hospital. In the meantime, I will do all I possibly can for you."

I was then brought back to the hospital cell and the next day I was examined by the commission and transferred to Matteawan Insane Asylum [Matteawan State Hospital for the Criminally Insane] on the following day.

On my arrival at this institution, I was brought into the private office of Superintendent Dr. Henry E. Allison, who began to examine me and

---

[109]Ambrose H. Purdy was an assistant district attorney in the 1880s and later a criminal defense attorney in New York. In 1894, he briefly allied himself with the anti-prostitution and anti-Tammany Hall campaign of the Reverend Charles Parkhurst and the City Vigilance League. Purdy served as Appo's counsel in 1895 when he was arrested for assaulting policeman Michael Rein and in 1896 when he was arrested for stabbing John Atwood.

try to find out what my insane delusions were. Whatever his conclusions were about my mental condition, I do not know.[110]

I was then taken to what is known as the Court Patients Ward. My good clothes were taken from me, [I was] given a bath and then a regulation hospital suit of clothes was handed to me by one of the attendants who stood and watched me very closely as I put them on. . . . I then stepped from the bathroom into the ward and took the first vacant chair I saw and sat down. I began to watch the actions of the poor, unfortunate, insane men who were walking up and down the floor, some of them singing hymns and others talking loudly to themselves and gesticulating to imaginary foes.

When I had been seated about twenty minutes, one of the patients came and took a seat beside me and said: "I guess you don't remember me, George. I used to work in the stove foundry when you were [a] runner for Paddy Mackin, the "screw" (keeper) at Sing Sing. That is many years ago. My name is Jimmie Reilly. You know me, don't you?"

"Oh, yes, I remember you well. You had a ten-year bit (sentence). How long have you been here in this place?" I asked.

"About seven years or more, and I guess I'll never get out of this rat hole."

"Why, you look well and all right mentally. If your time has expired, I don't see why the doctors hold you here."

He suddenly jumped from the seat and began to shout out his insane delusions about the doctors and judges conspiring against him and warning me to look out for all kinds of danger. He then began to walk rapidly up and down the ward floor, laughing to himself and shaking his finger at the attendant who was watching him closely. I mention this incident, as it was my first day's experience in an insane ward with a patient whom I really believed at first was as sane as a judge, so to speak. I never was more surprised to see how mistaken I was. After that, I was always very careful when a patient came to talk with me, to humor him.

On the next morning of my arrival and after breakfast, the head attendant of the ward I was in, named Maher, shouted out the order "Seats!" Every patient sat down in a chair, and then in came the doctor ([Robert

---

[110]Appo was admitted to Matteawan State Hospital for the Criminally Insane in Beacon, New York, on December 24, 1896. Dr. Henry Edward Allison (1851–1904) was appointed medical superintendent of the New York Asylum for Insane Criminals at Auburn Prison in 1889. He moved to Matteawan when it opened in 1892.

B.] Lamb)[111] and the supervisor with two attendants as bodyguards for the doctor, who passed and looked at each patient. Some the doctor would stop and talk to. Finally, he came to me and said: "What is your name and how much time have you to serve?" I gave him my name and told him I was a court patient. "Oh, yes, I remember you. How are you feeling?"

"Very well, in general, I thank you," said I.

"You look all right, I don't see anything the matter with you. How much time would you get if you were convicted on the charge against you?" asked the doctor.

I replied: "I don't know."

"Your father is here, would you like to see and have a talk with him?"

I replied: "Yes sir, with your permission."

"Well, I will let you know later on," said he, and then passed on to the other patients.

Every morning the same doctor with the supervisor and his attendants would visit the ward and as they stepped into the ward, the same order would be called out, "Seats!" When every patient would be seated, the doctor would make his rounds and view every patient as he passed them. Should a patient attempt to talk or complain to the doctor, the attendant would stop him.

When I had been there about three weeks, I was surprised, one afternoon, by my unfortunate father entering the ward and walking over to where I was seated, reading a book. He sat down on the chair next to me and began to talk very sensible and sane for about half an hour. Suddenly, I noticed a change in his actions and talk. He began to spring his insane delusions about his great wealth, and that he was the Commander of the Laws of Nature and was going to blow up all the prisons and with his army exterminate all keepers and doctors in them. I began to humor him, and in a few minutes he became normal and sensible in his talk once more. He then left the ward to attend to his work in the Imbecile Ward, where he acted in the capacity as nurse to poor, helpless patients unable to control themselves or leave their beds or chairs when necessary.

I was about fourteen months confined in the Court Patient's Ward, when one day the head attendant came to me. He told me I was to be transferred to another ward and took me with him to Ward No. 2 South,

---

[111]Dr. Robert B. Lamb was resident clinical assistant when Matteawan opened in 1892 and promoted to first assistant physician in 1896. Lamb succeeded Henry Allison as medical superintendent of Matteawan in 1904.

which was known as the Violent Ward. On entering this ward, I noticed many prison acquaintances. Some were violently insane, made so by the brutality and abuse inflicted on them during imprisonment under the silent system of Superintendent Louis D. Pilsbury's administration. Whenever I found any one of them in a normal state of mind, I would sit down, talk with them, keep them in good humor and play checkers with any who wanted to play. I could not understand why I was transferred to a violent ward. As I could get no satisfactory answer from any of the ward attendants or the visiting doctor (Dr. [Edgar J.] Spratling),[112] I asked permission to see the superintendent. I was told I would have to wait until he made his rounds of the wards, which was about once every three months, unless something special happened for his attention. I had to wait and be patient.

One day, about 3 p.m., the order was shouted, "Seats!" In walked the superintendent with his bodyguard. He passed and viewed each patient, some of whom would jump up and curse and call him all sorts of evil names, only to be grasped by the neck and thrown back into his chair again. Finally, the superintendent came to my seat and began to give me a searching look, and said to me, "How are you getting on over here?"

I replied, "Quite well. I cannot complain, but would be pleased to know why I was transferred from the Court Patients Ward to this ward."

"Oh, overcrowded there, I suppose."

"By the way, Doctor, I would ask your permission to write a letter to a lawyer and have my case looked after. I've been confined here now over sixteen months and during the course of that time, I am sure I have shown no sign of insanity. I have already written several letters to reliable friends outside and have received no response from them. I cannot account for their silence."

On the following day I received a sheet of writing paper and a pencil. I wrote to Ambrose H. Purdy, but never got one word in reply. In fact, the letters I had written never left the institution. Such was the red tape and rascality of the officials at Matteawan Asylum. I came to the conclusion that I was buried alive.

I began to use my wits, so to speak, to find a way out of the hole. After I had been there over two years, one day after finishing work up in the dormitory, I approached one of the sane patients named John Murphy whom I knew to be a good and all right fellow, a man who would not

---

[112]Appo misspelled Spratling as "Spradley." Spratling was named third assistant physician in 1895 and promoted to second assistant physician a year later.

tip off or squeal on another were he to see one trying to escape.[113] I needed his assistance in my efforts. I said to him: "Well, Johnny, we are all through work for the day. How long have you been here and what prospects have you of getting out of here? I see an opening to 'beat it' (escape) and if you want to take a chance with me, just say so and I will take all the chances and responsibility in case of a 'tumble' (discovery)."

"George, I just got a letter from my mother who is up in Albany now. I will be discharged from here in a week or so, but if I can help you to 'beat it' (escape) you can rely on me to do so. But take my advice, George, and not try it, unless you have got a sure thing of making it. I'll tell you why. Your prospects of getting out on the square are brighter than you think. The fact that the doctors allow you to come up here and do work in the dormitory without even an attendant to watch us is a sure indication that they have confidence in you, as being all right mentally. . . . Why, Campbell, the attendant, told me the other day that you was about as crazy as the superintendent himself. He could not understand why you are held here so long. Why, George, I am over seven months my full sentence of two years and six months. I was sent here from Auburn Prison where I got a tough deal for not being able to do my task in the foundry. I hit a 'screw' (keeper) with a hammer on the head and I was sent here as a 'bug' for it. Now George, take my advice and do nothing foolish . . . ," said he.

I thanked him and promised to wait a while and see how his expectations turned out. Sure enough, on the next week after our talk he told me his mother was coming to take him home in a couple of days and that if I wanted to get a letter out on the quiet, he would mail it for me safe. I then got a sheet of writing paper and wrote a letter to the Honorable Judge Goff and gave it to Murphy. The next day he was taken from the ward and discharged as cured.

Two weeks after Murphy's release, I was surprised by an attendant taking me from the ward to the private office of the superintendent, Dr. H. E. Allison, who greeted me in a very pleasant manner. "How are you feeling? How long have you been here now?"

I replied: "Very well in general, I thank you, and I have now been here two years, eight months and two weeks."

"Well," he said, "you appear in good condition both physically and mentally, and there has been no complaints made against your behavior

---

[113]No inmate named John Murphy appears in the Matteawan case files during Appo's period of treatment at the asylum. Appo may have confused him with an attendant by the name of John Murphy, who appears in the 1900 federal census.

since you have been here. You are discharged and the attendant here will have you dressed and see you to the station. If you want to see and have a talk with your father before you leave, you can do so."

I thanked him and left the office with the attendant who took me to a hallway and told me to wait there and he would bring my father so we could talk together in private. He then went to the Imbecile Ward and returned in about five minutes with my father who appeared rational and sane enough to talk to. I made sure not to excite him, and said, "How is everything with you? You are looking fine. Is there anything particular that you are in need of? I have just got good news from a friend. In a day or so I will be able to get you anything you need. I got the attendant, Mr. Mannix, to bring me here to see and have a talk with you. It was very good of Mr. Mannix to do so, wasn't it?"

He replied: "Oh, Mike Mannix is my friend and anytime you want to see me, just tell him and he will fix everything all right. I want you to get me a pair of good eyeglasses, No. 9, my sight is getting very bad. That is all I need."

After talking with him about twenty minutes and trying to get some information I needed concerning two brothers of my mother's, his whole demeanor changed. He began to pour out his insane delusions about his great wealth and his great army of soldiers and all the wonderful things he was going to do to benefit the unfortunate patients and convicts and blow up all the penal institutions, keepers and police with dynamite. . . .

I said goodbye once more and the attendant came and took me to the clothes room where I put on a suit of clothes. I then was brought to the clerk's office and signed some sort of paper and left the institution a free man once more [on June 14, 1899].[114] I feel quite certain that it was through the letter I had written and surreptitiously got out by the patient Murphy, who was discharged and mailed it for me that brought such good results and my freedom from a madhouse.

REFORM

On my arrival in New York [June 1899], I went direct from the Grand Central Depot down to Mott Street. After paying my railroad fare, I had but forty cents left to exist on, so I went to Mott Street to search for a friend from whom I could obtain a loan of a couple of dollars. Not seeing him around, I entered the saloon at 6 Mott Street and was surprised to

[114]Several repetitive sentences and some extraneous information have been deleted from this passage.

find Eddie Erwin in attendance behind the bar and the two false witnesses, Walsh and Hartigan, in front of the bar. Both of the latter men looked to be suffering in the last stages of consumption.

I was about to leave the place when I heard someone call out: "Hello there, George. When did you get out?" I turned and met Mr. Paddy Mullen the proprietor of the saloon, who with two other young men invited me to have a drink. I accepted and Mr. Mullen said to me: "What do you intend to do?"

I replied: "As soon as I can see my friend to borrow enough money to get out of New York, I will leave here for Philadelphia at once. I believed I would find my friend in here. That's why I drifted into the place."

"Oh, that's all right, George, how much money do you need?" inquired Mr. Mullen.

"Just my carfare, that's all," said I.

To my surprise he went down into his pocket and handed me $15, saying: "If you need more, say so."

I told him that the $15 was more than I needed, but he forced me to take it and forget all about it. So I took the $15 and thanked him, saying I would return the money with gratitude in a short time.

"Forget it, you owe me nothing," said Mr. Mullen.

During all the time that Mullen and I was talking there stood the three men, Erwin, Walsh and Hartigan, all of them employed about the place, with open-eyed wonder, at the kindhearted generosity of Mr. Mullen to one whom they so cowardly "framed" up to send to state prison after being assaulted by Ed Erwin.

I then left the place and went to Pennsylvania Railroad Station and took a train for Philadelphia. On arriving at Philadelphia, I started right in the crooked business again by working the "flimflam," or properly speaking, shortchanging businesspeople with a ten dollar bill by making them make a mistake in the change to their loss of $4.90. I remained in Philadelphia about three weeks and was quite successful during the course of that time.

One night while laying in an opium joint at 911 Race Street,[115] smoking the drug, I began to think what a fool I was to go back to the opium pipe after being away from it so long a time. As I had formed no habit for the drug as yet, I made up my mind to keep away from it entirely before it was too late. For three days I never went near or touched the drug, and during that time I felt no desire for it. Finally, that set me thinking

[115]Philadelphia's Race Street was populated by a significant number of Chinese immigrants and their offspring.

very deeply and the conclusion of my thoughts were that if I could break away so easily and so often as I had from the opium habit, why not muster up nerve enough to break away from a crooked life? I made up my mind to try again to get honest employment and to reform without fear or favor, not that I feared the discipline of a prison, nor did I favor it. I made up my mind to return to New York and make an effort to do right under all circumstances and conditions. . . .[116]

As I was completely without means of support and without a cent [in 1900], I began to search high and low, so to speak, for employment of some kind, but failed. Finally, I appealed to the Honorable Judge Goff, who sent me to the good lady, Mrs. Foster, and through her kind intercession for me, I obtained employment as a car cleaner at the Grand Central Railroad Station at Forty-Second Street, where I worked for two months. As it was in the wintertime, I was taken very sick and had to give up the hard work at the station. When I recovered my health and strength again, the good lady, Mrs. Foster, again obtained a situation for me in the Calvary Church at Fourth Avenue and Twenty-Second Street, where I worked from early spring until the cold weather set in. As I did not understand how to run a steam boiler and fire up during the cold wintertime, I had to vacate the position to make room for an engineer. In the meantime, I had secured work as a handyman around the machinery in the Sallade Dress Pleating Establishment, which was then located on Thirty-First Street near Broadway and worked steadily for this concern for a number of years. Finally, the business became so slack on account of dress pleating going out of fashion that the concern had to close up.

I was again out of work and remained idle for many months without a steady position, but owing to an occasional job given me by Mrs. [Mary F.] Sallade.[117] I managed to just exist through the kindly interest she still had for my welfare and she tried in every way to obtain a steady position for me after the failure of her own business, but was unsuccessful in her efforts for me. She then left New York for Lowell, Massachusetts.

I then began to search for work of some kind but met with no success. I finally made up my mind to hunt up George W. Lederer and try

[116]Appo confused the precise chronology of these events in his manuscript. He placed his encounter with Mullen, Erwin, Walsh, and Hartigan after his release from Matteawan (1899) but before his stage experience in *In the Tenderloin* (1894–1895).

[117]Appo referred to Mary F. Sallade as "Mrs. Salrade." By this time, she was married to Harrison Eugene Havens, a former Missouri congressman, attorney, railroad executive, and newspaper editor.

to have him pay me a portion of the money ($145) that he still owed me for my salary while on the stage. One day while on Broadway and Forty-Second Street watching for Lederer to appear, I was met by an old associate and a former burglar named Frank Taylor, alias "Brooklyn Beefer," whom I had not seen for over fifteen years. After we got over our surprise and hand shaking, he said to me: "What are you doing now?"

I replied: "Nothing, but at present I am looking for a square job at anything outside of graft. At this very moment I am trying to meet a theatrical fellow who owes me $145 and see if I can get some portion of it from him."

"You will never get a cent of it. . . . I am now in a business of my own in Philadelphia. Here is my business card and if you want to come to work for me, just say so and I will take you with me tomorrow to Philadelphia and put you right on the job," said Taylor.

"All right," said I, "when and where will I meet you tomorrow?"

"You can come now with me to my flat and I will introduce you to my wife and son. We then can make all arrangements and leave for Philadelphia the first thing in the morning. I have been very busy here in New York for the past ten days. I have tuned up and repaired thirty-two pianos in that time," said he.

On the following morning I called at the flat at 6:30 a.m. and found him up and making ready to leave for Philadelphia. We both then went down to the Pennsylvania Railroad Station and took the cars for Philadelphia.

On my arrival there, he brought me to his place of business on Fifteenth and Sansom Streets, where he had the whole house rented. On the ground floor he had six pianos of different makes, all in perfect order. In the rear room he had his shop where he put up a fine wood finish, under the name of "The Bull Dog Wood Finish." In fact, that finish could be applied to a nonstained floor and after two coats were applied, it would be perfectly dry in ten minutes and no smell of paint. The finished floor would look as bright as a polished piano and guaranteed to remain that way for two years.

I asked him who had learned him to tune and repair pianos and to make up the wood finish. He said about ten years previous he was arrested for burglary in the city of Baltimore, and being caught dead right, he pleaded guilty and was sentenced to a term of five years to the Maryland Penitentiary. He was assigned to work in the cabinet shop of the prison as an assistant to a German convict who had a fifteen-year sentence and who was a skilled cabinet and piano maker. This convict took an interest in Taylor and taught him the piano tuning business and gave him the formula to make up the wood finish. When he was released from the penitentiary, he gave up all crooked business and started right in making up the wood finish, and was very successful with it. He then bought himself a set of tools for the piano tuning and traveled all over the country tuning pianos and selling his wood finish. Finally, he established his business at Fifteenth and Sansom Streets, Philadelphia, where I worked with him for about three months.

During the course of that time he did a good business in the wood finish sales and I used to wonder why he was always in debt and could not pay his bills. But I soon learned that he was gambling his money away on the horses and faro. As a consequence, he had to close up the business on Sansom Street and go out on the road tuning pianos again.

I returned to New York and began a search for employment without any success. I was having a very hard time of it, being down and out, so to speak, and felt like the most forlorn of all God's creatures—a man without a single friend in all the world. This sense of feeling set me thinking very deeply about former friends who flutter around like butterflies for a season. When in prosperity, they can make use of one; but let misfortune overtake one, they soon forget you are alive. Still, I did not get discouraged and continued my search for employment.

One day while walking on Fourth Avenue and Twenty-Second Street, I was met by Mr. Alexander Hadden, a member of the Calvary Church on Fourth Avenue, where I used to work, who asked me what I was doing.[118]

I told him: "Looking for work."

"Can you address envelopes?" he asked.

I replied: "Yes, sir."

"Well, George, here is my address. You come up to my house at 9 a.m. tomorrow."

I thanked him and on the following morning, I called at his residence and was admitted at the basement gate to the dining room by a young man who placed a couple of boxes of envelopes and a list of names and addresses for me to copy. We both soon had the work done, and I was paid one dollar by the good gentleman, who took my address and said to me: "Whenever I have any work you can do, I'll let you know."

Soon after I received a postal card requesting me to call at another residence of his, and on my arrival there he asked me if I knew how to

[118]Alexander M. Hadden was a physician who was active in the Galilee Mission, a Christian benevolent organization founded in 1884 to provide "an evening home and ready, sympathizing help" to members of the "deserving poor." Hadden's interest in Appo may have partly originated with Calvary's ministry in the Chinese community, which included a Chinese Sunday school with English and religion classes.

stain and polish floors. I told him yes, and with two other men I helped to finish two floors and was paid two dollars for less than a day's work by Mr. Hadden. Soon after he went to Europe, and from London, sent me an Easter Card and another one on Christmas Day. Since then, [I] have heard no news of him, although I have written an acknowledgment of his kind remembrance of me in sending the cards.

Soon after this event, through the kind intercession and recommendation of my former employer, Mrs. Sallade, and Mr. Frank Moss and Dr. C. E. Bruce, who gave me a thorough physical examination and his favorable decision, I secured a steady position with the Society for the Prevention of Crime, where I have been employed for the past few years and up to the present time.

GOOD FELLOWS

During the course of my unfortunate criminal life, I have received many violent assaults with weapons in the hands of unprincipled men, with whom I was forced to associate and come in contact with in my daily routine of graft. My head, face and body still show the scars conspicuously as the results of their cowardly assaults on me for no provocation other than that I was a "good fellow" which is a very bad thing to be. What constitutes a good fellow in the eyes and estimation of the underworld is a nervy crook, a money getter and spender, and particularly one who will foolishly stand the consequences and punishment of an arrest for some other fellow's evil doings both inside and out of prison. I've seen many so-called good fellows go through the mill under the [Thomas] Byrnes and [William] Devery[119] police administrations and the tyrannical discipline of Louis D. Pilsbury's silent system then in vogue in the state prisons of New York. Some of these good fellows were buried alive for ten and fifteen years in state prison, *entirely innocent,* for being a good fellow. Some are now insane at the Matteawan Asylum or in their graves there from the inhuman treatment at the state prisons under the silent system.

One of my experiences for being a good fellow with one of my associates came near causing me the loss of an eye. This man was known by

---

[119]William S. "Big Bill" Devery (1854–1919) was born in New York City and appointed to the police force in 1878. In 1891, he was promoted to captain in the Tenderloin district. Devery's toleration of prostitution and gambling drew extensive criticism. After 1894, he was indicted six times for corruption and failure to suppress disorderly houses, but he was never convicted. In 1898, he was named chief of police, a position he held until his retirement in 1902.

the name of Dick Cronin, and had the reputation of being a fighter.[120] In fact, most everyone who knew him, was afraid of him, and to make matters worse he was so ignorant that he could not read or write. Jim McNally, the financial backer of the green goods business, had Cronin around him as a sort of bodyguard and no one in the business could afford to send him out of town to bring in a victim (come-on), because the few he did go after refused to do business after meeting Cronin.

It was December 1892 when McNally was forced to move his business over to Jersey City, New Jersey. Therefore, we all had to follow and do our business over there with him. So one cold stormy winter's night, I received a telegram stating: "Come to Green Street, Jersey, *at once*," signed "Jim." I made all haste and arrived at the meeting place on Green Street, New Jersey, where I met Jim McNally's salesman (or turner) who said to me: "You will have to go to Elizabeth, New Jersey, tonight.[121] So wait over in the saloon until I get the 'pointers' for you to land the 'guy' (victim) and have him here the first thing in the morning."

I then went to the saloon and entered the place by the rear door and was somewhat surprised to see standing at the rear end of the bar an old-time crook known as "Old Boston" who had only been out of prison a couple of days after serving a four-and-a-half-year term. Naturally, I was pleased to meet him and we drank and talked together on old times. As I knew he was financially broke, I slipped him a five dollar bill and he began to tell me how a fellow by the name of Dick Wolcott was the unintentional cause of his arrest and conviction. Every time he would mention the name of this fellow he would say "*Dick*." Now there was a screen partition that enclosed the entire rear of the barroom, unknown to me, in the front end of the bar, stood Dick Cronin and another fellow talking and drinking together.

Suddenly, Cronin appeared behind the screen where Boston and I were and said to Boston: "What are you talking about me for. I'll break your jaw," and at the same time made a swinging blow at Boston.

I quickly jumped between them, pushed Cronin away, saying: "Why, Dick, you are mistaken, the man don't know you. He was talking about another fellow named Dick Wolcott, not you," and in the meantime I had signaled old man Boston to clear out of the place.

Cronin said to me: "You lie. What have you got to say about it," and at the same time he made a blow at my face with his clinched fist. I dodged the blow and clinched him and we both fell to the floor with me on top and a grip on his throat. Suddenly I was struck a violent blow on my

---

[120]Dick Cronin was associated with Barney Maguire's gang during the 1880s.
[121]Appo erroneously believed this event took place in December 1891.

left eye with a large-size Wilson's whiskey bottle, cutting me badly and fracturing the bone of the upper eyelid and rendering me unconscious.

When I came to my senses again, I found myself on the operating table at the Christ Hospital and the good doctor sewing up the gash over my eye.[122] When he had finished, a policeman in uniform brought into the operating room Dick Cronin and asked me: "Is this the man who struck you?"

I replied: "No, I do not know what hit me." Then the doctor told the nurse to put me to bed, and as my clothes had already been removed, I was taken to the ward. When I reached the bed, I said to the nurse: "I am feeling all right, give me my clothes. I want to get home as soon as possible."

He replied: "Well, I'll see," and finally came back with my clothes. I dressed myself and as I missed my necktie I asked the nurse what had become of it and my diamond stud and $62.

He said: "You had no tie when you were brought here and the only amount of money you had was $7 and here it is," handing me an envelope with the $7 inside.

I thanked him and said: "Well, this money will get me home safe, so I am lucky to be left that amount." I said goodbye to him and left the hospital with my head all bandaged up, out into the snowstorm.

When I got to the ferry for Cortlandt Street, New York, I met Mr. Dalton, the railroad detective at the ferry, who asked me what was the matter and how I got hurt.[123] I told him everything and also about the diamond stud valued at $250 and the balance of the $62 I lost, and said to him: "If you can get the diamond back from the person who stole it from me, I will make you a present of it, and I am quite certain that neither Dick Cronin nor the officer who brought me to the hospital took it."

"Well," said Dalton, "I'll look it up," and sure enough about ten days after, I again met the detective at the Pennsylvania ferry house with the diamond stud in his tie. He told me that the nurse at Christ Hospital had it and told him that after I had left the hospital, he (the nurse) found my tie and diamond on the floor of the clothes room, but did not find my money. So I said nothing more about the loss and soon forgot the misfortune.

Of course, I went looking after the fellow who struck me with the bottle and was told that he was a western crook known only by the name

[122]Christ Hospital was founded in 1873 in Jersey City and operated by the Episcopal Church.

[123]William H. "Billy" Dalton was an Irish immigrant who joined the Jersey City police force in 1871. Dalton was later charged with allowing James McNally's green goods operation to operate in Jersey City.

of "Pete" and a stranger in New York, and just happened to be in Dick Cronin's company that night in the barroom. Cronin was jealous of my success in the business and blamed me for his failure. Consequently, [he] tried to make everything disagreeable for me whenever he got the chance, and as I was shot down about one month after and laid up in prison for nine months and ten days waiting for a decision in my case from the court of appeals, I never heard again or seen Cronin until I learned of his death from consumption on the day of my release from state's prison [on December 5, 1893].

I have had many other assaults inflicted on me with deadly weapons in the hands of enraged men. Most of whom were strangers to me. I still bear the scars on my head, neck and body, where I was struck five different times on the head, with blackjacks and other blunt weapons. My neck [was] slashed with a knife and [I was] shot on two occasions, once in the lower part of the stomach, and as I said before, my right eye shot out. All these assaults were done by big, able-bodied men who were too cowardly to use their hands. The only provocation I had given them was for being a good fellow.

I will give an instance of what I mean by being a good fellow. In 1899, while in the city of Philadelphia, I used to visit every evening a friend's house on South Eighth Street, just below Locust Street, where him and his wife lived and used to receive many visitors, most of whom were people who were connected with the theatrical and circus business. One afternoon, I called and my friend's wife, Mrs. Neal Murphy, met me at the door and showed me into the dining room, where I was introduced to two big six-foot men and two young girls. The men were both connected with the Forepaugh Circus and their names were Big Jack White and Sam Gibbons. Both were under the influence of drink and using very insulting language to the girls. Finally, one of the girls, Miss Ida Rice, a chorus singer, got up from her chair to leave the dining room very indignant. Jack White grasped her by the arm and violently pushed her on the chair. She jumped up and threw the chair at White and ran into the kitchen with White after her. Seeing that he meant to strike her, I followed him to try and prevent trouble, as the two girls were frightened out of their wits. Gibbons was too drunk and when I reached the kitchen, White had the frying pan from the stove in his hand and raised to hit the girl.

I jumped between them and tried to talk to White and cool him off. At the same instant, he made a smash at me with the frying pan. I caught the blow on my left arm and quickly grabbed a quart bottle of bluing[124]

---

[124]A substance used to whiten clothes or give them a bluish tinge.

from the washtub and smashed it in half on top of White's head. We then clinched each other and both of us fell down the small stoop that led into the backyard, I on top of White with half of the bottle still in my hand. But as White weighed nearly 200 pounds and I only 118 pounds, he soon had me off of him, jumped up, closed in on me and slashed me across the neck with a penknife. I struck him on his hand with the broken bottle.

In the meantime, the girls' screaming aroused Sam Gibbons, who seeing his partner White's condition, grabbed up a poker to strike me with. A policeman came just in time and took Gibbons, White and me to the police station where we were locked up. But Gibbons sent a messenger and he was soon released on bail. White and me, after the doctor dressed our wounds, were locked up in a cell for the night to await a hearing in the morning.

In about one hour after Gibbons got released, he came and visited White and me at our cell doors and asked me how the trouble came about and who was the cause of it all. I told him the circumstances and said to him that he or White need have no fear, for I would take all the blame and turn them both out on the street in the morning. He was pleased and seemed greatly relieved. . . . When we were brought to court before the magistrate, the officer made the charge of drunk and disorderly. The judge, looking at me, asked me: "What have you to say and how were you hurt?"

I replied: "It was all my fault and I accidentally hurt myself, Your Honor and these two men are not to blame."

"I'll fine you ten dollars," said the judge. As I was about to pay the fine, Gibbons stepped up and paid the ten dollar fine himself for me. We three left the courtroom together and on reaching the street, Gibbons invited me to have a drink. When we got into the saloon, he gave White a sound lecture about using a knife on me. After a friendly talk, we three parted good friends. . . . That was the last I ever seen or heard of them.

In about two weeks my neck got better and I left Philadelphia for Baltimore, where I visited a young friend who was serving a five-year sentence at the penitentiary there under the name of Jacob Brown for robbing jewelry stores by the system known as the penny-weight. When the keeper brought him to the visiting room and he took a seat beside me on the bench, the keeper took a high stool and seated himself directly in front of us where he could see and hear everything done or said between us. I was surprised to see the sad change in Jake's physical condition and asked him how he was getting along and what was the cause of him looking so bad. He told me that he was often getting flogged with the lash for not being able to do his task in the contract shop where he worked. His back was all bruised and marked from the flogging. I told him I would see and talk to the warden and see what could be done to stop the abuse.

So when the half hour allowed for visitors was nearly over, I asked him what things he needed. When he mentioned them I got up and said goodbye, and then asked the officer in charge of the outer office for permission to see the warden. He said to take a seat and in about ten minutes the warden entered and said: "Do you wish to see me?"

"Yes sir," said I.

"Warden, I just came from visiting my friend inside Jacob Brown and noticing his sickly appearance and condition in general, I naturally asked the cause for it. He tells me that he is being often flogged for not being able to do his task, as he is too weak. If he could get some lighter work to do, he would appreciate it and gladly do his best. He tells me that his body is all marked up from the lash. Now, Warden, I would not care to have his folks learn about this abuse, and I trust you will look into the matter."

The warden then said: "How much time has this man Brown?" I replied: "He has about eight months yet to serve out of a five-year sentence."

"Well," said the warden, "I'll see what can be done." He put the name of Jacob Brown on a piece of paper and handed it to the officer. Turning to me, he said: "All right, what's your business?"

I told him: "A printer." I then thanked him and left the prison and then purchased everything that Jake needed and left them at the prison office for delivery to him.

In about two weeks after I learned that he was assigned to lighter work and better work and the next thing I heard of Jake about two years after was that he went to Philadelphia from Baltimore after his release and was arrested and sentenced to a term of fifteen years at the Eastern Penitentiary in Philadelphia for the same offense (penny-weight). The reason he got so severe a sentence was that twenty prominent jewelers of Philadelphia identified him as the man who robbed them. I was greatly surprised about four years after I met him in New York and he told me that by good conduct he was released after serving only three years and six months of the fifteen-year sentence. He was through with the graft, and since released from the penitentiary, he had married a good girl and was working at his trade opening oysters.

He said, "You may think because I am now working on the square, that I have lost my nerve through fear of the rough deal I got while in prison, but it is not so. I have a good wife and I mean to do right by her in all things through life and be guided by her advice in all matters and forget the past."

I mention the above fact of Brown's determination to lead an honest life to show that the influence of a good woman or a kindly act from any person of influence will do more toward the reformation of an unfortunate fellow creature whose mind and body is not wrecked by the brutality and tyrannical discipline that had been in vogue and practiced in the state prisons and penitentiaries throughout the United States by a gang of political leachers, who make criminals and insane degenerates out of really innocent persons from the brutal tyrannical discipline and the inhuman punishments of the paddle, the dark cell with its iron knobbed floor and the two ounces of bread and a gill of water per day, the ball and chain with iron shackles and the iron head cage with its five-pound lock resting on chest day and night, eating and sleeping and working with it on for weeks at a time. This latter punishment was inflicted on one for merely talking in the shop or turning one's head from his work. The above punishments were in practice during the administration of the *immoral* tyrant, Superintendent Louis D. Pilsbury who filled the state prisons with a gang of upstate politicians, particularly from Troy and Albany as keepers, some of whom were robbing the contracts and doing all sorts of graft and practicing immorality on young, innocent convicts.[125] Such was the system in practice to reform convicts from 1873 to 1881 to my own personal knowledge and bitter experience.

REFLECTIONS

During the administration of chief of police [Thomas] Byrnes, it was the common question among his detectives when they would meet each other: "How is everything coming with you?" And the answer would be: "Well, I put so many years (thirty, forty or more) for the state this week," meaning that he had brought about convictions of persons which amounted to thirty or forty years for contract labor in the state prisons. When these unfortunates would arrive at the prisons, one could hear

[125]As late as 1892, at least fifty-one of fifty-seven appointed employees of Clinton Prison were Democrats, forty of whom were appointed by "Boss" Edward Murphy of Troy. Well into the 1920s, the warden of Sing Sing was a political appointee, usually a patronage position for Westchester County.

the keepers ask each other: "How many fresh fish today?" and when they were told so many, I heard them say: "Well, the more the merrier for us," and talk of the convicts under their charge as though they were a lot of cattle and treat them as such for the least provocation. . . .

One time I was put in a cell with a very clever safe burglar at Sing Sing. I noticed he would never go to Sunday service at the chapel. So one Sunday on coming from the chapel to my cell, I said to him after the doors were closed and locked: "Harry, you ought to have gone to the chapel and heard the sermon given by an outside minister today. He made everybody laugh. He told a story about one bad apple in a barrel of good ones spoils and rottens the whole barrel. Why is it you never go to Sunday service, Harry?"

"Oh," said he, "I don't believe in such talk one hears there. In fact, I don't believe in any kind of religion. I used to, but what I have seen of such people in the prisons I've been in got me thinking very deeply on such matters. I am now firmly convinced that religious teachings are all superstition, and I can convince any minister or anybody else that there is no hereafter and that the only hell we will ever experience is right here in the prisons. We need fear no future punishment after the life leaves the body," said the safe burglar, Harry Jacques.

I became interested in so strange a subject and began to ask him the following questions. "Then what is this life and who is the creator of it and the earth?"

He replied: "Nature created life and life is matter and matter is life. We cannot go any further and there is nothing dead or living that can go to waste on this earth. Nature governs all things."

"Then," said I, "who governs Nature and her laws?"

"Who do you believe?" asked he.

"Why, God, the Supreme Being," I replied.

"Who governs God?" asked he.

"Why, God Himself," I replied.

"Then why cannot nature govern itself? Now, listen," said he, "we are told by the preachers of the Gospel, that God is all merciful and all powerful; that He knows everything before and hereafter. And that if we break His commandments and do not repent, we will be thrown into an eternal hell of fire and brimstone after we leave this life. Now does it stand to reason, George, that He being so merciful, that He would put us on this earth knowing before we were born just what sort of life we were going to lead, and that the willpower which He gave us was insufficiently strong enough to resist the temptations to do evil, and He knew just what our end would be. Do you mean to say that He would put us on this earth to die and go to an eternal hell? In fact, George, He knew before we were born that we both would be locked up together in this stone box of a cell. This prison is the only hell you or I need ever be afraid of," said he.

"Well, Harry," said I, "you give a good appearing argument on your belief, but I am going to be on the safe side all the time. When my end comes, [I'll] try not to leave any dirt behind me, after this life."

The above statement is one of the religious instructions I received from a well-educated burglar, name Harry Jacques, who was serving a five-year term at Sing Sing in 1877. I have been doubled up in the same cell with many educated crooks who had similar and more strange beliefs of this life and the hereafter, but in all my prison experience, I never had a chaplain of a prison come to my cell and talk to me or to any other convict, not even at the deathbed in the prison hospital. The convict died in those days without any religious consolation just like an animal. I have seen a few of them die from the abuse received at the hands of petty tyrants and political leeches and the chaplain of the prison said nothing to stop the abuse. . . .

One day a poor fellow was hung up by the thumbs and his cries from pain: "Oh, my arms! Let me down!" reached the ears of the chaplain who went from his office to the guard room and asked the deputy warden: "What is the trouble with him?"

"Oh," replied the deputy, "he says the work is too hard for him."

And with a laugh, said the chaplain, "Maybe he would like to be a clerk in my office." Such sarcastic remarks made by a minister while an unfortunate creature is being punished and tortured by a brutal official soon spreads throughout the prison, among the convicts. When they are in the chapel at Sunday service, listening to him preaching the Gospel of Christ, I have frequently heard them say: "He is a hypocrite and not on the level."

I mention the above fact about the chaplain (Mr. [Silas W.] Edgerton) merely to show how small an interest he had in the redemption of a crook. I have known many prisoners, appeal to him for relief, but in vain. He would tell them to call and see the doctor, who by the way was nicknamed "the Butcher," and the only satisfaction and relief the doctor would give them who were really in need of medical aid, was: "Oh, I guess you can do that work. Give him a little paregoric and ginger." Should the prisoner still persist in his appeal and not take the medicine ordered, he would be locked up in the dark cell and put under a diet of a gill of water and two ounces of bread every twenty-four hours until he submitted. In a word, the state prisons of New York State were nothing

more than factories for turning criminals and insane out of really innocent persons in those days under the contract slave system particularly.

Now I look back to the scenes of inhuman treatment and cruelty
inflicted on prisoners I have witnessed and experienced myself at the
hands of brutal keepers who are placed in such positions and power
through political influence. Many [were] the pickings from the bar-
rooms of the saloons of the country towns and villages along the Hudson, particularly Albany and Troy, where I have met several of them who
were under the influence of liquor and in the company of fast women,
having a jolly good time as they called it. One night, two Sing Sing keepers had the nerve to make a night of it on the Bowery in New York and
were seen by three ex-convicts who gave them a terrible beating up and
never was caught for doing so. The names of both these keepers were
Mr. [Thomas] Mulligan and Mr. [James] McCormick.[126] This fact goes
to show that fear of the then brutal system never reformed any man
whom I knew of during all my prison experience. Instead, the brutal
discipline made them worse criminals after their release from that gall-
ing yoke of servitude.

A few of them [prison inmates and criminals] with whom I was intimately acquainted from boyhood ended their careers on the gallows
and the electric chair. The names of three of these unfortunates were
Danny Driscoll, Danny Lyons and Tommy Tobin.[127] All three [were]
born and raised in the then-known "bloody Sixth Ward" which environment at that time was a nest of crime, so to speak, and turned out many
clever crooks of the youth of the neighborhood. Most of them are now
dead or in the insane asylum. Now as I look back on the past, I wonder
how I ever lived through it all and escaped the many close calls of death
from the knife, blackjacks and pistol shots I received. . . .

Such inhuman treatment never did any good toward the reformation
of me or any other so-called criminal. A word of sympathy or a kindly
act will go further toward that end than all the instruments of torture,
such as the paddle, the lash, the thumbscrew, the head cage, the ball
chain and shackles and the "bed of roses" in the "black hole" (dark cell)
on two ounces of bread and a gill of water every twenty-four hours. All

[126]James McCormick was a Sing Sing keeper from 1876 to 1880, and again from 1882
to at least 1893. Thomas Mulligan was appointed Sing Sing keeper in 1884 and remained
in Sing Sing until at least 1893. Appo misspelled McCormick as "McCormack."

[127]Daniel Driscoll (1855–1888) was the leader of the Whyo gang and a prominent
Five Points figure. He was hanged in the Tombs on January 23, 1888. Daniel Lyons
(1857–1887) was a pickpocket and an acquaintance of Appo, as well as a member of the
Whyo gang and an associate of Driscoll.

these tortures were practiced during my prison experience from 1873 to 1884. <u>Fear of these</u> will and <u>never</u> did reform any man. . . . The best proof that the fear of such tyranny did no good, I and the other men always returned to a life of a crook as soon as discharged and soon again back serving another term.

I really believe were I not fortunate enough to meet good people who took a kindly interest to secure honest employment for me, I don't know what would have become of me. Now for nearly twenty years I have managed to live honest and keep on the right road of life. But during the course of that time I have had many obstacles to contend with in my early efforts to break away from my former crooked life and naturally made many of my former associates very unfriendly and suspicious. Above all, I was hounded by some of the old-time detectives under Chief Byrnes and Devery's administration who feared I knew too much about their crooked dealing with the "sure thing grafters" who worked under their protection in those days. Consequently, life for me was made very disagreeable by them and some of the "sure thing crooks" under their protection aided them. . . .

I can truthfully say that during all my unfortunate crooked life in and out of prison, there is not one of my former associates can say I ever wronged them in any manner, shape or form. I always tried to do what was considered the right thing by them and took all kinds of chances and risks to be strictly on the level, and as they call, a good fellow, but generally got the worst of it for doing so in the end. Of course, I have met some good, principled men leading a crook's life, both in and out of prison who would go to extremes to render aid to one in misfortune and I have come in contact with some who would stoop to any meanness to benefit their own selfish desires. These latter class of men I always avoided when I found them so in order to keep out of trouble and misfortune in those days now past and gone, and it is now over twenty years ago since I first started to lead a better life.

It was my great fortune to be brought as a witness before the Lexow Investigating Committee and after I left the witness stand, after three long hours of being questioned by the Honorable John W. Goff and Mr. Frank Moss, counselors for the committee, I was made glad to learn that through their kind intercession for me to the good Christian lady, Mrs. Foster, I obtained honest employment and secured the first start on the right road to a better life. Ever since I have continued to lead an all honorable life up to the present year 1916, and notwithstanding the many obstacles that have been thrown in my way by unscrupulous persons to upset my efforts to live honest.

I came out on the right side and an example that a criminal can be reformed, not through fear of brutal prison discipline, but by a kind and encouraging word and a friendly act. I can only hope one day to be able to have those good people know, who had confidence in me, that the fruits of their kindness have not been sown in a barren soil, and that to them alone rebounds the credit of snatching an unfortunate fellow creature from the life of misery and shame into which he had so unresistingly permitted himself to be carried. Such good people who so kindly recognized my honest endeavors to lead a better life and had sufficient confidence to secure for me honest employment were very few and hard to find in those days. Were it not for the Lexow Investigation, I don't know what would have become of me. . . .

Many times I have been assaulted by would-be toughs and I have defended myself and never howled for the police for satisfaction in the courts, even when I got the worst of the fight. That was the way I was taught and brought up from boyhood down in the old Sixth Ward where in them days the word *fear* was not known among the crooks who were my boyhood associates. I was always good-hearted and generous with plenty of energy in my way of doing business and I never had a partner "drop" from me during my whole life as a crook. I was the one who took all the chances and consequences of an arrest and conviction, and in many ways and means have done good for others whenever chance came my way to render aid to those in need and misfortune.

In conclusion of this truthful statement of my life up to the present time, I am glad to be able to say that for nearly eighteen years I have lived an honorable life and for several of these recent years I have had steady employment through the kindness of the good Christian people connected with the S.P.C. [Society for the Prevention of Crime], and I am extremely grateful to them for their kindly interest and the confidence placed in me. During the course of these years I worked faithfully and endeavored to have these good people know that the fruits of kindness had not been sown in a barren soil.

George Appo

PART THREE

Related Documents

1

George Appo in His Words and Those of Others

1

LOUIS J. BECK

New York's Chinatown

1898

Louis J. Beck (1867–?) was a reporter who wrote the first book on New York's Chinatown neighborhood. He supposedly befriended Appo in the 1890s, but his description of Appo is hardly positive and reflects the sensationalized and racially charged journalism common during this era. In the following excerpt, Beck's account of Appo's Poughkeepsie trial introduces Lena Miller as Appo's "common-law wife." Miller is never mentioned in Appo's autobiography and may have been hired by Appo's attorneys to impersonate his wife and make him a more sympathetic defendant.

Chapter XXVIII: George Appo — Born to Crime

THE SON OF A MURDERER, AFTER SPENDING HALF HIS LIFE IN PRISON, FOLLOWS IN THE FOOTSTEPS OF HIS FATHER TO A CELL FOR THE INSANE.

George Appo was born in New York City, July 4, 1858,[1] and is therefore an American citizen, and should be a patriotic one, but is not. His father was a full-blooded Chinaman and his mother an Irish woman. He was an

---

[1] Although Appo gives his birth year as 1858 in his autobiography, he was actually born in 1856.

From Louis J. Beck, *New York's Chinatown: An Historical Presentation of Its People and Places* (New York: Bohemia, 1898), 250–52, 254–61.

exceedingly bright child, beautiful to look upon, sharp-witted and quick of comprehension. For ten years he was the pet of the neighborhood where his parents dwelt, and during that time had abundant opportunity to acquaint himself with many forms of vice. After a careful consideration he selected some of these as his own. At the age of ten he became a pickpocket. The reference to his beauty is no exaggeration. Throughout his long and varied career of crime he retained the handsome features and charming manners which characterized him as a boy, and were it not for the scars of knife and bullet wounds that are visible on his face he would now be a handsome man of striking appearance.

To-day there are scores of little half breeds playing about the streets and doorways of the Chinese quarter, but in the 60's the Appo boy was looked upon as one of the curiosities of the neighborhood, and among his playfellows in the Oliver Street School[2] he was regarded as a sort of juvenile hero, partly on account of his eastern ancestry and partly because of his nerve and cunning. He was a bright child, tricky and fearless, and as he grew into manhood he drifted naturally into one of the numerous gangs of roughs and loafers that were at that time so common in the lower wards. . . .

While still very young he had learned to smoke and prepare the opium for the pipe, and it was through him that many New York roughs and crooks began to use the "dope" themselves and to spread the taste for it among their associates. They began to seek out the places in which smoking might be enjoyed, and in 1880, or thereabouts, there were a score of joints in full blast in Pell, Mott, and Doyers Streets and in the lower Bowery, and not one of these but what had its quota of Caucasian smokers of both sexes, most of whom belonged to the criminal or dissolute classes. There were other visitors, too—actors, actresses, clubmen and those who dropped in from time to time for the fun of the thing and because they found a peculiar charm in the heavy, pungent, soothing atmosphere, and in the outspoken frankness and freedom which distinguished the conversation of the regular habitués. . . .

The opium habit has always been a dominant influence in the career of this man, and it was through his indulgence in it that he came upon the great opportunity of his life, one which led to his leaving the business of picking pockets, which, after all, required only digital expertness and occasional fleetness of foot, and embarking in the beautiful green-goods profession, which called into play all the mental cunning and duplicity

---

[2] Appo claimed that he never attended school during his childhood.

which he had inherited from his father, as well as the general "flyness"[3] which came partly from his mother and partly from his long association with New York toughs, and in which he was an adept of the highest order and greatest proficiency.

Barney McGuire [*sic*], at that time the acknowledged king of the green-goods men, was not only an habitual opium smoker himself, but was the proprietor of a joint of his own on Crosby Street, which was the favorite resort of some of the most agile artists in his line of business. Barney and his craftsmen were not slow to recognize in Appo the qualities which have already been alluded to, and which they know could be successfully applied to their peculiar calling. They said as much to him on more than one occasion, and it was not long before Appo began operations as a regular dealer in phantom counterfeit bills. . . .

George wanted to be famous, but fame came to him first in an unlooked for and wholly undesired manner, in the winter of 1893. It was early in February of that year that he went up to Poughkeepsie to meet an ancient and seedy "come-on" and his friend who had left their rural homes in the mountains of North Carolina, impelled by some alluring essays on the advantage of using counterfeit money, mailed to them by Mr. Appo, who had written them in a strain of imaginative beauty, such as can be found only in the "Arabian Nights." These "come-ons" wore long whiskers and had large rolls of good money secreted in their waistbands. They met their tempter in a room in a Poughkeepsie hotel, and the latter, finding his victims loath to part with their money, became threatening in his manner. He was promptly shot in the eye and the bullet went through his head. All hands were put under arrest, and Appo was removed to a hospital, where he . . . attempted to take his own life. It was thought at first that his wound would prove fatal to his reason, if not his life, but he recovered his senses in a day or so and was visited by a woman named Lena Miller, his common-law wife, and a gentleman who represented himself as a wealthy manufacturer from Block Island, a place which fairly teems with factories as every summer visitor knows.[4] His sweetheart wept when she saw the stricken crook, and the wealthy manufacturer inquired, with considerable anxiety, whether George had "given anything away." The wealthy manufacturer was none other than Walter McNally, brother of the notorious king of green-goods men, Jimmy McNally, now serving a term in state's prison in Illinois. Appo's

---

[3] "Fly" was a slang expression for being clever, ingenious, artful, or cunning.
[4] Beck is writing tongue-in-cheek. Block Island was largely a summer resort and had no factories.

nerves were in a horrible condition for want of opium, and he expressed himself with much bitterness in regard to his associate in the enterprise whom he referred to as "Dolph," and who, he declared, had sneaked off and left him to his fate. The Dolph referred to was Dolph Sanders [*sic*], an associate and steerer for the notorious McNally green-goods gang. If it had not been for the influence of the Miller woman, who relieved his sufferings with small pellets of opium which she had brought with her, it is probable that he would have betrayed the members of the gang, as he claimed at the time it was a put-up job to do him. Three months later he got out of the hospital and was sentenced to a year's imprisonment. And sometime afterward, while being transferred from Sing Sing to Danamora [*sic*] in charge of Detective Jackson of Sing Sing prison, he again attempted suicide. On his release he declared openly that the man who shot him was what was called a "dummy come-on," who had been hired by James McNally to put him out of the way, as McNally bore him a grudge. . . . It was this suspicion on Appo's part, according to the testimony of some who know him, that led him to give away the operations of the gang at the Lexow investigation.

. . . As a study in the heredity and racial traits and tendencies, George Appo's character is one which is well worth investigating, not only because of the way in which his peculiar talents have been applied to the business of money-getting, but also because he is the first one of the new hybrid brood to which he belonged who has come into popular notice. The question which naturally presents itself to the thinker is:

"What part will the rest of his tribe take in our national development?"

There is no doubt that many of the half-breeds will be heard of the same as was Appo. But it must be remembered that they are not all common, ignorant laundrymen and sailors, these pig-tailed aliens. Some of them are men of education, and even wealth, who have been brought up in their own native land as merchants or professional men, and there are many among them who would be termed, in Mr. Appo's picturesque lingo, "Fly mugs" (gamblers and sharpers), who surpass in cunning and mendacity the average confidence men of upper Broadway, and who journey from one city to the other playing faro as well as fan-tan, and fleeing those with whom they come in contact without regard to race or creed. Verily it is an interesting quarter of the town in which young men of the George Appo type are growing up, and we shall hear more from its half-breeds as time rolls on. . . .

To attempt, according to the records of the much abused science of criminology, to trace a physical resemblance between father and son would be a superfluous task. Whether George Appo's insanity is the natural result of a career of vice and dissipation, or whether its seed was an inheritance long latent, is a question for alienists.[5] The secret of his career is so simple that a child can see it. For George Appo to have led a pure and noble life would have required the moral strength of a Savanarolla, the genius of a Cromwell and the patience of a Job, qualities inconceivable in one man.[6] For him to have lived as he did was—Human.

When George Appo gives up the ghost it will be the greatest benefit he ever conferred on his fellow man—more worthy of record than any or all of his long count of misdeeds. The approach of his death is in itself almost too trite a matter for comment. He has all his life been an enemy to all that is good and true in the world. He has done nothing but harm. He is so constituted that were he to be at liberty for a hundred years to come he would continue to do nothing but harm. In all fairness, such a man is better dead. But George Appo, insane, is another matter. With the loss of his reason he assumes a value that otherwise he could never have acquired. He teaches a wonderful lesson. If there is in all the world a human being who will profit by it, George Appo's appalling wickedness has not been in vain.

---

[5] Psychiatrists.

[6] Girolamo Savonarola was a fifteenth-century Italian reformer. Oliver Cromwell was a seventeenth-century English revolutionary and leader. Job is a Biblical character and the namesake of *The Book of Job*.

2

GEORGE APPO

Letter to Governor Theodore Roosevelt

May 9, 1899

In 1896, Eddie Erwin and John Atwood assaulted George Appo outside a saloon, allegedly for his testimony before the Lexow Committee (Document 8), and Appo stabbed Atwood in self-defense. Appo's attorney, Ambrose H. Purdy, feared for his client's life if he was incarcerated in Sing Sing. Purdy requested a medical examination of Appo, which concluded that the defendant suffered from "a form of mental derangement known as Monamania [sic] of the type called persecutive."[1] This convinced the presiding judge, Martin T. McMahon, to declare Appo temporarily insane and send him to the Matteawan State Hospital for the Criminally Insane for treatment. Appo thus became one of the first individuals subjected to a psychological examination before sentencing, one of the principles of Progressive Era criminology. Defendants judged to be "certifiably insane" avoided conviction but remained under indictment. After more than two years in Matteawan, Appo petitioned for his release in a letter to the governor of New York, Theodore Roosevelt. The letter reveals Appo's state of mind, his belief in his rights as a citizen, and his hope that Roosevelt's reputation as an opponent of police and municipal corruption would render a sympathetic hearing.

MAY 9, 1899

Dear Sir:

I beg for permission to address and make following remarks. I have been here for two years four months and two weeks and previous to my arrival here was three months in the "Tombs" City Prison and

---

[1] Statement of Dr. Joseph Terriberry, October 9, 1896, in *People v. George Appo*, July 24, 1896, Case #9126, New York Supreme Court Cases, unprocessed collection, New York County District Attorney Indictment Papers, New York City Municipal Archives and Records Center.

George Appo to Governor Theodore Roosevelt, May 9, 1899, Governor's Executive Clemency and Pardon Case Files (series A0597), New York State Archives, Albany.

two months at the Bellevue Hospital Prison ward under care of Physicians all that time. I now believe I have fully recovered my mental and bodily health and should again be set free from this Hospital. I am now entirely without means to engage a Lawyer which is absolutely necessary for me to get to court. I have already applied for aid and relief from Recorder John W. Goff and Rev. C. H. Parkhurst and secured answer from Recorder Goff that he would look into my case and he has recently written to Dr. H. E. Allison concerning my general condition. Also Rev. Parkhurst had informed me by letter that he would refer my case to the "Society for Prevention of Crime" in the city of New York. Since Feb. 16th last I have heard no news from them. Now I humbly appeal and beg you Governor—if such is possible—to exercise your charity and kindness towards me by communicating with Dr. H. E. Allison calling his attention to my demand to be returned to court for trial where I am confident my innocents [*sic*] can be proven. Should you desire details of my case and the circumstances which have consigned me to this Institution I will willingly tell them to you and answer all questions candidly and truthfully and if necessary under oath.

Permit me to recall to your memory that I was a witness for the former "Lexow" Investigating Committee and before said Honorable Body gave truthful testimony, and to beg you Governor in the Hope that Your favor will be granted me. I am

Respectfully
George W. Appo.

3

DR. HENRY E. ALLISON

Report on George W. Appo

1899

Dr. Henry E. Allison (1851–1904) was the medical superintendent of Matteawan State Hospital for the Criminally Insane during Appo's time there. Allison was trained at Dartmouth Medical College, graduated in 1878, and eventually specialized in psychiatry. In 1889, he was named medical superintendent of the New York Asylum for Insane Criminals at Auburn Prison. Three years later, the new Matteawan State Hospital opened in Beacon, New York. Allison's medical diagnosis describes Appo as violent and "beyond . . . rational," and presents a different picture of Appo from the one found in Appo's letter to Theodore Roosevelt (Document 2).

George W. Appo

The Commission appointed to examine this patient stated that he believed himself to be the victim of police persecution, far beyond what is rational. One specification was that he was poisoned by his enemies or at their instigation. He is said to have attacks of dizziness in which he has fallen to the ground. About three months after admission he suddenly assaulted a patient without apparent provocation. Appo stated, however, that the patient had been calling him vile names in a low whisper (Appo is quite deaf and unable to hear any sound like a whisper).

Some time after this, he complained that another patient on the ward was conspiring against him and was talking about him to various persons and "throwing glances" at him, all of which the patient himself denied. He has imagined from time to time that various people here are "down on him." That their object was to injure him. His conduct, however, has on the whole been very good. He has been on both the disturbed and the quiet wards; at present he is on one of the quietest wards

---

Report of Dr. Henry E. Allison, Medical Superintendent of Matteawan State Hospital for the Criminally Insane, on George W. Appo, May 16, 1899, Governor's Executive Clemency and Pardon Case Files (series A0597), New York State Archives, Albany.

in the house and latterly has not made any complaint or evidenced any active ideas of persecution on the part of others. He is as well very much improved physically. His previous convictions have been as follows:—

Sing Sing Prison, 1st term, under the name of George Dixon, Attempted Petty Larceny from Person, sentenced April 13, 1874, from N.Y. County by Hon. Mr. Hackett;

Sing Sing Prison, 2nd term, under the name of George Wilson, Grand Larceny, sentenced Jan. 10, 1877, from N.Y. County by Judge Gildersleeve;

Sing Sing Prison, 3d term, George Appo, Grand Larceny, sentenced April 26, 1882, from N.Y. County by Judge Smyth;

Sing Sing Prison, 4th term, under the name of George Albrow [sic], Attempted Fraud, sentenced April 25, 1893, from N.Y. County by Judge Guernsey;

N.Y. County Penitentiary, under the name of George Leon, Petit Larceny, sentenced June 2, 1890, at a Court of General Sessions, N.Y. County, by Judge Martine;

N.Y. County Penitentiary, George W. Appo, Assault, 3d degree, sentenced October 3, 1895, at a Court of General Sessions N.Y. County, by Judge Cowing.

Very respectfully,
H. E. Allison
Medical Superintendent.

N.B. This patient is not a convict but having been found insane while under a criminal charge his trial was suspended and he was committed here to remain until recovered. H.E.A.

4

LEWIS E. LAWES

Twenty Thousand Years in Sing Sing

1932

Lewis E. Lawes (1883–1947) was the warden of Sing Sing from 1920 to 1941. He began his career in corrections as a guard at Clinton Prison in Dannemora, New York, in 1905. He then worked at Auburn Prison, Elmira Reformatory, the New York City Reformatory on Hart Island (superintendent), and the Massachusetts State Prison (warden). In 1920, New York governor Al Smith appointed Lawes warden of Sing Sing. Lawes rejected the harsh and often violent methods of inmate control. Instead, he emphasized raising inmate morale as a way to maintain prison peace and security. For a brief period, Lawes's brand of penology was a national model. He wrote several books, including Twenty Thousand Years in Sing Sing *(1932), in which he examined the history of the prison and quoted Appo's unpublished account of his experience there in order to illustrate the horrors of the nineteenth-century penitentiary and the need for reform.*

Such was the Sing Sing of the Nineteenth Century. A hopeless, oppressive, barren spot. Escapes were frequent, attempts at escape almost daily occurrences. Suicides were common. Prisoners were considered a tough and dangerous lot of men. The kneading process of the prison made them still more dangerous and tougher. The whole theory of the prison was to inure the prisoner to hardship and suffering.

The prison warden is primarily a custodian. His function under the law is to keep his men within the confines of his prison. They are his stock in trade. His stock must always be properly accounted for. And so wardens looked with some degree of misgiving at the many escapes and the frequent attempts to leave their bailiwick. Naturally, the first thing that occurred to them was security. The institution must be made foolproof. Sing Sing needed a wall. Wardens for twenty years advocated

---

From Lewis E. Lawes, *Twenty Thousand Years in Sing Sing* (New York: A. L. Burt, 1932), 88–94.

the building of a stone wall around the prison grounds. Every annual report prayed for this relief. Finally in 1877, the wall was completed, the one that now surrounds the old prison. Twenty feet high, punctuated here and there with guard posts from which armed keepers could view the prison grounds and buildings. But life within the prison continued along traditional lines. The warden was now sure that his subjects could not escape him. They would be there to receive their dues. And so the shower drenched its unending victims; the ball and chain restrained rebellious spirits; men continued to languish in weary abandon within the dark recesses of inaccessible dungeons. All this despite the legislative prohibition of 1870 against corporal punishment.

Is this picture overdrawn? Is it a fact that these harsh measures hardened prisoners and officers alike? Let me lay aside for a moment the prison volumes which, for the first time, are now seeing the light of day. A prisoner by the name of George Appo found himself in Sing Sing in 1874. Appo had served three prison terms between 1874 and 1883. He had been a witness before the Lexow Investigating Committee. John W. Goff and Frank Moss became interested in the discharged prisoner and obtained honest employment for him. Sixteen years after his last prison term he wrote the story of his prison experiences. It is a voluminous document but has never been published. We find therein a vivid picture of prison life and discipline of the period.

Those were the days of contract labor. Contractors bought labor. The income went to the State. The prisoner got nothing. Appo tells of his experiences.

"I was at work only three days when the paid instructor of the contractor put a dozen shirts on my table. 'You will have to do these shirts today,' he said, 'and see that you do them perfect or I'll know the reason why.'

"I told him I would do my best. I finished two shirts, but unfortunately while on the third shirt, I had to go and get a hot iron. Before using it I dipped it in water to cool off. Then I started to iron the sleeve of the shirt and accidentally scorched it. I reported the accident to the citizen instructor. He went to the keeper and told him I willfully burned the shirt. The keeper said to me: 'Get your hat and coat.' I did so. He and the instructor took me to the guard room to the Principal Keeper and reported me to him as deliberately burning shirts.

"'What have you to say about that?' the Principal Keeper asked. 'It was an accident and I couldn't help it,' I said.

"'Accident, hey! Couldn't help it, hey! Well, we'll make you be more careful after this. Take off your clothes,' he shouted.

"'Take off your clothes,' he again demanded and when I did not respond quickly enough he shouted, 'Seize him.' Two big six-foot keepers grasped me by the throat, tore off my coat and pants, knocked out my front teeth by shoving me violently over the paddle board, pulled my hands behind my back, handcuffed me and pulled them up behind my back, as I lay across the paddle board, by a small tackle attached to a frame work on sides of the paddle board. After securing me, this six-foot keeper took a board shaped just like a canoe paddle with small holes in the blade and swung it over his shoulders and brought it down with all his might on my bare back and spine. I counted nine blows before I became insensible. When I came to, I was lying on the floor. I heard the Doctor say, 'he's all right now.' The Principal Keeper said to me: 'Do you think you can go back and do your work all right now? If you don't, we have a way to make you.' I replied, 'You punished me for nothing and the next time I am brought here, you will punish me for something.' 'No insolence; take him back to the shop.'

"When I got back to the shop, with my teeth knocked out and my body black and bruised from the paddle, I took the shirts that were on my table to iron across the shop to the stove, kicked open the stove door, put the shirts into the fire and slammed the door shut again.

"I was again brought over to the guard room and asked why I did it. I would not answer. The Principal Keeper said, 'Put him in again.' But the Doctor objected. 'No, lock him up in the dungeon.' So they took me to the dark cell.

"I lay there for fourteen days on two ounces of bread and a gill of water every twenty-four hours. When I was taken from the dark cell, I was carried to the hospital injured for life. . . ."

Appo was discharged, but his resumption of stealing soon returned him to Sing Sing. "On my arrival at Sing Sing Prison," he tells us, "I found a new Warden in charge, but the discipline was just as severe and brutal and the food and everything in general unfit for the lowest animal life. In fact, there was a general epidemic among the prisoners caused by rotten and filthy meat and other foodstuffs they had to eat, and during the whole course of my first two terms, I never saw or knew of a place to bathe after a hard day's work in the Stove Foundry."

I found in Appo's story an incident that brings out in a forceful manner the nature and extent of the silent system, as it then prevailed at Sing Sing. A system that was for almost a century the "Pride" of American penal administration.

"In this shop (the plumbing shop) was a convict by the nickname of 'Ginger.' He was there under the name of Thompson, with a five year sentence to serve. This convict had occasion to speak to the convict who worked next to him on the work bench. One was instructing the other how to finish a piece of work. The keeper, one Tierney, saw Ginger talking to his neighbor and rushed over with his big stick and poked Ginger in the neck. 'Stop your talking.' Ginger, who happened to have his working hammer in his hand, was taken by surprise. He jumped from his bench with the hammer in his hand, tried to explain that he had to instruct the other man, but Tierney, with another jab of his stick, told Ginger to 'shut up,' put his hammer down and not give him any back talk. Ginger jumped back, and the keeper pulled out his gun and shot him dead. Afterward Tierney claimed that he shot poor Thompson in self-defence. Nothing was said or done to Keeper Tierney. Thompson had no relatives or even a good friend in the outside world to take an interest in the case. He was only twenty-seven years of age at the time and was raised up from boyhood down in the fourth ward. The prison authorities nailed his body in a pine box and buried him up on the hill, or as the graveyard is called by convicts, '25 gallery,' without even a prayer from the so-called Chaplain."

What a forbidding picture was the Sing Sing of the Nineteenth Century! Conceived along the lines of Dante's imaginative Inferno. A procrustean world. Sensitive souls were hardened. Strong men rendered weak and helpless. As an "example" it failed miserably of its purpose. Crime continued. As a deterrent, it was futile. New laws created new crimes. In 1902, the number of laws violated had risen to forty-eight. By 1926 they totalled sixty. Sing Sing's population continued to grow.

It was then hardly realized that the prison was only a link in the scheme of crime prevention. Origins, sources, motivating forces did not concern the administrator, prosecuting or judicial agencies. Nor was a consideration given to the fact that prisoners were a continuing social problem. When, finally, administrators timidly called for modifications in prison routine, it was with the apologetic suggestion that they would make their own task easier. Brutalizing prisoners worked havoc with their keepers. It was then a case of brute against brute. Why not tame the animal?

5

BRONX HOME NEWS

Obituary of George Appo
June 15, 1930

Little is known about Appo after 1910. He died on May 17, 1930, just two months shy of his seventy-fourth birthday, of general arteriosclerosis. Three days later, he was interred in Mount Hope Cemetery in Hastings-on-Hudson, New York. Some obituaries portrayed Appo as a romantic figure. This one from the Bronx Home News *describes him as "one of the wiliest of pickpockets, burglars and confidence men up to the time he reformed in the late 90's." Another depicted him as "the finest crook that ever turned a new leaf." These descriptions sharply contrast with the images of Appo given by Louis Beck (Document 1) and Dr. Henry Allison (Document 3) during his lifetime.*

George Appo, Famous Criminal of Late 90's, Called Man of Fine Sensibilities by Bronxite

Born the son of a Chinese father and an Irish mother, the toughest of Cherry Hill toughs at the age of ten, and considered one of the wiliest of pickpockets, burglars and confidence men up to the time he reformed in the late 90's, George Appo died recently at the age of 72 [*sic*], leaving a case history which is a seemingly incredible social paradox.

When he died, a tired and somewhat befuddled old man, his reputation for honesty was almost as firmly established as his previous notoriety as one of the craftiest swindlers ever fingerprinted by the Police Department.

Few knew George Appo better in the latter years of his life than Howard C. Barber, 1592 University Ave., near Featherbed Lane, superintendent of the Society for the Prevention of Crime.

Barber, a tall, angular outspoken man, was the ex–bunco man's friend and adviser until the day the ex-convict died at Ward's Island from heart

---

Bronx Home News, June 15, 1930, box 32, Society for the Prevention of Crime Papers, Rare Book and Manuscript Library, Columbia University, New York.

trouble. Barber first met him 17 years ago, when he became superintendent of the society.

At the time the Bronxite met him, Appo was no longer the spry,
gaminesque, fearless lawbreaker whose exploits had set New York agog
before he reformed. He was a subdued man, blind in one eye from a bullet wound. He was seeking honest work.

DEVELOPED CLOSE FRIENDSHIP

The superintendent's friendship meant much to the man who once was
described as "one of the unfortunate wretches against whom all mankind seems to turn." Time and again he would pay visits to Barber at the
headquarters of the society at 133 William St.

"George," Barber stated ruminatively, "was a man of unusually sensitive temperament. He was loyal to the core. He was one of the most
fearless men I had ever known."

In the latter years of his life the man who spent 22 years in prison
for crimes whose very audacity betrayed him, always turned to Barber
when he was in need. At the time of his death he was a withered little
man, almost totally blind and hard of hearing.

He had strange mental lapses which were attributed to hereditary
insanity. Barber is inclined to discredit this report. Appo, he said, merely
suffered from the affliction of his age—senility.

PLASTICITY AMAZING

To Barber the most amazing quality of the man was his plasticity after
40 years as a social outcast hounded relentlessly by the police since the
age of 14 when he was first placed in prison for picking pockets.

He was the son of Chang Quimbo Appo, who was born in Ning-po
and who had a particularly ferocious record of violent crimes. Chang
spent 35 years in prison, and died at 90 in Matteawan State Hospital for
the Criminally Insane in 1912.

George's mother, Katherine Fitzpatrick, was born in the slums of
London, and at an early age came to live in the slums of New York.
Chang was accused of killing his wife, but Barber declares that this mur-
der was never established.

George, the superintendent said, had said that his mother was
drowned while en route to California to visit her brother. George,
according to the story told by the reformed criminal, had been rescued
by a sailor and eventually found himself back in New York.

BECAME THIEF AT TEN

He took up pocket-picking at the age of ten, when his mother's death left him to shift for himself. He grew up with the toughs of the Fourth and Sixth Wards.

Progressing from pocket-picking to burglary, he began about 1894 to assume importance in the world of confidence games. He became an expert in "sure thing" grafts—bunco, dice, short cards, flim flam, fake jewelry and "green goods."

For years his hands were in other people's pockets. His long deft fingers assumed a peculiar shape, and he constantly practised the delicate maneuvers which caused portly gentlemen to lose their watches and flustered matrons to seek their pocketbooks. The cries of "Thief, thief!" would send him scurrying through the crowds like a water rat under rocks.

He gained great unpopularity with his fellow criminals—and the police and prison authorities—in 1894 when the Lexow Committee got him to tell of the methods of swindlers and conditions in State prisons.

REFORMATION AMAZED POLICE

After he reformed in 1894 his amazing conversion to scrupulous honesty amazed both the police and social students. Barber vouches that even in times of dire need, George successfully combatted the latent impulse of turning to petty thievery until he could find honest work.

Despite the fact that he had no schooling in childhood, the ex-convict, in an amazingly brief time, picked up the rudiments of spelling and grammar and was even able to leave a long account of his criminal experiences.

There was a streak of the poet in him. Barber has in his possession some of the ex-convict's efforts. They are elementary, crude, but express a depth of emotion and even idealism which seem incongruous in view of his life record. One, containing his reflections on prison life, is as sad as a dirge.

In the last few years of his life he was supported by the Society for the Prevention of Crime. He had a dread of institutions, and fought all efforts to have him committed. He had spent too many years in Clinton Prison and Sing Sing.

He was saved from a grave in Potter's Field through the society. Barber arranged for his interment in Mt. Hope Cemetery.

2

Subcultures of Crime

6

GEORGE W. MATSELL

Vocabulum; or, The Rogue's Lexicon

1859

George Washington Matsell (1811–1877) was a police official, judge, bookstore owner, and the first commissioner of the New York City Police Department (1845–1857). The offspring of English immigrants, Matsell apprenticed in his father's bookstore and later opened his own establishment, which was known for selling freethinking and "racy," or obscene, publications. He was active in Democratic party politics and became a police magistrate in 1840. Matsell actively promoted police reforms that led to the passage of the Municipal Police Act of 1844, which created a professional police force in New York City. As police chief, Matsell introduced uniforms, improved patrol methods, imposed strict discipline, and created a special police division to patrol waterfront neighborhoods. He left his post to become editor of the National Police Gazette *in 1857, but returned as superintendent of police from 1873 to 1875 and briefly as president of the board of police commissioners in 1874. Matsell's career embodied the overlapping relationships among police officers, journalists, politicians, and criminals. His* Vocabulum *(1859) was among the first exposés of the oral culture and distinctive language of the urban underworld.*

From George W. Matsell, *Vocabulum; or, The Rogue's Lexicon* (New York: George W. Matsell, 1859), iii–vi, 105.

Preface

... The rogue fraternity have a language peculiarly their own, which is understood and spoken by them no matter what their dialect, or the nation where they were reared. Many of their words and phrases, owing to their comprehensive meaning, have come into general use, so that a Vocabulum or Rogue's Lexicon, has become a necessity to the general reader, but more especially to those who read police intelligence.

Occupying the position of a Special Justice, and Chief of the Police of the great Metropolis of New York, where thieves and others of a like character from all parts of the world congregate, and realizing the necessity of possessing a positive knowledge of every thing connected with the class of individuals with whom it was my duty to deal, I was naturally led to study their peculiar language, believing that it would enable me to converse with them more at ease, and thus acquire a knowledge of their character, besides obtaining from them information that would assist me in the position I occupied, and consequently be of great service to the public. To accomplish this task was no mean undertaking, as I found that it required years of diligent labor to hunt up the various authorities, and these when found proved only partially available, as much of the language in present use was unwritten, and could only be obtained by personal study among first-class thieves who had been taught it in their youth. The difficulties surrounding it, did not deter me from following out my resolution, and by closely pursuing it, I had opened up to me a fountain of knowledge that I could not have obtained if I had not possessed a clear understanding of this peculiar dialect. Experience has since demonstrated to me that any man engaged in police business can not excel without understanding the rogues' language, in the study of which they will find this Lexicon of invaluable service.

It is not, however, to policemen alone that this book will be of service, as these cant[1] words and phrases are being interwoven with our language and many of them are becoming recognized Anglicisms. It is not unusual to see them in the messages of presidents and governors—to hear them enunciated at the bar and from the pulpit, and thus they have come to be acknowledged as appropriately expressive of particular ideas; so that while they are in common use among the footpads[2] that infest the land, the *élite* of the Fifth Avenue pay homage to their worth, by frequently using them to express thoughts, that could not, otherwise, find a fitting representative. The vocabulary of the rogue is

[1] The private language of the underworld.
[2] Thieves who prey on pedestrians.

not of recent date; although it is mainly made up of arbitrary or technical words and phrases, while others are of a purely classical origin. It is a language of great antiquity, and may be dated back to the earliest days of the roving gipsy [Gypsy] bands that infested Europe, from whom the greater portion of it has been derived. It might more properly be termed the Romany or Gipsy language, adapted to the use of modern rogues in all parts of the world, and in which the etymologist will find words drawn from every known language. Some of these words are peculiarly national, but as a general thing the language of the rogue in New-York is the language of the rogue the world over.

Among policemen, not only in this city but in different parts of the United States, the cant language of thieves is attempted to be used; but there being no standard they are unable to do so understandingly, and each one gives to the words the corrupted sense in which he received it; thus speaking as it were, a miserable *"patois,"*[3] to the exclusion of the true "Parisian French." This departure from the true meaning of the words used is mischievous in its tendency, as it is calculated to mislead and bewilder, so that rogues might still converse in the presence of an officer, and he be ignorant of what they said. This I have endeavored to correct, and although I may not claim fallibility in these matters, yet I believe that I have arrived at as high a degree of perfection as is now attainable. . . .

Geo. W. Matsell.
New-York, 1859.

Examples

Tim Sullivan buzzed a bloke and a shakester of a reader. His jomer stalled. Johnny Miller, who was to have his regulars, called out, "cop-bung," for as you see a fly-cop was marking. Jack speeled to the crib, when he found Johnny Doyle had been pulling down sawney for grub. He cracked a casa last night, and fenced the swag. He told Jack as how Bill had flimped a yack, and pinched a swell of a spark-fawney, and had sent the yack to church, and got half a century and a finnif for the fawney.

TRANSLATION

Tim Sullivan picked the pockets of a gentleman and lady of a pocket-book and purse. Tim's fancy-girl stood near him and screened him from

---

[3] A dialect, jargon, provincial forms of speech.

observation. Johnny Miller, who was to have a share of the plunder, called out to him: "Hand over the stolen property—a detective is observing your maneuvers." Sullivan ran immediately to his house, when he found Johnny Doyle had provided something to eat, by stealing some bacon from a store-door. Doyle committed a burglary last night, and disposed of the property plundered. He told Sullivan that Bill had hustled a person, and obtained a watch, and also robbed a well-dressed gentleman of a diamond ring. The watch he sent to have the works taken out and put into another case, or the maker's name erased and another inserted; the ring realized him fifty-five dollars.

7

NEW YORK STATE ASSEMBLY

Report of the Select Committee Appointed by the Assembly of 1875 to Investigate the Causes of the Increase of Crime in the City of New York

1876

Crime, political corruption, and urban disorder became increasing concerns among municipal and state officials during the nineteenth century. In 1874, Tammany Hall leader and state senator William "Boss" Tweed was convicted for various charges of political corruption. The following year, the New York Assembly appointed a select committee to examine "the causes of the increase of crime" in New York City, one of the first legislative investigations into urban disorder and criminal activity. The committee held public hearings for several months and finally issued a report that criticized the management and sometimes the integrity of various municipal agencies, including the police department, court system, coroner's office, district attorney, board of excise, and city prisons. Charges of collusion between public officials and criminals, illegal appropriation of public funds, and other forms of political malfeasance

From New York State Assembly, *Report of the Select Committee Appointed by the Assembly of 1875 to Investigate the Causes of the Increase of Crime in the City of New York*, Assembly Document 106 (New York: Martin B. Brown, 1876), 1, 7, 8–9, 10–11, 15–16, 30–34, 76.

remained a mainstay of urban reform efforts and political debate throughout the Gilded Age and Progressive Era. The committee also offered a rare public examination of prostitution, with a recommendation for legalization and police regulation. Many of these issues would be revisited twenty years later in the Lexow Committee investigation (Document 8) and would remain the subject of various Progressive Era municipal reforms.

NEW YORK, *FEBRUARY* 11, 1876.

Hon. James W. Husted,
    Speaker of the Assembly of the State of New York:
    The undersigned, members of the select committee appointed by the Assembly of 1875, to investigate the causes of the increase of crime in the city of New York, respectfully report as follows: . . .

Inefficiency and Corruption of the Police

Among the most potent causes of the increases of crime in the city of New York has been, without a doubt, the inefficiency and the corruption of the police force, which is demonstrated by the existence and flourishing of certain classes of crime to which we would more particularly invite the attention of the Legislature. The common pickpocket, the forger, the counterfeiter, and the burglar are of course more or less under the dominion of the police, and can be more or less restrained as the police are more or less honest or efficient; but that they will exist, no matter how powerful and how upright the police force is, is no matter of doubt. But certain other classes of crime peculiar to great cities, and almost indeed peculiar to this city, depend for the breath of life upon the connivance or the imbecility of the police force. . . .

Prostitution

. . . While we do not doubt that prostitution necessarily will exist, we also do not doubt but that the police authorities can prevent its open, indecent and offensive manifestations. Street-walking, soliciting, indecent exposure from windows of houses, noise, drunkenness, and confusion can be prevented by police authorities, as can also the existence of houses of the most beastly and degraded character. It seems, however, from the whole testimony before us, that in but few, if any, precincts of the city, had any such measures been taken by the police authorities as would prevent these occurrences prior to the time that the sessions of this committee began, and even after its sessions had commenced a great many things continued to go on which a well governed police force would never allow. . . . But, instead of suppressing and preventing these outward and offensive manifestations of prostitution, there is but too much reason to fear that the police have used the prohibition of the law against houses of prostitution, systematically to extort money from the keepers and inmates of those places.

. . . Many of these houses are conducted for the purpose of having the most obscene exhibitions, a fact which cannot fail to be known to the police, and yet on account of which they are rarely interfered with. Indeed, one captain testified before the committee that no such places existed in his precinct, and on the very night that he gave that testimony the committee had no difficulty whatever, through a head-quarters detective, in finding five such houses in a row within one-eighth of a mile of that captain's station-house. . . .

Houses Owned by Respectable Citizens

Among the other curious elements that enter into this subject of prostitution, is the fact that a number of houses in the Eighth and Fifteenth wards, which are let and occupied as low dens, are owned by highly reputable people, some of them pillars of the Church and State. . . . Quite a number of these persons have been indicted, but the indictments appear to be mere matter of form, as one of the parties against whom these indictments had been found, testified before the committee, that he was then serving on the grand jury himself. It is not a pleasing subject for contemplation, that these most disreputable houses should carry grist to the mills of highly reputable citizens, nor is it an agreeable thought for citizens of New York that an indictment stands on record against an ex-mayor of the city for owning a house of prostitution. . . .

Detective Force

That all other classes of crime have received at times the earnest support of the police, will appear by looking at the detective system of the police force of the city of New York. The detective system of the city is divided into two branches, the head-quarters detectives and the ward detectives, although the latter do not seem to be expressly recognized by that name, and are variously styled at times in the testimony as "ward detectives," "special duty men," "detailed men" and by various other appellations. The head-quarters detective force consisted of about twenty-five men under the command of a captain up to January, 1875. The ward detectives were about two in number, in each precinct, although varying; there being sometimes only one and sometimes three or four. The duties of the head-quarters detectives were the investigation of crimes assigned to them for that purpose by the superintendent.

The duties of the ward detectives were also the investigation of crimes in the precincts, and in this respect they and their captains at times clashed with the head-quarters detectives; and they were also understood to be in general supervision of, and acquaintance with, criminals, thieves, prostitutes and gamblers, in their respective precincts. In addition to this, a very important branch of their business seems to have been the management of the financial relations between the dishonest captains and the criminal classes under their control. This latter fact will be found reiterated again and again, with greater or less emphasis in different portions of the committee's testimony, and of the fact there can be no question whatever. The ward detectives are selected by the captains from the patrolmen under their command, a most ingenious method of making them the absolute tools of their captains. Indeed, at various times, the captain, on moving from one precinct to another, appears to have taken his ward man along with him, and the same firm has set up business in a new sphere of operations. That ward detectives are eminently desirable, that their local knowledge and constant activity, would be of great benefit to the police force, your committee cannot question, but that a more hopelessly ridiculous means of appointing them, than now exists, could be devised, we do not believe. . . .

Prostitution

In approaching the discussion of this subject the committee are aware that it is a most delicate topic, and that the mere mention of it seems, to many people, an insult to the morality of a nation. . . . The evidence . . . shows, what every man knows to be the fact, that there are large numbers of houses of prostitution in the city of New York, containing many inmates, and also a large number of individuals who, living in their own apartments, continue to prostitute themselves there; that these places are scattered all over the city, in many instances being found in some of the most fashionable and respectable quarters; that many of them are absolute eye-sores to their respectable neighbors, carrying on their infamous business, not in quiet and obscurity, but flauntingly, openly, indecently and offensively and that attempts to check even this latter class are very irregular and inefficient. The law, construed to its letter, looks upon all prostitutes as disorderly persons. . . . They are under the absolute ban of the law, and . . . it being within the power, and being in a strictly legal sense the duty, of a captain of police to suppress every house of prostitution in his precinct, it has come to be a custom for the proprietors of these places to pay blackmail to captains in order to secure immunity. The committee do not wish to be understood as saying that this prevails without exception; they are assured to the contrary; but that in many cases such has been the result. . . . Under the law as it now stands, no power of classification, no power of localization, no power of restriction or control or inspection is legitimately given to the police authorities. Their theoretical duty is to *suppress* prostitution. It is a fact, however, which the experience of all mankind proves, that laws of this sort are dead letters upon the statute book. Human nature is so constituted that prostitution will continue in the future as it has in the past, no matter what laws are fulminated against it, and no matter how strictly they are sought to be enforced. . . .

Brought face to face with this fact, the question remains for the legislative body of this State to decide whether or not it is wise to continue the nominal, legal ban under which prostitution is placed, to close the eyes of the law-making power to a fact which their hearts cannot ignore, and putting aside all considerations of local welfare, of the greatest happiness of the greatest number, to go on in the future as they have in the past, taking no steps toward permanent or healthy reforms. . . . The committee are willing to take it upon themselves in earnestly recommending to the Legislature the regulating or permitting, or, if the word be not deemed offensive, the licensing of prostitution. . . .

Now, what would be the good effects of placing prostitution in the city of New York under police regulation? In the first place the houses could be located; the keepers could be required to remain in certain localities. Respectable people, living quietly in their homes with their families, would no longer be annoyed by disreputable neighbors, and would be no longer constrained to run from police captain to Police Court, from Police Court to district attorney, and from district attorney to police commissioner, and back again throughout the circle, as the witnesses before the committee have testified that they have been compelled to do, without obtaining redress in the end. In the second place, the whole temptation as to bribery of police officers would cease at once. Prostitution being indirectly recognized by law [and] the houses and inmates being registered, the police captain's only authority over them would be to see that they lived harmlessly and in obedience to the law. At the same time, such a system would prevent all street walking, all indecent exposure of every kind, all offensive demonstrations from windows. Any prostitute who was guilty of such an offense, should have her permit taken away, should be sent to jail; and every house whence such demonstrations issued should have its permit taken away and its inmates dispersed. In addition to these reasons, the institution should be under medical supervision. The doctors attached to the police department should examine the inmates, and when they are found to be afflicted with contagious diseases, they should be removed to the hospital. . . .

For many years prostitution has been under rigorous regulation in Paris, in Hamburgh [sic], in Berlin, in Vienna, and in others of the large cities of Europe. Despite the immense amount of prejudice to the contrary, it has even been regulated, and with eminent success, in the English garrison towns, such as Portsmouth. . . . The same system was introduced with great success in the city of St. Louis. . . .

In the interest of the well-being, the decorum, the decency of society, in the interest of the peace and happiness of by far the greatest number of people, in the interest of the preservation of the purity of the guardians of the public peace, in the interest of public health, . . . the committee earnestly urge upon the Legislature, as the only means of grappling with the social evil, the granting to the police the power of regulation, of localization, and medical visitation. . . .

> Very respectfully submitted,
> THOS. COOPER CAMPBELL,
> LEO C. DESSAR,
> JOHN T. MCGOWAN,
> JACOB HESS,
> *Committee.*

8

NEW YORK STATE SENATE

Report and Proceedings of the Senate Committee Appointed to Investigate the Police Department of the City of New York

1895

Police malfeasance, investigated by the New York Assembly in 1875 (Document 7), was revisited two decades later when, in 1894, the New York Senate formed a special committee chaired by Republican Clarence Lexow (1852–1910) (known as the Lexow Committee) to investigate police misconduct in New York City. The privately financed, Republican-led investigation was a response to the corruption charges against Tammany Hall, the dominant faction within New York's Democratic party and municipal government. From March to December 1894, the committee called 678 witnesses, including George Appo, and produced more than 5,700 pages of testimony and documentary evidence relating to election fraud, blackmail, and extortion by police officials. The corruption extended beyond simple toleration of unlicensed saloons, brothels, and gambling dens. Police officials also resorted to "terror" in extorting payments from many merchants engaged in licensed activities or in need of "protection" from various criminals. The investigation revealed how law enforcement was frequently an inconsistent and personalized series of informal negotiations among police officials, judges, and criminals. The Lexow Committee report generated a national debate about policing and disorder in American cities, foreshadowing the "white slavery" and antiprostitution campaigns of the Progressive Era.

Taken as a whole, the record upon this point discloses the fact that the police department, from the highest down to the lowest, was thoroughly impregnated with the political influence of Tammany Hall, and that the suppression and repression of crime depended, not so much upon the

From New York State Senate, *Report and Proceedings of the Senate Committee Appointed to Investigate the Police Department of the City of New York*, Senate Document 25 (Albany: James B. Lyon, 1895), 1:19, 21, 24, 25, 27, 28–29, 32–34, 40.

ability of the police to enforce the law, but rather upon the will of that organization or faction to have the law enforced. . . .

. . . The testimony of this kind, in fact, showed throughout, an extraordinary disinclination on the part of the police, so efficient in other respects, to display any desire or activity in the suppression of certain descriptions of vice and crime, a disinclination so strong that others attempting to perform that function found the police arrayed against them and experienced greater embarrassment from this circumstance than from any difficulty connected with the suppression of the vice itself. It indicated the amazing condition that in most of the precincts of the city, houses of ill-repute, gambling houses, policy shops, pool rooms and unlawful resorts of a similar character were being openly conducted under the eyes of the police, without attempt at concealment, so publicly, in fact, that the names of the persons and the street numbers of the houses were not only known throughout the community, but were published in the daily prints, and yet they remained open and ostentatiously flourished. . . .

. . . It seemed, in fact, as though every interest, every occupation, almost every citizen, was dominated by an all-controlling and overshadowing dread of the police department. If this was true with reference to legitimate business and wealth and station in metropolitan life, how much stronger necessarily was that condition of fear and servitude with reference to those in the humbler walks of life, those who shared the protection of neither wealth nor station, and more especially those who came in daily contact with the police force of the city, under its surveillance, conducting unlawful avocations, or engaged in the commission of licensed crime? There was only one method available, and that was to impress upon the minds of those who had suffered from the extortions, exactions and terrorism of the police, the conviction that the reign of terror had come to an end and that the authority of your committee . . . was superior to that of the police of the city. . . .

Those in the humbler walks of life were subjected to appalling outrages which to some extent continued, even to the end of the investigation. They were abused, clubbed, and imprisoned, and even convicted of crime on false testimony by policemen and their accomplices. Men of business were harassed and annoyed in their affairs, so that they too, were compelled to bend their necks to the police yoke, in order that they might share that so-called protection which seemed indispensable to the profitable conduct of their affairs. People of all degrees seemed to feel that to antagonize the police was to call down upon themselves the swift judgment and persecution of an invulnerable force, strong in itself, banded together by self-interest and the community of unlawful gain, and so thoroughly entrenched in the municipal government as to defy ordinary assault. Strong men hesitated when required to give evidence of their oppression, and whispered their stories; tricks, subterfuges and schemes of all kinds were resorted to to withhold from this committee and its counsel the fact that they had knowledge of acts of corruption or oppression by the police. The uniform belief was that if they spoke against the police, or if the police discovered that they had been instrumental in aiding your committee, or had given information, their business would be ruined, they would be hounded from the city and their lives, even, jeopardized. . . .

The poor, ignorant foreigner residing on the great east side of the city has been especially subjected to a brutal and infamous rule by the police, in conjunction with the administration of the local inferior criminal courts, so that it is beyond a doubt that innocent people who have refused to yield to criminal extortion, have been clubbed and harassed and confined in jail, and the extremes of oppression have been applied to them in the separation of parent and child, the blasting of reputation and consignment of innocent persons to a convict's cell.

The co-ordination of all the departments of city government, under the sway of the dominant Democratic faction in that city, has produced a harmony of action operating so as to render it impossible for oppressed citizens, particularly those in the humbler walks of life, the poor and needy, to obtain redress or relief from the oppression or the tyranny of the police. Their path to justice was completely blocked. . . .

In conclusion, your committee expresses the conviction that the testimony taken conclusively establishes an indictment against the police department of the city of New York as a whole. It establishes the necessity for a radical and basic reorganization by the elimination of those elements which may be found to be untrustworthy, inefficient, and corrupt. The conclusion which has impressed itself upon your committee, however, is that the disorganizing elements at work in the police department are such that operate from the higher officials down, rather than from the patrolmen up. . . .

It is a significant fact that but little corruption has been traced into the pockets of the ordinary patrolman, and that such sins as may be laid at his door largely consist in abuse of physical force, infringement upon the rights and privileges of private citizens, and omission to disclose the criminal conduct of his superiors. It is probable and even certain from the testimony, that a large number of patrolmen have paid sums averaging $300 for appointment. It is not strange that starting in this way, some of them have imitated the examples of their superiors and should have become victims to a most pernicious and criminal practice. But it would be manifestly unfair, because of the proof of isolated cases to arraign all the force under one general charge. On the contrary, your committee believes that a very large proportion of the patrolmen of the city, and a considerable number of their superiors are good officers and true, reliable and incorruptible men, whose conduct in guarding their honor, despite the example set by their superiors and their associates, marks them as men to be especially commended, and in any reorganization of the force to be particularly honored by retention and promotion, and we recommend that in any plan of reorganization which may be adopted, special stress should be laid upon this, because, in this way more than in any other, will the esprit de corps and the future efficiency of the force be subserved. . . .

Disorderly Houses

. . . The testimony upon this subject, taken as a whole, establishes conclusively the fact that this variety of vice was regularly and systematically licensed by the police of the city. The system had reached such a perfection in detail that the inmates of the several houses were numbered and classified and a reliable charge placed upon each proprietor in proportion to the number of inmates, or in case of houses of assignation the number of rooms occupied and the prices charged, reduced to a monthly rate, which was collected within a few days of the first of each month during the year. This was true apparently with reference to all disorderly houses, except in the case of a few specially favored ones. The prices ran from $25 to $50 monthly, depending upon the consideration aforesaid, besides fixed sums for the opening of new houses or the resumption of "business" in old or temporarily abandoned houses, and for "initiation fees" designed as an additional gratuity to captains upon their transfer into new precincts. The established fee for opening and initiation appears to have been $500. . . .

Detectives, Pawnbrokers, and Thieves

It has been conclusively shown that an understanding existed between headquarters' detectives, pawnbrokers, and thieves, by which stolen property may be promptly recovered by the owner on condition that he repay the pawnbroker the amount advanced on the stolen property. In every such case, which appears in evidence, the detective seems to have acted rather in the interest of securing the pawnbroker's advances than of securing the absolute return of the stolen property. . . .

In almost every instance it also appears that the detective, acting between the owner and the pawnbroker, receives substantial gratuities from the owner of the property for the work done in his official capacity. In some cases these gratuities were received without demand. Others were the result of demand on the part of the detectives. In very many cases, the amount of the pawnbrokers' advances added to the gratuities paid to the detectives, equalled, and, in some cases, exceeded the value of the article recovered.

9

THOMAS BYRNES

Professional Criminals of America

1886

Thomas Byrnes (1840–1910) was a famous New York City police detective. An Irish immigrant, he joined the police force in 1863 and quickly rose through the ranks, eventually serving as chief of detectives (1880–1892) and superintendent of police (1892–1895). During his tenure, he instituted a number of high-profile reforms. In 1880, he established the "dead line," which authorized police to arrest any criminal suspect south of Fulton Street; overnight Byrnes became a hero to Wall Street businessmen. He required "professional criminals," upon entering the city, to appear before him and promise not to engage in any criminal activity while in New York. In 1892, the New York Tribune *wrote that Byrnes had "effected a complete revolution in the criminal outlook and statistics of this city. The thieves at once dread and respect him."* [1] *Byrnes's methods, however, came under increasing attack. In 1895, he was forced to*

[1] *New York Tribune,* January 10, 1892.

From Thomas Byrnes, *Professional Criminals of America* (New York: Cassell, 1886), 1, 30–32, 34–37.

resign when Theodore Roosevelt was appointed president of the New York City board of police commissioners. Byrnes authored numerous widely read works on crime promoting his methods and ideas. Professional Criminals of America *(1886), his best-known publication, identified the nation's leading lawbreakers — male and female alike — and their distinctive criminal activities.*

Bank Burglars

The ways of making a livelihood by crime are many, and the number of men and women who live by their wits in all large cities reaches into the thousands. Some of the criminals are really very clever in their own peculiar line, and are constantly turning their thieving qualities to the utmost pecuniary account. Robbery is now classed as a profession, and in the place of the awkward and hang-dog looking thief we have to-day the intelligent and thoughtful rogue. There seems to be a strange fascination about crime that draws men of brains, and with their eyes wide open, into its meshes. Many people, and especially those whose knowledge of criminal life is purely theoretical, or derived from novels, imagine that persons entering criminal pursuits are governed by what they have been previously, and that a criminal pursuit once adopted is, as a rule, adhered to; or, in other words, a man once a pickpocket is always a pickpocket; or another, once a burglar is always a burglar. Hardly any supposition could be more erroneous. Primarily there are, of course, predisposing influences which have a certain effect in governing choice. . . .

Shoplifters and Pickpockets

Holiday week is the shoplifters' harvest. The ladylike and gentlemanly pilferers of the city know this. They feel that Christmas comes but once a year, and before and after opportunities for spoliation are most abundant. So the shoplifter sallies forth and the pickpocket wends his way with keen eyes and ready hand among the throng — wends her way perhaps it should be put, for of the shoplifters who infest the city the large majority are females. There are various reasons for this. The work of shoplifting is comparatively easy, it is sometimes remunerative, and above all it is congenial. There are few ladies to whom the visitation of the shops and the handling of the wares are not joys which transcend all others on earth. And the female shoplifter has that touch of nature left in her which makes a clothing store, variety bazaar or jewelry establishment the most delightful spot to exercise her cunning. . . .

There are generally but two classes of shoplifters—the regular criminal professional and the kleptomaniac. The very poor classes seldom take a hand in it. Poverty is held by the world to be the badge of crime, and the poor slattern who enters a store is sure to be so carefully watched that larceny is next to impossible. The shoplifter is always a person of fair apparel and she generally has a comfortable home. If she be a professional she may be one of a criminal community and her home may be shared by some other engaged in equally evil ways. If she be a kleptomaniac—and in shoplifting the word has peculiar significance—she is possibly a woman whose life in other respects is exemplary. It does seem strange that a wife and mother whose home is an honest one, who attends religious services regularly, and who seems far removed from the world of crime, should be so carried away by her admiration of some trinket or knickknack as to risk home, honor, everything to secure it. But the annals of metropolitan offenses are full of instances of just this kind. It is the sex's fondness for finery that nine times out of ten gets them in trouble. A woman who has left a home happy and well provided for goes shopping. She buys the necessary article she first started to procure after a good deal of selecting and chaffering.[2] Then she has time to look about her and goes counter-gazing. That is the fatal moment. She has already spent the contents of her purse, and she cannot honestly possess it. But the object every moment gains new fascination. She must have it. Then comes the temptation. It is so exposed. There is no one about. It would be such a simple thing to take it and conceal it. Conscience stifled by cupidity is dormant, and the lust of possession is all that possesses her. A moment more and the article is under her cloak, and all of a tremble she is edging away, half frightened, half regretful, yet wholly swayed by the securing of the moment's idol. Then comes detection. Everything about her rises to betray her—her frightened glance, her sneaking attitude, the close clutch she has upon her cloak. She is accosted, questioned, and then every thought of home, family, and the disgrace that threatens rises before her, and she summons all the pluck there is in her poor, fluttering heart, and denies.

Fatuous soul! She forgets that the sanctity which a moment since surrounded her as an honest woman is now stripped from her. She is

---

[2] Haggling or negotiating.

searched. The stolen article is found upon her, and she stands there drooping and despairing—a proven thief.

Every year, repeated over and over again, is this sad scene produced. Kleptomania is a by-word applied to Heaven knows how many forms of crime. But among the shoppers of New York there are more women who have had a passion for larceny bred in them than perhaps anywhere else in the world. . . .

Pickpockets

Pickpockets are an interesting class of thieves, and among the men and women who pursue that particular phase of crime there is much diversity of standing. The male operators all dress well and display considerable jewelry, but the females, while pillaging, generally appear in humble attire. Professional pickpockets are naturally great rovers and are continually traveling over the country to attend large gatherings. It is in crowds that these dexterous rascals successfully practice their nefarious calling. They are to be found one day among the assemblage present at the inauguration of the president of the United States, another at the funeral obsequies of some distinguished person, and the next at a country fair. A year ago members of the light-fingered fraternity flocked from all parts of the country to New York City, expecting to reap a rich harvest among the immense gathering at the funeral of ex-President Ulysses S. Grant. The perfect police arrangements, however, frustrated the plans of these rogues, and notwithstanding the fact that there were hundreds of thousands of people that day along the route of the funeral procession, not a single watch or pocket-book was stolen. Never before in the history of the Police Department had there been such a clean record. The day before the funeral all the professional pickpockets then in the city were arrested upon suspicion, and the police magistrates, when the precautionary scheme was explained to them, concurred in the flank movement against the rogues and held the prisoners. The alarm was then raised, and just as soon as the news had spread beyond the limits of the city, the hundreds of criminals on their way to New York gave up the project, left the trains and scattered in another direction. A few, however, who were reckless enough to attempt to reach the metropolis, found detectives awaiting them at the several depots. They were taken in charge and were kept safely housed at the Police Central Office, the various precinct station-houses and the Tombs prison until the funeral was over and all the strangers had departed for their homes. When there was no one to prey upon the disgusted rogues were liberated. The effort made to thwart the many bands of pickpockets upon that occasion was truly a bold one, but the end certainly justified the means.

Of professional pickpockets there are several types, and their peculiarities and characteristics are imperfectly understood by the general public. Odd are the notions that some people entertain of the personal appearance of criminals of that class. Some believe them to be a forbidding and suspicious-looking set but the photographs in this book will convince them that they are not unlike ordinary individuals, and that unless their faces are known, their appearance or dress would not excite curiosity. Still between the several classes of operators there is a vast and striking difference. The pickpocket, either male or female, who dexterously abstracts a purse or captures a watch or diamond pin on any of the principal thoroughfares, in a street car, train, or church, does not in any way resemble the person who will perform the same operation in a side street or at an enthusiastic gathering. Various as are the dispositions of these robbers also are their methods in getting possession of a pocket-book or valuables. Those who seek only large plunder are entertaining conversationalists and easy in their manners. They are generally self-possessed fellows, and are dexterous and cautious operators. Women make the most patient and dangerous pickpockets. Humble in their attire, and seemingly unassuming in their demeanor, without attracting any notice or particular attention, they slip into an excited crowd in a store or in front of a shopwindow. A quick eye or a delicate touch will locate for them without difficulty the resting-place of a well filled purse. That discovered, they follow the victim about until the proper opportunity presents itself and they capture the prize. Sometimes they go off on thieving excursions in pairs, but an expert female pickpocket invariably prefers to work alone. The latter class are difficult to run down because of their craftiness and closeness. Men, after committing a large theft, are in nearly all instances extravagant and reckless, but women have no such reputation. On the contrary, they are careful of the money they have stolen, and have been known to remained concealed for a long time. . . .

Some expert pickpockets ply their vocation alone. One of this class succeeded in stealing a valuable timepiece from the vest pocket of a distinguished jurist some time since while the latter was viewing a procession in front of a leading hotel. Another class of pickpockets are to be found in churches and at funerals. Women generally do the stealing, and they pass the plunder to their male confederates, who disappear with the watch or pocket-book the moment it has been captured. The men as a rule are old thieves who have lost their nerve and are unable to work themselves. Those that operate in conjunction with an assistant always require the latter to do the pressing or engage the attention of the intended victim while his pocket is being plundered. A "mob" is always composed of not less than three men working in harmony. Just as soon as a watch or pocket-book has been stolen by one of these men the thief hands the plunder to his accomplices, who passes it to the third or fourth man, as the case may be. This style of thieving is to protect the rogue, and only yields small profits on account of the number engaged in the crime. Should the victim discover on the spot that his pocket had been picked and cause the arrest of the robber standing alongside or in front of him, the failure to find the plunder upon the prisoner would create a serious doubt as to his guilt. Cunning old professionals, veritable Fagins[3], are the brains of these "mobs." They delegate a daring young man with quick hands to do the stealing, and the instant the purse, timepiece or jewel has been passed to them they disappear. If it is a purse that has been taken, it is promptly rifled and the "leather" thrown into an ash-barrel or sewer. The veteran first divides with himself the lion's share of the booty, and afterwards splits up the remainder with the other members of the gang. . . .

The favorite method of robbery by the men who operate upon trains has been described in this way. When a mob of pickpockets start out to "work a crowd" on a train they break into twos. The part of one is to ascertain the location of his victim's money. He gets alongside the man whose pocket is to be picked, and with rapid movement he dexterously passes his fingers over every pocket. His touch is so delicate that it enables him to locate the prize, and to ascertain its character, whether a roll, a purse, or a pocket-book. The surging of the crowd, especially on the railroad train, accounts to the suspicious traveler for the occasional jostling he receives. It is found that the most common receptacle for the pocket-book is the left trousers pocket. When the victim is selected, the second man plants himself squarely in front of him, while the other crowds up behind him on the right side. The operator in front, under a cover of a newspaper or coat thrown over his arm, feels the pocket, and if the victim is a straight-backed man, in standing position, he finds the lips of the pocket drawn close together. In such a case it is dangerous to attempt the insertion of the hand. A very low-toned clearing of the throat, followed by a gutteral [sic] noise, is the signal for his confederate

---

[3] Individuals who, like the character in Charles Dickens's novel *Oliver Twist*, instruct others in crime.

to exert a gentle pressure upon the victim's right shoulder. This is so gradually extended that the traveler yields to the pressure without knowing it, and without changing the position of his feet. This throws the lips of the pocket conveniently open for the operator in front, who does not insert his hands to draw the book out, but works upon the lining. He draws it out a little at a time, without inserting his fingers more than half way. Should this process of drawing the contents of the pocket to its mouth be felt by the victim, another low clearing of the throat gives the sign to the confederate, and the game is dropped. If the victim's suspicions are not aroused, the pickpocket continues at his work of drawing the lining out until the roll of bills or pocket-book is within reach of his deft fingers. The successful completion of the undertaking is indicated by a gentle chirrup, and the precious pair separate from their victim to ply the same tricks upon the next one.

10

LINCOLN STEFFENS

The Underworld

1931

Lincoln Steffens (1866–1936) was an American journalist who, along with Ida Tarbell and Ray Stannard Baker, pioneered an early form of investigative journalism in the late nineteenth century known as muckraking. Steffens wrote for the New York Evening Post *and edited* McClure's Magazine *and* American Magazine. *His articles vilified municipal government and political corruption and were later collected and revised in two books,* The Shame of the Cities *(1904) and* The Struggle for Self-Government *(1906). His two-volume autobiography, published later in his life and excerpted here, discussed his investigations of city police forces and the urban underworld at the turn of the twentieth century. Steffens relied on his interview with New York police superintendent Thomas Byrnes, author of* Professional Criminals of America

From Lincoln Steffens, *The Autobiography of Lincoln Steffens* (New York: Harcourt, Brace, 1931), 1:221–25.

(Document 9), to explain how police officials developed relationships with criminals that enabled them to solve crimes on one hand, but compelled them to tolerate illegal activities and behaviors (pickpocketing, prostitution, and homosexuality, for example) on the other (Documents 7 and 8).

The inspector, [Thomas] Byrnes, was cultivating my friendship, and he did it by letting me in to a view of his relations with thieves and the underworld generally. . . . Before he was promoted to be Superintendent of Police, he had been for years the inspector in charge of the detective bureau. He had enjoyed that work, evidently, and his many miraculous services to prominent people who had been robbed had made him loom in their imagination as the man of mystery and of marvelous effects. They all knew him in Wall Street; big men down there envied me the privilege of knowing personally "the inspector," as they still called him. . . .

. . . Even those he had helped out of trouble rarely met him personally. It was his pose to remain in the background, receiving communications through others—detectives and attorneys—and working in the dark, suddenly hand out his results. You saw only the hand and the restored property. Bankers told me tales of how somebody's house had been robbed; the inspector had been told about it, and having listened in silence a moment, had said, "Enough. Your diamonds will be delivered at your house within three days." And on the third day—not on the second or fourth, but exactly when this amazing man had promised—your diamonds were handed in by two startling men "with the compliments of the inspector." . . .

While I was pondering these questions he did one [a favor] for me. Drawing my salary one Saturday afternoon, I went home and took my wife out for dinner. As I was about to pay the waiter, I discovered that my pay envelope with the money was gone. My pocket had been picked. I complained to Byrnes by 'phone; he asked how much was in the envelope, how the envelope was addressed, and what lines of cars I had used to go home and to dinner. When I had answered all his questions, he said, "All right. I'll have it for you Monday morning." And on Monday morning Byrnes handed me the envelope with the money just as I had received it from my paper. . . .

. . . Crime was a business, and criminals had a "position" in the world, a place that was revealing itself to me. I soon knew more about it than

[Jacob] Riis did, who had been a police reporter for years; I knew more than Max [Fischel][4] could tell Riis, who hated and would not believe or even hear the "awful things" he was told. Riis was interested not at all in vice and crime, only in the stories of people and the conditions in which they lived. I remember one morning hearing Riis roaring, as he could roar, at Max, who was reporting a police raid on a resort of fairies.[5]

"Fairies!" Riis shouted, suspicious. "What are fairies?" And when Max began to define the word Riis rose up in a rage. "Not so," he cried. "There are no such creatures in this world." He threw down his pencil and rushed out of the office. He would not report that raid, and Max had to telephone enough to his paper to protect his chief.

There were fairies; there were all sorts of perverts; and they had a recognized standing in the demi-world;[6] they had their saloons, where they were "protected" by the police for a price. That raid Riis would not report was due to a failure of some one to come through with the regular bit of blackmail overdue. And so with prostitution, so with beggars, so with thieves, as I gradually learned, first from the reporters, then from police officers I came to know well, then from the crooks themselves who learned to trust me, and all the while from Byrnes. When he discovered that, while and because I did not write criminal news, he could interest and trust me with it, he used to call me in and tell me detective stories of which he was the hero. He was bragging, and he was inventing, too. This I knew because I had found out where he hid the detective story-books he was reading, and borrowing them when he was not looking, I read and recognized in them the source of some of his best narratives. Thus I discovered that instead of detectives' posing for and inspiring the writers of detective fiction, it was the authors who inspired the detectives. . . .

The police all over the world caution citizens who are robbed to report to headquarters and never to the press. They explain that detectives can work better if the thieves are not warned by the newspapers that the police are after them. This is absurd, of course. Thieves always know when the police are looking for them after a crime. The true reason of the police for privacy is that they don't like to have the public know how many unsolved crimes are committed, and they do like to deal privately and freely with the criminals. My detective assumed that I understood this; he assumed that I knew everything. His next assumption was that

[4] A young reporter who was Riis's chief assistant.
[5] Slang for a male homosexual.
[6] Underworld.

I knew that detectives specialized, as criminals do, in one class of crime, and that the detective's trade consists not in pursuing but in forming friendships with criminals.

11

WILLIAM T. STEAD

King McNally and His Police

1898

William T. Stead (1849–1912) was a British journalist who attracted international attention by exposing female trafficking and prostitution in his book The Maiden Tribute of Modern Babylon, *which was serialized in London's* Pall Mall Gazette *in 1885. He later coauthored* In Darkest England and the Way Out! *(1890) with Salvation Army founder William Booth. After visiting the World's Columbian Exposition in Chicago in 1893, Stead published* If Christ Came to Chicago! *(1894), a sensational and inflammatory exposé of the city's political corruption and underground economy. The book reportedly sold 70,000 copies on its publication day. Stead continued his muckraking journalism in* Satan's Invisible World Displayed; or, Despairing Democracy: A Study of Greater New York *(1898), which chronicled similar themes in North America's largest city. In this excerpt, Stead details the green goods confidence game and James McNally, one of its most successful practitioners and for a time George Appo's employer. Stead died on the* Titanic *in 1912.*

The Confidence Trick is perhaps the form of crime that would most naturally commend itself to the police banditti [bandits] of New York. For the force was engaged all day long in playing a gigantic Confidence Trick upon the citizens. The gold brick which the swindlers sold to the credulous countryman was hardly more mythical than the enforcement of the law which was supposed to be secured by the organisation of the

From William T. Stead, "King McNally and His Police," in *Satan's Invisible World Displayed; or, Despairing Democracy: A Study of Greater New York* (London: Mowbray House, 1898), 107–10, 112, 115–18.

City police. It is therefore not surprising to learn that the police were hand-and-glove with the gang of swindlers which, under King [James] McNally, carried on the Green Goods trade in the City of New York. It was one of the most lucrative of all the crimes which were carried on under police protection, and one of the safest. Few of all the stories told before the Lexow Committee display quite so unblushing a co-partnership between the lawbreakers and the law officers as was revealed in this Green Goods swindle. The rascality of the rogues was so audacious that it provokes a laugh. For it is possible to carry impudence to a point where indignation is momentarily submerged by the sense of the ludicrous. Sheer amazement at the existence of such preposterous villains begets such a sense of its absurdity, that any censure seems as much out of place as in the nonsense tales of the nursery. . . .

Green Goods are forged or counterfeit bank notes. The pretence is either that there has been an over-issue of certain denominations of paper money by the Treasury, or that the plates have been stolen from the Government, and by this means it is possible to sell ten dollars for one.

McNally, the King of the Green Goods men, employed at times a staff of thirty-five men. He began his career some twenty years ago as a bully who was kept by a prostitute. He swindled out of all her money a mistress of his who kept a restaurant, and started an Opium Joint. He then embarked in the Green Goods business, kept his carriage, and made his fortune.

The men who work this Confidence Trick seem to have carried their organised system of swindling to a very high pitch of perfection. Their master-stroke, however, was the admission of the police to a working partnership, which enabled them not merely to carry on their swindling with impunity, but also stood them in good stead whenever a victim had to be bullied and driven out of the city. . . .

. . . A Green Goods gang in full operation is constituted as follows:—

(1) The Backer or Capitalist, who supplies the bank roll—a roll of 10,000 genuine dollar bills, which are shown to the victim. He receives fifty per cent, out of which he pays the police, and so guarantees the protection of the gang.

(2) The Writer, who addresses the wrappers in which the circulars, bogus newspaper-cuttings, etc, are enclosed. He receives the other fifty per cent, out of which he has to pay the percentage due to the rest of the gang.

(3) The Bunco Steerer, who is sent to meet the victim at some hotel, fifty to a hundred miles distant from the city. He is the

messenger who gives the victim the pass-word, and then leads him to the Joint or den where the swindle is completed. He receives five per cent of the plunder.

(4) The Old Man, a respectable-looking older gentleman, who says nothing, but who sits solemnly in the Joint when the "beat"[7] is being carried through. He receives five dollars.

(5) The Turner, who is represented as the son of the old man, and does the selling of the bogus notes. His fee is ten dollars.

(6) The Ringer, a confederate behind the partition, who dexterously replaces the good money shown in the bank roll by the bundles of bogus notes. His fee is five dollars.

(7) The Tailer, who remains on guard at the railway station, personating a policeman, for the purpose of bullying any victim who discovers he has been swindled, and returns to try to recover his money. This gentleman is also paid five dollars a victim.

With this staff, and the protection of the police, the Green Goods business can be carried on very successfully. McNally used to take as much as £1,600 in a single day. Fortunes of £40,000 were accumulated by the leading backers, although McNally's pile was not estimated at more than £20,000.

The first step is the obtaining of directories and the arranging for the despatch of circulars. The circulars were of the familiar kind, printed as if typewritten, and addressed by a staff of writers, of whom McNally had eight or ten kept constantly at work. Enclosed in the envelope with the circular were slips printed as if they were cut out of newspapers, the same with intent to deceive, the slip being carefully written by Mr. McNally, or some member of his gang, for the purpose of giving the reader to understand that the offer of the circular was *bona fide* and reliable. These were sent out by thousands, the printer executing orders for 200,000 sets at a time. A slip was also included giving the address to which a telegram should be sent, in order to secure the advantageous offer made to the victim by the circular. These addresses were usually vacant lots in the city, but arrangements were made by bribing the officials of the telegraph company to hold all telegrams sent to such fictitious addresses until called for.

. . . A writer would send out 10,000 circulars or more a day. One, or perhaps two, of those would hook a victim, who would telegraph, making

---

[7] The con game or swindle.

an application for the money offered him at such tempting terms. This victim would belong to the writer of the circular by which he had been caught. Having thus hooked a victim, he had to be landed, and for this purpose he had to be brought to town and personally conducted by a bunco steerer to the den or joint, where three confederates fooled the victim to the top of his bent, and usually succeeded in fleecing him by one form or another of the confidence trick.

The victim, who was known as a "Come On" or as a "Guy," was swindled by a variety of methods. One favourite plan was to undertake to sell the credulous rustic 10,000 dollars for 650 dollars. For less than 650 dollars he was told he could not have the "State rights." The monopoly for his own State was promised to the favoured individual, whose 650 dollars had to be paid down on the spot. A locked box was then given him within which he was assured there were 10,000 dollars in coin. In reality, there was a brick, which was all the poor victim got for his money. . . .

Some such methods are probably familiar to the police of all the cities in the world, but that which was peculiar to New York was the arrangement made for carrying on this business, not merely with the cognizance of, but with the active co-operation of the police. . . .

Every now and then, when the newspapers made too much fuss concerning the scandals of the Police Department, the authorities would order what is known as a "general shake-up" — *i.e.*, the captains would be shifted all round, the assumption being that a new broom would sweep clean, and that by changing the captains from one precinct to another the abuses that had created any fuss would be rectified. Unfortunately the whole system of blackmail and corruption was so elaborately organised that the shifting of the captains made no change. Each newcomer succeeded to the business, and carried on the collection of blackmail without losing a single day. "Business carried on as usual during alterations" might have been posted up over every police-station in New York; but in the case of Green Goods men, their business was too profitable to be lost by the captain who had once got hold of it. The consequence was that, when the shake-up took place, and Captain [William] Meakin was transferred from the "down-town precinct" to Harlem at the other end of the island, he carried all the Green Goods men with him up to his new station. As soon as the order was given that the shake-up was to be enforced, Captain Meakin sent word to McNally that he must follow him to Harlem. . . .

The only terror which seemed to haunt the mind of the Green Goods men was that of being shot down by some sharper who made himself up as a guy in order to possess himself of the bank-roll of genuine money. Appo, a man who spent most of his life in picking pockets when he was at liberty, and in doing time in gaol[8] when he was caught, had a rough experience of the murderous possibilities that the Green Goods man has to face. On one occasion a Tennessee detective made himself up as a country bumpkin. When the critical moment came, he clapped his revolver at the head of Appo, shot out his eye, lodged the bullet in his skull, from which it was never extracted, and made off with all the money at that time on Appo's person. . . .

Another ingenious precaution which was taken by McNally was to have the detectives at the various railway stations surrounding New York in his pay, so that in case any Guy were to discover that he had been swindled, and make a fuss at the station, he could be promptly arrested for holding counterfeit money, and so bullied as to make him thankful to get home without saying more about it. The detective at the Central Depot was paid £10 a month for his services. . . .

The principle of territorial jurisdiction is so deeply rooted in the American mind that the New York police seem to have acted upon it in all their dealings with the criminals with whom they shepherded. For instance, they appear to have parcelled Broadway into blocks, allotting each block to a different thief, who, of course, paid quit rent[9] for his district to the police. The understanding was that the policeman was to be free to arrest the thief if there was a complaint made by the victim, but that so long as no complaints were made the policeman would "close the other eye" and allow the pickpocket a free run. Mr. [John] Goff stated that there was once a fight between the thieves; that one trespassed upon the other's domain and went to a pawnshop about it, and the authorities at police headquarters threatened to send the first thief up the river if he ever invaded the second thief's privileges.

This reverent regard for territorial landmarks is very touching. The New York police appear to have been as much opposed to poaching as are English gamekeepers.

---

[8] Jail.
[9] A bribe. A quitrent was originally the compensation masters were required to pay indentured servants at the end of their term of servitude during the seventeenth and eighteenth centuries.

3

The Criminal in Popular Culture

12

ILLUSTRATED AMERICAN

Review of In the Tenderloin

1895

When George Appo testified before the Lexow Committee in June 1894, he described his role in the green goods game. Later that summer, he was invited by attorney and playwright Edmund E. Price to play himself in a dramatic production titled In the Tenderloin. *The melodrama portrayed various elements of New York's underworld, including the green goods game. It opened in New Haven, Connecticut, before moving to Brooklyn, New York, and then the People's Theatre on the Bowery in Manhattan. The production traveled to Syracuse, New York; Youngstown, Ohio; and Indianapolis before abruptly closing. Appo's role was minimal but nevertheless attracted reviews from New York's theater critics. In this excerpt from the* Illustrated American, *an anonymous reviewer laments the "moral effect" of popular entertainments that glorified criminal and illicit behavior (Documents 7, 8, and 11). Such criticism had little impact, and the genre persisted for more than a century thereafter.*

The production in New York of such a play as "In the Tenderloin" has an importance out of all proportion to the merits of the performance. Considered artistically, the production had no merits. The melodrama was bad, the actors were bad, and the audience was such a one as might be expected at the People's Theatre on the Bowery. It is significant,

From "Plays and Players," *Illustrated American*, January 5, 1895, 6–7 however, that shrewd managers who know what their public demands should invest money in putting on the boards what is avowedly an attempt to depict the lowest forms of vice to be found in New York. And more significant still is the probability that these far-seeing gentlemen will make handsome earnings!

What is the substance of "In the Tenderloin"? A succession of living pictures of metropolitan infamy. Throughout the four acts there pass before the audience, in shameless review, ugly specimens of the dregs and slums that taint Manhattan Island. There are thieves, thugs, assassins, fallen women, and the brutes who exploit them, gamblers, painted men, dive-keepers and the low company they harbor — cunning scoundrels whose trade is to lure men into their dens and despoil them; infamous creatures who traffic in the dishonor of young girls, "green goods" men, confidence men — all the foul brood of carrion birds that gorge themselves in the moral cesspools of a sinful city. Such is the "play" this high-minded "playwright," Mr. E. E. Price has "constructed"! Such is the play that will possibly make a "barrel of money" for the philanthropists who have mounted it! . . .

Is there, then, no point at which the line shall be drawn in theatrical representations? Shall the craze for realism force reputable actors and actresses to divide the roles with men who belong in State prison and women who were better dead? If genuine dive-keepers, burglars, "green goods" men and bruisers are to be exhibited on the stage, why not genuine bawds and murderers? Why not have a man killed, say, at every hundredth performance, instead of giving away souvenir spoons? As long as we have started on a campaign of brutality and shamelessness, what matters a little more or less?

There may be a fortune awaiting the manager who will turn to account the heroes and heroines of our police courts and divorce courts in the cause of stage sensationalism. How vivid to have as the heartless lover in a play the actual seducer fresh from a real breach of promise case! Think of the free advertising the newspapers would have given him and how angry they would be to have thus ground a theatrical ax without getting any revenue for it! Or again, a girl elopes from a luxurious home with the family coachman. A few weeks later, finding themselves in want, the impoverished pair accept large salaries to do an "eloping act" in some popular melodrama. Wouldn't that be splendid, wouldn't it "draw"? And, if worse came to worst, the rich old father could be made to "come down" handsomely rather than have his name further disgraced. What is there to prevent a manager with "In the Tenderloin" instincts from advertising for would-be suicides and offering them superior inducements to do their little razor or revolver specialties as thrilling climaxes in the death scenes! As long as there are miserable wretches who will kill themselves, why not utilize them? The more one thinks of it, the more possibilities one sees in this new departure in realism!

Do I hear some one suggest that such people could not act? Ah, the merry humor of that objection! How many of the tribe of bridge-jumpers, pugilists, scandal-branded wives, and "gentlemen" like Messrs. "Tom" Gould and George Appo were ever accused of knowing how to act? Many other offenses against laws human and divine they have, doubtless, on their consciences, but the sin of acting—*jamais!*

To speak more seriously, the trouble with art nowadays, not only on the stage but along many lines, is that those who devote themselves to it are led aside from high ideals by the sordid spirit of this age and land, the spirit that judges all things by one single standard: "Is there money in it?" No one any longer desires to lead the public taste in unremunerative efforts toward better things, but all slavishly follow it, eager to anticipate, to exaggerate, to stimulate each new vanity and weakness, regardless of the moral effect, provided always that the money-bags keep jingling.

While it is true that the successful playwrights of the hour show a tendency to weave into their dramas moral questions that are apparently of burning moment to the race, the fact is their morality is one of show, not of reality, of tinsel, not of gold. They care at heart for the subjects of their plays no more than our popular newspapers care for the poor when they champion some philanthropic scheme—because it will "catch on" and boom their circulations. There is no longer any fixedness of purpose, any earnestness of conviction, whether among playwrights, novelists, musicians, or painters. Each makes his "inspiration" harmonize with the greedy policy of the business office. Each asks: "Will it pay?" before lifting pen or brush. Does anyone believe that the masters of creative art in the past were thinking all the time as their work advanced toward completion: "I wish I could do so and so, for that would be grand; but I will do just the contrary, for that will be lucrative"?

How can anyone expect fine results from such a prostitution of talent? Artists must be great before they can produce great work. There is a profound lesson to be learned from this unworthy production, "In the Tenderloin."

A Quimbo and George Appo Chronology
(1820s–1930)

1820s   Chang Quimbo Appo, known as Quimbo, born in China.

1847–
1849   Quimbo migrates from China to San Francisco, establishes tea business, and then moves to northern California to prospect for gold.

1853   Quimbo shoots two Mexicans in self-defense as they rob and kill his partner; flees to East Coast.

1854   Quimbo and Catherine Fitzpatrick meet and marry.

1855–
1856   Quimbo operates successful tea store in New Haven, Connecticut.

1856   George Appo born on July 4 in New Haven; family later moves to New York City.

1859   George Matsell publishes *Vocabulum; or, The Rogue's Lexicon.*

1859–
1860   Quimbo commits murder and is sentenced to death by hanging; Governor Edwin Morgan later commutes sentence to ten years in Sing Sing.

1861–
1871   George grows up in Donovan's Lane in the Five Points neighborhood of New York; works as newsboy and learns to pickpocket.

1869   Quimbo released from Sing Sing.

1870s–
1890s George addicted to opium.

1871–
1872   George, under alias George Leonard, convicted of pickpocketing and sentenced to school-ship *Mercury* for two years; travels to Canary Islands, Brazil, Barbados, and St. Thomas; escapes from ship upon returning to New York.

1872   Quimbo convicted of assault and sentenced to five years in Sing Sing.

1874   George, under alias George Dixon, arrested for pickpocketing and sentenced to two and a half years in Sing Sing; meets Quimbo there.

Tammany Hall leader and state senator William "Boss" Tweed convicted on various charges of political corruption.

1875   Quimbo sent to Auburn Prison Hospital for the Criminally Insane; released later that year.

New York Assembly appoints select committee to examine crime in New York City, one of the first legislative investigations of urban disorder and criminal activity.

1876   George released from Sing Sing, moves to Philadelphia, and then returns to New York, where he is shot after pickpocketing $150 from man on Fulton Street.

Quimbo convicted of assault and sentenced to seven years in Sing Sing.

New York Assembly releases report on crime in New York City.

1877   George, under alias George Wilson, convicted of pickpocketing and sentenced to two and a half years in Sing Sing. George and Quimbo in Sing Sing together for brief time in January. George later sent to Clinton Prison in Dannemora, New York.

1878   Quimbo admitted to Auburn Prison Hospital for the Criminally Insane.

1879   George discharged from Clinton Prison.

1880   George stabs Jack Collins in self-defense in Bayard Street saloon; acquitted of attempted murder; goes to work for Tom Lee, "the Mayor of Chinatown," and later Barney Maguire in green goods game.

1882   George convicted of pickpocketing and sentenced to three and a half years in Sing Sing; involved in graft in stove production there.

1884   George released from Sing Sing.

1885–
1893   George works as green goods steerer for Eddie Parmeley and James McNally.

1886   George, under alias George Leon, arrested for petty larceny in Philadelphia and sentenced to Eastern State Penitentiary for one year.

Thomas Byrnes's *Professional Criminals of America* published.

1887   George released from Eastern State Penitentiary; travels around United States with Tom Wilson (alias Woods).

1890   George, under alias George Leon, convicted of petty larceny and sentenced to Blackwell's Island Penitentiary.

1893   George shot in head in Poughkeepsie by Ira Hogshead; survives but loses eye; tried under name George Albow and convicted of fraud; conviction is later overturned by New York Court of Appeals.

1894   George works for Mike Ryan in green goods game; testifies before Lexow Committee on June 14; later assaulted at least three times by underworld rivals.

1894–
1895   George plays himself onstage in *In the Tenderloin*.

1895   George stabs policeman Michael J. Rein in self-defense during fight defending actor Theodore Babcock; later pleads guilty and is sentenced to six months in Blackwell's Island Penitentiary.

1896   George stabs John Atwood in self-defense; attorney Ambrose H. Purdy convinces judge to declare him insane; sent to Matteawan State Hospital for the Criminally Insane, where he sees Quimbo.

1898   William T. Stead's *Satan's Invisible World Displayed; or, Despairing Democracy: A Study of Greater New York* and Louis J. Beck's *New York's Chinatown* published.

1899   George released from Matteawan and moves to Philadelphia; later returns to New York and works in a variety of menial service occupations.

1911–
1916   George employed as undercover agent by Society for the Prevention of Crime.

1912   Quimbo dies on June 23 at Matteawan State Hospital (reportedly age ninety).

1915–
1916   George writes autobiography.

1930   George dies of general arteriosclerosis on May 17 at Manhattan State Hospital, a psychiatric hospital on Wards Island in the East River (age seventy-three); buried in Mount Hope Cemetery, Hastings-on-Hudson, New York.

Questions for Consideration

1. What kind of picture of crime does George Appo present? Positive? Negative? Romantic? Horrifying?
2. What social forces led Appo to a life of crime?
3. What does Appo's childhood reveal about the treatment of children in nineteenth-century cities?
4. What is a "good fellow"? How does Appo define that term?
5. How effective was prison in rehabilitating Appo? Explain.
6. How "organized" was the crime described by Appo (part two)? By Thomas Byrnes (Document 9)? By Lincoln Steffens (Document 10)? By William T. Stead (Document 11)? Compare their descriptions of the criminal underworld. How are they similar or different?
7. Is there such a thing as an "underworld subculture," with its own values and ideas, distinct mentality, and moral economy (or immoral economy)?
8. Does Appo's criminal behavior represent that of a "social bandit" whose goal is to avenge social injustice and challenge the dominant culture?
9. What was the role of ethnicity, race, gender, or religion in Appo's life and his description of the nineteenth-century underworld?
10. How would you analyze *The Autobiography of George Appo* (part two) as a form of autobiographical literature? Is it comparable to Charles Dickens's *Oliver Twist*? Victor Hugo's *Les Misérables*?
11. In 1932, Sing Sing warden Lewis E. Lawes quoted extensively from Appo's autobiography (Document 4). Why? What image of Sing Sing during the nineteenth century did Lawes emphasize or convey?
12. Why did Appo write to New York governor Theodore Roosevelt in 1899 (Document 2)? What does the letter reveal about Appo? How does Matteawan medical superintendent Henry E. Allison's medical diagnosis (Document 3) depart from the state of mind displayed in Appo's letter to Roosevelt?
13. Compare Louis J. Beck's description of Appo in 1898 (Document 1) with Appo's obituary from the *Bronx Home News* in 1930 (Document 12).

How does Beck describe Appo? How does the obituary describe him? What was responsible for any differences? How do these accounts of Appo differ from his autobiography?

14. According to George W. Matsell (Document 6), what was distinctive about the criminal underworld? What does Matsell's account reveal about the underworld? Do any of the other accounts corroborate or refute Matsell's?

15. Compare the legislative investigative reports published in 1876 and 1895 (Documents 7 and 8). What kinds of crime do they emphasize? What do they conclude about the problem of crime? How are they similar or different in what they emphasize?

16. What policies and changes did some elected officials recommend to address the problem of prostitution in the 1870s? Why? What does this reveal about the role of government in city life?

17. How does Thomas Byrnes address criminal behavior in Document 9? What does this reveal about defendants' rights in the nineteenth century?

18. How does Byrnes distinguish between male and female criminals?

19. The legislative investigative reports, Thomas Byrnes, and Lincoln Steffens discuss certain kinds of sexual behavior and female crime. What do they reveal about nineteenth-century sexuality?

20. Why was Appo invited to play himself onstage in *In the Tenderloin*? How did reviewers react? Why was this the case?

21. Why were sensational accounts of the underworld such as *In the Tenderloin* so popular?

22. How did Progressive reform address the problem of crime and criminal behavior?

Selected Bibliography

PRINTED CRIMINAL MEMOIRS

Berkman, Alexander. *Prison Memoirs of an Anarchist*. New York, 1912.
Bidwell, George. *Forging His Chains: The Autobiography of George Bidwell*. Chicago, 1888.
Black, Jack. *You Can't Win*. New York, 1926.
Boxcar Bertha: An Autobiography. As told to Dr. Ben L. Reitman. New York: Amok Press, 1988. Originally published in 1937 as *Sister of the Road*.
The Con Game and "Yellow Kid" Weil: The Autobiography of the Famous Con Artist. As told to W. T. Brannon. New York, 1948.
Guerin, Eddie. *I Was a Bandit*. Garden City, N.Y., 1929.
The Autobiography of a Thief. Recorded by Hutchins Hapgood. New York, 1903.
Hawthorne, Julian. *The Subterranean Brotherhood*. New York, 1914.
Lyons, Sophie. *Why Crime Does Not Pay*. New York, 1913.
Moreau, William B. *Swindling Exposed: From the Diary of William B. Moreau, King of the Fakirs*. Syracuse, N.Y., 1907.
Sutherland, Edwin Hardin. *The Professional Thief: By a Professional Thief*. Chicago, 1937.

PRINTED PRIMARY SOURCES

Brace, Charles Loring. *The Dangerous Classes of New York, and Twenty Years' Work among Them*. New York, 1872.
Buel, James. *Mysteries and Miseries of America's Great Cities: Embracing New York, Washington City, San Francisco, Salt Lake City, and New Orleans*. St. Louis, 1883.
———. *Sunlight and Shadow of America's Great Cities*. Philadelphia, 1889.
Buel, James, and Joseph A. Dacus. *A Tour of St. Louis; or, the Inside Life of a Great City*. St. Louis, 1878.
Buntline, Ned [Edward Zane Carroll Judson]. *The Mysteries and Miseries of New York: A Story of Real Life*. New York, 1848.
———. *Mysteries and Miseries of New Orleans*. New York, 1851.
Byrnes, Thomas. *Professional Criminals of America*. New York, 1886.

Campbell, Helen, Thomas W. Knox, and Thomas Byrnes. *Darkness and Daylight; or, Lights and Shadows of New York Life*. Hartford, Conn., 1891.

Comstock, Anthony. *Frauds Exposed; or, How the People Are Deceived and Robbed, and Youth Corrupted*. New York, 1880.

Crapsey, Edward. *The Nether Side of New York; or, the Vice, Crime and Poverty of the Great Metropolis*. New York, 1872.

Eldridge, Benjamin P., and William B. Watts. *Our Rival, the Rascal: A Faithful Portrayal of the Conflict between the Criminals of This Age and the Defenders of Society, the Police*. Boston, 1897.

Farley, Phil. *Criminals of America; or, Tales of the Lives of Thieves*. New York, 1876.

Flynt [Willard], Josiah. *Tramping with Tramps: Studies and Sketches of Vagabond Life*. New York, 1899.

———. *The World of Graft*. New York, 1901.

Foster, George. *New York by Gas-Light, with Here and There a Streak of Sunshine*. New York, 1853.

Howe, William F., and Abraham H. Hummel. *In Danger; or, Life in New York: A True History of a Great City's Wiles and Temptations*. New York, 1888.

Lawes, Lewis E. *Life and Death in Sing Sing*. Garden City, N.Y., 1928.

———. *Twenty Thousand Years in Sing Sing*. New York, 1932.

Lippard, George. *The Empire City; or, New York by Night*. New York, 1853.

———. *New York: Its Upper Ten and Lower Million*. Cincinnati, 1854.

———. *The Quaker City; or, the Monks of Monk Hall: A Romance of Philadelphia Life, Mystery, and Crime*. Philadelphia, 1845.

Ludlow, Fitz Hugh. *The Hasheesh Eater: Being Passages from the Life of a Pythagorean*. New York, 1857.

Matsell, George W. *Vocabulum; or, The Rogue's Lexicon*. New York, 1859.

McAdoo, William. *Guarding a Great City*. New York, 1906.

McCabe, James D., Jr. *Lights and Shadows of New York Life; or, The Sights and Sensations of the Great City*. Philadelphia, 1872.

———. *New York by Sunlight and Gaslight, A Work Descriptive of the Great Metropolis*. Philadelphia, 1881.

Moss, Frank. *The American Metropolis*. 3 vols. New York, 1897.

Osborne, Thomas Mott. *Society and Prisons: Some Suggestions for a New Penology*. New York, 1916.

———. *Within Prison Walls*. New York, 1914.

Parkhurst, Charles H. *Our Fight with Tammany*. New York, 1895.

Pinkerton, Allan. *Criminal Reminiscences and Detective Sketches*. New York, 1878.

———. *Professional Thieves and the Detective*. New York, 1880.

———. *Thirty Years a Detective*. Chicago, 1884.

Smith, Matthew Hale. *Sunshine and Shadow in New York*. Hartford, Conn., 1868.

Stead, William T. *If Christ Came to Chicago!* Chicago, 1894.

————. *Satan's Invisible World Displayed; or, Despairing Democracy: A Study of Greater New York.* London, 1898.

Sutton, Charles. *The New York Tombs: Its Secrets and Its Mysteries.* New York, 1874.

Walling, George W. *Recollections of a New York Chief of Police.* New York, 1887.

Wilkes, George. *The Mysteries of the Tombs: A Journal of Thirty Days Imprisonment in the New York City Prison.* New York, 1844.

Willemse, Cornelius W. *Behind the Green Lights.* New York, 1931.

Wines, Enoch Cobb, and Theodore W. Dwight. *Report on the Prisons and Reformatories of the United States and Canada.* Albany, N.Y., 1867.

SECONDARY SOURCES

Ayers, Edward L. *Vengeance and Justice: Crime and Punishment in the 19th-Century American South.* New York: Oxford University Press, 1984.

Bell, Daniel. "Crime as an American Way of Life." *Antioch Review* 13 (1953): 131–54.

Blok, Anton. "The Peasant and the Brigand: Social Banditry Reconsidered." *Comparative Studies in History and Society* 14 (1972): 494–505.

Cohen, Patricia Cline. *The Murder of Helen Jewett: The Life and Death of a Prostitute in Nineteenth-Century New York.* New York: Alfred A. Knopf, 1998.

Cohen, Patricia Cline, Timothy Gilfoyle, and Helen Lefkowitz Horowitz. *The Flash Press: Sporting Men's Weeklies in the 1840s.* Chicago: University of Chicago Press, 2008.

Courtwright, David T. *Dark Paradise: Opiate Addiction in America before 1940.* Cambridge, Mass.: Harvard University Press, 1982.

————. *Violent Land: Single Men and Social Disorder from the Frontier to the Inner City.* Cambridge, Mass.: Harvard University Press, 1996.

Czitrom, Daniel. *Media and the American Mind: From Morse to McLuhan.* Chapel Hill: University of North Carolina Press, 1982.

————. "Underworlds and Underdogs: Big Tim Sullivan and Metropolitan Politics in New York, 1889–1913." *Journal of American History* 78 (1991): 536–58.

Foucault, Michel. *Discipline and Punish: The Birth of the Prison.* Translated by Alan Sheridan. New York: Vintage, 1977.

Franklin, H. Bruce. *Prison Literature in America: The Victim as Criminal and Artist.* New York: Oxford University Press, 1989.

Friedman, Lawrence M. *Crime and Punishment in American History.* New York: Basic Books, 1993.

Gilfoyle, Timothy J. *A Pickpocket's Tale: The Underworld of Nineteenth-Century New York.* New York: W. W. Norton, 2006.

————. *City of Eros: New York City, Prostitution, and the Commercialization of Sex, 1790–1920.* New York: W. W. Norton, 1992.

Gorn, Elliott J. *The Manly Art: Bare-Knuckle Prize Fighting in America.* Ithaca, N.Y.: Cornell University Press, 1986.

Harring, Sidney. *Policing a Class Society: The Experience of American Cities, 1865–1915.* New Brunswick, N.J.: Rutgers University Press, 1983.

Hirsch, Adam J. *The Rise of the Penitentiary: Prisons and Punishment in Early America.* New Haven, Conn.: Yale University Press, 1992.

Hobsbawm, Eric J. *Bandits.* New York: Pantheon, 1981.

Johnson, David R. *Illegal Tender: Counterfeiting and the Secret Service in Nineteenth-Century America.* Washington, D.C.: Smithsonian Institution Press, 1995.

————. *Policing the Urban Underworld: The Impact of Crime on the Development of the American Police, 1800–1887.* Philadelphia: Temple University Press, 1979.

Johnson, Marilynn S. *Street Justice: A History of Police Violence in New York City.* Boston: Beacon Press, 2003.

Jonnes, Jill. *Hep-Cats, Narcs, and Pipe Dreams: A History of America's Romance with Illegal Drugs.* Baltimore: Johns Hopkins University Press, 1996.

Katz, Jack. *Seductions of Crime: Moral and Sensual Attractions in Doing Evil.* New York: Basic Books, 1988.

Katz, Michael B., ed. *The "Underclass" Debate: Views from History.* Princeton, N.J.: Princeton University Press, 1993.

Keller, Lisa. *Triumph of Order: Democracy and Public Space in New York and London.* New York: Columbia University Press, 2009.

Lane, Roger. *Murder in America: A History.* Columbus: Ohio State University Press, 1997.

————. *Policing the City: Boston, 1822–1885.* Cambridge, Mass.: Harvard University Press, 1967.

————. *Violent Death in the City: Suicide, Accident, and Murder in Nineteenth-Century Philadelphia.* Cambridge, Mass.: Harvard University Press, 1979.

McLennan, Rebecca M. *The Crisis of Imprisonment: Protest, Politics, and the Making of the American Penal State, 1776–1941.* New York: Cambridge University Press, 2008.

Mihm, Stephen. *A Nation of Counterfeiters: Capitalists, Con Men, and the Making of the United States.* Cambridge, Mass.: Harvard University Press, 2007.

Miller, Wilbur R. *Cops and Bobbies: Police Authority in New York and London, 1830–1870.* Chicago: University of Chicago Press, 1973.

Monkkonen, Eric H. *The Dangerous Class: Crime and Poverty in Columbus, Ohio, 1860–1885.* Cambridge, Mass.: Harvard University Press, 1975.

————. *Murder in New York City.* Berkeley: University of California Press, 2001.

————. *Police in Urban America, 1860–1920*. New York: Cambridge University Press, 1981.

Morris, Norval, and David J. Rothman, eds. *The Oxford History of the Prison*. New York: Oxford University Press, 1997.

Reynolds, David. *Beneath the American Renaissance: The Subversive Imagination in the Age of Emerson and Melville*. New York: Alfred A. Knopf, 1988.

Richardson, James F. *The New York Police: Colonial Times to 1901*. New York: Oxford University Press, 1970.

Rothman, David. *Conscience and Convenience: The Asylum and Its Alternatives in Progressive America*. Boston: Little, Brown, 1980.

————. *The Discovery of the Asylum: Social Order and Disorder in the New Republic*. Boston: Little, Brown, 1971.

Stansell, Christine. *American Moderns: Bohemian New York and the Creation of a New Century*. New York: Metropolitan Books, 2000.

Steinberg, Allen. *The Transformation of Criminal Justice: Philadelphia, 1800–1880*. Chapel Hill: University of North Carolina Press, 1989.

Willrich, Michael. *City of Courts: Socializing Justice in Progressive Era Chicago*. New York: Cambridge University Press, 2003.

Acknowledgments (*continued from p. iv*)

Figure 1. Undated photograph of George Appo. Society for the Prevention of Crime Papers, Rare Book and Manuscript Library, Columbia University. Used by permission of Columbia University.

Main document. *The Autobiography of George Appo.* Society for the Prevention of Crime Papers, Rare Book and Manuscript Library, Columbia University. Used by permission of Columbia University.

Document 2. Letter of George Appo to Gov. Theodore Roosevelt of New York, May 9, 1899, Governor's Executive Clemency and Pardon Case Files (series A0597), New York State Archives, Albany, N.Y.

Document 3. Report of Dr. Henry E. Allison, Medical Superintendent of Matteawan State Hospital for the Criminally Insane, on George Appo, May 16, 1899, Governor's Executive Clemency and Pardon Case Files (series A0597), New York State Archives, Albany, N.Y.

Document 4. Lewis E. Lawes. Pages 88–94 from *Twenty Thousand Years in Sing Sing* (New York: A.L. Burt and Company). Copyright © 1932 by A.L. Burt and Company. Used by permission of Joan Lawes Jacobsen.

Document 5. Obituary of George Appo from *Bronx Home News*, June 15, 1930. Society for the Prevention of Crime Papers, Rare Book and Manuscript Library, Columbia University. Used by permission of Columbia University.

Document 10. Excerpts from *The Autobiography of Lincoln Steffens*. Copyright © 1931 by Houghton Mifflin Harcourt Publishing Company. Copyright © renewed 1959 by Peter Steffens. Reprinted by permission of Houghton Mifflin Harcourt Publishing Company. All rights reserved.

Index